CASENOTE® Legal Briefs®

CRIMINAL LAW

Keyed to Courses Using

Kaplan, Weisberg, Binder, and Gruber's Criminal Law, Cases and Materials Tenth Edition

Authored by: Publisher's Editorial Staff

ASPEN PUBLISHING

To contact Customer Service, e-mail customer.service@aspenpublishing.com, call 1-800-950-5259, or mail correspondence to:

Aspen Publishing
Attn: Order Department
1 Wall Street
Burlington, MA 01803

Printed in the United States of America.

1 2 3 4 5 6 7 8 9 0

ISBN 979-8-8941-0388-4

ABOUT ASPEN PUBLISHING

Aspen Publishing is a leading provider of legal education content and digital learning solutions in the United States and globally. Our innovative products and platforms—designed based on best practices in learning science—engage students and enhance outcomes. From textbooks and audiobooks authored by renowned experts to digital platforms and products like LEAF, Connected eBooks, Connected Quizzing, PracticePerfect, and JD-Next, we empower the next generation of legal professionals with innovative, trusted, and accessible resources.

The Aspen Casebook Series, affectionately known as the "red and black" casebooks among law faculty and students, includes hundreds of highly regarded textbooks across more than 80 disciplines. These range from foundational courses like Torts and Contracts to emerging electives such as Sustainability and the Law of Policing. Our study aids, including the popular *Examples & Explanations* series, help law students master complex topics with clarity and confidence.

Aspen's expertise extends to undergraduate education with our Paralegal, Criminal Justice, and Business Law series, offering the same hallmark quality to a broader audience. JD-Next, our groundbreaking online law school prep course and admissions test, provides a realistic preview of law school, equips students with essential skills for academic success, and evaluates their readiness for legal studies.

Aspen Publishing Is Proud to Be a UWorld Company

Since 2003, UWorld has been a global leader in developing high-quality learning tools for students preparing for high-stakes exams. With a commitment to excellence, UWorld has helped millions of students in undergraduate, graduate, and professional programs in fields such as medicine, nursing, finance, and law achieve their academic and career goals.

Founded by Chandra S. Pemmasani, M.D., during his medical residency, UWorld began focusing on medical education and has since expanded into various academic fields, including law. In 2020, UWorld launched its Legal vertical, starting with its comprehensive Multistate Bar Exam (MBE®) Question Bank, followed by the acquisition of Themis Bar Review, which integrated resources to provide a complete bar exam preparation experience. In 2024, UWorld expanded its offerings by acquiring Aspen Publishing, enhancing its suite of legal education products.

Today, UWorld offers an unparalleled range of study materials that blend active learning methods with expert content, ensuring students and educators can access the most effective resources. From bar preparation to law school success, UWorld is committed to supporting the next generation of legal professionals. Learn more at uworld.com.

Format for the Casenote® Legal Brief

Nature of Case: This section identifies the form of action (e.g., breach of contract, negligence, battery), the type of proceeding (e.g., demurrer, appeal from trial court's jury instructions) or the relief sought (e.g., damages, injunction, criminal sanctions).

Fact Summary: This is included to refresh your memory and can be used as a quick reminder of the facts.

Rule of Law: Summarizes the general principle of law that the case illustrates. It may be used for instant recall of the court's holding and for classroom discussion or home review.

Facts: This section contains all relevant facts of the case, including the contentions of the parties and the lower court holdings. It is written in a logical order to give you a clear understanding of the case. The plaintiff and defendant are identified by their proper names throughout and are always labeled with a (P) or (D).

Issue: The issue is a concise question that brings out the essence of the opinion as it relates to the section of the casebook in which the case appears. Both substantive and procedural issues are included if relevant to the decision.

Palsgraf v. Long Island R.R. Co.

Injured bystander (P) v. Railroad company (D)

N.Y. Ct. App., 248 N.Y. 339, 162 N.E. 99 (1928).

NATURE OF CASE: Appeal from judgment affirming verdict for plaintiff seeking damages for personal injury.

FACT SUMMARY: Helen Palsgraf (P) was injured on R.R.'s (D) train platform when R.R.'s (D) guard helped a passenger aboard a moving train, causing his package to fall on the tracks. The package contained fireworks which exploded, creating a shock that tipped a scale onto Palsgraf (P).

RULE OF LAW

The risk reasonably to be perceived defines the duty to be obeyed.

FACTS: Helen Palsgraf (P) purchased a ticket to Rockaway Beach from R.R. (D) and was waiting on the train platform. As she waited, two men ran to catch a train that was pulling out from the platform. The first man jumped aboard, but the second man, who appeared as if he might fall, was helped aboard by the guard on the train who had kept the door open so they could jump aboard. A guard on the platform also helped by pushing him onto the train. The man was carrying a package wrapped in newspaper. In the process, the man dropped his package, which fell on the tracks. The package contained fireworks and exploded. The shock of the explosion was apparently of great enough strength to tip over some scales at the other end of the platform, which fell on Palsgraf (P) and injured her. A jury awarded her damages, and R.R. (D) appealed.

ISSUE: Does the risk reasonably to be perceived define the duty to be obeyed?

HOLDING AND DECISION: (Cardozo, C.J.) Yes. The risk reasonably to be perceived defines the duty to be obeyed. If there is no foreseeable hazard to the injured party as the result of a seemingly innocent act, the act does not become a tort because it happened to be a wrong as to another. If the wrong was not willful, the plaintiff must show that the act as to her had such great and apparent possibilities of danger as to entitle her to protection. Negligence in the abstract is not enough upon which to base liability. Negligence is a relative concept, evolving out of the common law doctrine of trespass on the case. To establish liability, the defendant must owe a legal duty of reasonable care to the injured party. A cause of action in tort will lie where harm, though unintended, could have been averted or avoided by observance of such a duty. The scope of the duty is limited by the range of danger that a reasonable person could foresee. In this case, there was nothing to suggest from the appearance of the parcel or otherwise that the parcel contained fireworks. The guard could not reasonably have had any warning of a threat to Palsgraf (P), and R.R. (D) therefore cannot be held liable. Judgment is reversed in favor of R.R. (D).

DISSENT: (Andrews, J.) The concept that there is no negligence unless R.R. (D) owes a legal duty to take care as to Palsgraf (P) herself is too narrow. Everyone owes to the world at large the duty of refraining from those acts that may unreasonably threaten the safety of others. If the guard's action was negligent as to those nearby, it was also negligent as to those outside what might be termed the "danger zone." For Palsgraf (P) to recover, R.R.'s (D) negligence must have been the proximate cause of her injury, a question of fact for the jury.

ANALYSIS

The majority defined the limit of the defendant's liability in terms of the danger that a reasonable person in defendant's situation would have perceived. The dissent argued that the limitation should not be placed on liability, but rather on damages. Judge Andrews suggested that only injuries that would not have happened but for R.R.'s (D) negligence should be compensable. Both the majority and dissent recognized the policy-driven need to limit liability for negligent acts, seeking, in the words of Judge Andrews, to define a framework "that will be practical and in keeping with the general understanding of mankind." The Restatement (Second) of Torts has accepted Judge Cardozo's view.

Quicknotes

FORESEEABILITY A reasonable expectation that change is the probable result of certain acts or omissions.

NEGLIGENCE Conduct falling below the standard of care that a reasonable person would demonstrate under similar conditions.

PROXIMATE CAUSE The natural sequence of events without which an injury would not have been sustained.

Party ID: Quick identification of the relationship between the parties.

Concurrence/Dissent: All concurrences and dissents are briefed whenever they are included by the casebook author.

Analysis: This last paragraph gives you a broad understanding of where the case "fits in" with other cases in the section of the book and with the entire course. It is a hornbook-style discussion indicating whether the case is a majority or minority opinion and comparing the principal case with other cases in the casebook. It may also provide analysis from restatements, uniform codes, and law review articles.

Holding and Decision: This section offers a clear and in-depth discussion of the rule of the case and the court's rationale. It is written in easy-to-understand language and answers the issue presented by applying the law to the facts of the case. When relevant, it includes a thorough discussion of the exceptions to the case as listed by the court, any major cites to the other cases on point, and the names of the judges who wrote the decisions.

Quicknotes: Conveniently defines legal terms found in the case.

Note to Students

Aspen Publishing is proud to offer *Casenote® Legal Briefs*—continuing thirty years of publishing America's best-selling legal briefs.

Casenote® Legal Briefs are designed to help you save time when briefing assigned cases. Organized under convenient headings, they show you how to abstract the basic facts and holdings from the text of the actual opinions handed down by the courts. Used as part of a rigorous study regimen, they can help you spend more time analyzing and critiquing points of law than on copying bits and pieces of judicial opinions into your notebook or outline.

Casenote® Legal Briefs should never be used as a substitute for assigned casebook readings. They work best when read as a follow-up to reviewing the underlying opinions themselves. Students who try to avoid reading and digesting the judicial opinions in their casebooks or online sources will end up shortchanging themselves in the long run. The ability to absorb, critique, and restate the dynamic and complex elements of case law decisions is crucial to your success in law school and beyond. It cannot be developed vicariously.

In addition to *Casenote® Legal Briefs*, Aspen Publishing offers the following study aids:

- *Casenote® Legal Briefs*
- *Emanuel Law Outlines®*
- Emanuel® *Law in a Flash Flash Cards*
- Emanuel *CrunchTime® Series*

Each of these series is designed to provide you with easy-to-understand explanations of complex points of law. Each volume offers guidance on the principles of legal analysis and, consulted regularly, will hone your ability to spot relevant issues. We have titles that will help you prepare for class, prepare for your exams, and enhance your general comprehension of the law along the way.

To find out more about our law school tools for success, visit us at *www.AspenPublishing.com* or e-mail us at *customer.service@aspenpublishing.com*. We'll be happy to assist you.

How to Brief a Case

A. Decide on a Format and Stick to It

Structure is essential to a good brief. It enables you to arrange systematically the related parts that are scattered throughout most cases, thus making manageable and understandable what might otherwise seem to be an endless and unfathomable sea of information. There are, of course, an unlimited number of formats that can be utilized. However, it is best to find one that suits your needs and stick to it. Consistency breeds both efficiency and the security that when called upon you will know where to look in your brief for the information you are asked to give.

Any format, as long as it presents the essential elements of a case in an organized fashion, can be used. Experience, however, has led *Casenote® Legal Briefs* to develop and utilize the following format because of its logical flow and universal applicability.

NATURE OF CASE: This is a brief statement of the legal character and procedural status of the case (e.g., "Appeal of a burglary conviction").

There are many different alternatives open to a litigant dissatisfied with a court ruling. The key to determining which one has been used is to discover *who is asking this court for what.*

This first entry in the brief should be kept as *short as possible.* Use the court's terminology if you understand it. But since jurisdictions vary as to the titles of pleadings, the best entry is the one that addresses who wants what in this proceeding, not the one that sounds most like the court's language.

RULE OF LAW: A statement of the general principle of law that the case illustrates (e.g., "An acceptance that varies any term of the offer is considered a rejection and counteroffer").

Determining the rule of law of a case is a procedure similar to determining the issue of the case. Avoid being fooled by red herrings; there may be a few rules of law mentioned in the case excerpt, but usually only one is *the* rule with which the casebook editor is concerned. The techniques used to locate the issue, described below, may also be utilized to find the rule of law. Generally, your best guide is simply the chapter heading. It is a clue to the point the casebook editor seeks to make and should be kept in mind when reading every case in the respective section.

FACTS: A synopsis of only the essential facts of the case, i.e., those bearing upon or leading up to the issue.

The facts entry should be a short statement of the events and transactions that led one party to initiate legal proceedings against another in the first place. While some cases conveniently state the salient facts at the beginning of the decision, in other instances they will have to be culled from hiding places throughout the text, even from concurring and dissenting opinions. Some of the "facts" will often be in dispute and should be so noted. Conflicting evidence may be briefly pointed up. "Hard" facts must be included. Both must be *relevant* in order to be listed in the facts entry. It is impossible to tell what is relevant until the entire case is read, as the ultimate determination of the rights and liabilities of the parties may turn on something buried deep in the opinion.

Generally, the facts entry should not be longer than three to five *short* sentences.

It is often helpful to identify the role played by a party in a given context. For example, in a construction contract case the identification of a party as the "contractor" or "builder" alleviates the need to tell that that party was the one who was supposed to have built the house.

It is always helpful, and a good general practice, to identify the "plaintiff" and the "defendant." This may seem elementary and uncomplicated, but, especially in view of the creative editing practiced by some casebook editors, it is sometimes a difficult or even impossible task. Bear in mind that the *party presently* seeking something from this court may not be the plaintiff, and that sometimes only the cross-claim of a defendant is treated in the excerpt. Confusing or misaligning the parties can ruin your analysis and understanding of the case.

ISSUE: A statement of the general legal question answered by or illustrated in the case. For clarity, the issue is best put in the form of a question capable of a "yes" or "no" answer. In reality, the issue is simply the Rule of Law put in the form of a question (e.g., "May an offer be accepted by performance?").

The major problem presented in discerning what is *the* issue in the case is that an opinion usually purports to raise and answer several questions. However, except for rare cases, only one such question is really the issue in the case. Collateral issues not necessary to the resolution of the matter in controversy are handled by the court by language known as *"obiter dictum"* or merely *"dictum."* While dicta may be included later in the brief, they have no place under the issue heading.

To find the issue, ask *who wants what* and then go on to ask *why did that party succeed or fail in getting it.* Once this is determined, the "why" should be turned into a question.

The complexity of the issues in the cases will vary, but in all cases a single-sentence question should sum up the issue. *In a few cases,* there will be two, or even more rarely, three issues of equal importance to the resolution of the case. Each should be expressed in a single-sentence question.

Since many issues are resolved by a court in coming to a final disposition of a case, the casebook editor will reproduce the portion of the opinion containing the issue or issues most relevant to the area of law under scrutiny. A noted law professor gave this advice: "Close the book; look at the title on the cover." Chances are, if it is Property, you need not concern yourself with whether, for example, the federal government's treatment of the plaintiff's land really raises a federal question sufficient to support jurisdiction on this ground in federal court.

The same rule applies to chapter headings designating sub-areas within the subjects. They tip you off as to what the text is designed to teach. The cases are arranged in a casebook to show a progression or development of the law, so that the preceding cases may also help.

It is also most important to remember to *read the notes and questions* at the end of a case to determine what the editors wanted you to have gleaned from it.

HOLDING AND DECISION: This section should succinctly explain the rationale of the court in arriving at its decision. In capsulizing the "reasoning" of the court, it should always include an application of the general rule or rules of law to the specific facts of the case. Hidden justifications come to light in this entry: the reasons for the state of the law, the public policies, the biases and prejudices, those considerations that influence the justices' thinking and, ultimately, the outcome of the case. At the end, there should be a short indication of the disposition or procedural resolution of the case (e.g., "Decision of the trial court for Mr. Smith (P) reversed").

The foregoing format is designed to help you "digest" the reams of case material with which you will be faced in your law school career. Once mastered by practice, it will place at your fingertips the information the authors of your casebooks have sought to impart to you in case-by-case illustration and analysis.

B. Be as Economical as Possible in Briefing Cases

Once armed with a format that encourages succinctness, it is as important to be economical with regard to the time spent on the actual reading of the case as it is to be economical in the writing of the brief itself. This does not mean "skimming" a case. Rather, it means reading the case with an "eye" trained to recognize into which "section" of your brief a particular passage or line fits and having a system for quickly and precisely marking the case so that the passages fitting any one particular part of the brief can be easily identified and brought together in a concise and accurate manner when the brief is actually written.

It is of no use to simply repeat everything in the opinion of the court; record only enough information to trigger your recollection of what the court said. Nevertheless, an accurate statement of the "law of the case," i.e., the legal principle applied to the facts, is absolutely essential to class preparation and to learning the law under the case method.

To that end, it is important to develop a "shorthand" that you can use to make marginal notations. These notations will tell you at a glance in which section of the brief you will be placing that particular passage or portion of the opinion.

Some students prefer to underline all the salient portions of the opinion (with a pencil or colored underliner marker), making marginal notations as they go along. Others prefer the color-coded method of underlining, utilizing different colors of markers to underline the salient portions of the case, each separate color being used to represent a different section of the brief. For example, blue underlining could be used for passages relating to the rule of law, yellow for those relating to the issue, and green for those relating to the holding and decision, etc. While it has its advocates, the color-coded method can be confusing and time-consuming (all that time spent on changing colored markers). Furthermore, it can interfere with the continuity and concentration many students deem essential to the reading of a case for maximum comprehension. In the end, however, it is a matter of personal preference and style. Just remember, whatever method you use, underlining must be used sparingly or its value is lost.

If you take the marginal notation route, an efficient and easy method is to go along underlining the key portions of the case and placing in the margin alongside them the following "markers" to indicate where a particular passage or line "belongs" in the brief you will write:

N	(NATURE OF CASE)
RL	(RULE OF LAW)
I	(ISSUE)
HL	(HOLDING AND DECISION, relates to the RULE OF LAW behind the decision)
HR	(HOLDING AND DECISION, gives the RATIONALE or reasoning behind the decision)
HA	(HOLDING AND DECISION, applies the general principle(s) of law to the facts of the case to arrive at the decision)

Remember that a particular passage may well contain information necessary to more than one part of your brief, in which case you simply note that in the margin. If you are using the color-coded underlining method instead of marginal notation, simply make asterisks or checks in the margin next to the passage in question in the colors that indicate the additional sections of the brief where it might be utilized.

The economy of utilizing "shorthand" in marking cases for briefing can be maintained in the actual brief writing process itself by utilizing "law student shorthand" within the brief. There are many commonly used words and phrases for which abbreviations can be substituted in your briefs (and in your class notes also). You can develop abbreviations that are personal to you and which will save you a lot of time. A reference list of briefing abbreviations can be found on page x of this book.

C. Use Both the Briefing Process and the Brief as a Learning Tool

Now that you have a format and the tools for briefing cases efficiently, the most important thing is to make the time spent in briefing profitable to you and to make the most advantageous use of the briefs you create. Of course, the briefs are invaluable for classroom reference when you are called upon to explain or analyze a particular case. However, they are also useful in reviewing for exams. A quick glance at the fact summary should bring the case to mind, and a rereading of the rule of law should enable you to go over the underlying legal concept in your mind, how it was applied in that particular case, and how it might apply in other factual settings.

As to the value to be derived from engaging in the briefing process itself, there is an immediate benefit that arises from being forced to sift through the essential facts and reasoning from the court's opinion and to succinctly express them in your own words in your brief. The process ensures that you understand the case and the point that it illustrates, and that means you will be ready to absorb further analysis and information brought forth in class. It also ensures you will have something to say when called upon in class. The briefing process helps develop a mental agility for getting to the *gist* of a case and for identifying, expounding on, and applying the legal concepts and issues found there. The briefing process is the mental process on which you must rely in taking law school examinations; it is also the mental process upon which lawyers rely in serving their clients and in making a living.

Abbreviations for Briefs

acceptance	acp
affirmed	aff
answer	ans
assumption of risk	a/r
attorney	atty
beyond a reasonable doubt	b/r/d
bona fide purchaser	BFP
breach of contract	br/k
cause of action	c/a
common law	c/l
Constitution	Con
constitutional	con
contract	K
contributory negligence	c/n
cross	x
cross-complaint	x/c
cross-examination	x/ex
cruel and unusual punishment	c/u/p
defendant	D
dismissed	dis
double jeopardy	d/j
due process	d/p
equal protection	e/p
equity	eq
evidence	ev
exclude	exc
exclusionary rule	exc/r
felony	f/n
freedom of speech	f/s
good faith	g/f
habeas corpus	h/c
hearsay	hr
husband	H
injunction	inj
in loco parentis	ILP
inter vivos	I/v
joint tenancy	j/t
judgment	judgt
jurisdiction	jur
last clear chance	LCC
long-arm statute	LAS
majority view	maj
meeting of minds	MOM
minority view	min
Miranda rule	Mir/r
Miranda warnings	Mir/w
negligence	neg
notice	ntc
nuisance	nus
obligation	ob
obscene	obs
offer	O
offeree	OE
offeror	OR
ordinance	ord
pain and suffering	p/s
parol evidence	p/e
plaintiff	P
prima facie	p/f
probable cause	p/c
proximate cause	px/c
real property	r/p
reasonable doubt	r/d
reasonable man	r/m
rebuttable presumption	rb/p
remanded	rem
res ipsa loquitur	RIL
respondeat superior	r/s
Restatement	RS
reversed	rev
Rule Against Perpetuities	RAP
search and seizure	s/s
search warrant	s/w
self-defense	s/d
specific performance	s/p
statute	S
statute of frauds	S/F
statute of limitations	S/L
summary judgment	s/j
tenancy at will	t/w
tenancy in common	t/c
tenant	t
third party	TP
third party beneficiary	TPB
transferred intent	TI
unconscionable	uncon
unconstitutional	unconst
undue influence	u/e
Uniform Commercial Code	UCC
unilateral	uni
vendee	VE
vendor	VR
versus	v
void for vagueness	VFV
weight of authority	w/a
weight of the evidence	w/e
wife	W
with	w/
within	w/i
without	w/o
without prejudice	w/o/p
wrongful death	wr/d

Table of Cases

CHAPTER 1

The Purposes and Limits of Punishment

Quick Reference Rules of Law

Kansas v. Hendricks

State (P) v. Child molester (D)

521 U.S. 346 (1997)

NATURE OF CASE: Certiorari review of a Kansas Supreme Court decision.

FACT SUMMARY: Kansas enacted a Sexually Violent Predator Act (the Act), which it invoked for the first time in committing Hendricks (D) to a mental hospital when he was scheduled for release from prison. The Kansas Supreme Court invalidated the Act. The United States Supreme Court granted certiorari review.

RULE OF LAW

A statute is constitutional if it provides for civil commitment and long-term treatment of persons who have been convicted of sexually violent offenses, who suffer from mental abnormalities or personality disorders that make them likely to engage in predatory behavior.

FACTS: Hendricks (D) had a long history of molesting children. He had been incarcerated on several occasions and, upon release, had molested more children. In 1984, he was convicted of "taking indecent liberties" with two teenaged boys. Hendricks (D) was scheduled for release after serving about ten years of his sentence, which was about the same time the Kansas Legislature passed the Sexually Violent Predator Act (the Act) to address repeat sexual offenders. His scheduled release prompted the State (P) to file a petition seeking his civil commitment under the Act. Hendricks (D) agreed with his diagnosis of pedophilia and did not believe he could be treated. A jury found beyond a reasonable doubt that Hendricks (D) was a sexually violent predator and Hendricks (D) appealed. The Kansas Supreme Court found that the Act was unconstitutional. The United States Supreme Court granted certiorari review.

ISSUE: Is a statute constitutional if it provides for civil commitment and long-term treatment of persons who have been convicted of sexually violent offenses, who suffer from mental abnormalities or personality disorders that make them likely to engage in predatory acts?

HOLDING AND DECISION: (Thomas, J.) Yes. A statute is constitutional if it provides for civil commitment and long-term treatment of persons who have been convicted of sexually violent offenses, who suffer from mental abnormalities or personality disorders that make them likely to engage in predatory behavior. Hendricks (D) first asserts the Sexually Violent Predator Act (the Act) violates substantive due process, but states can forcibly restrain persons who are a danger to society because of an inability to control behavior. Hendricks (D) next argues that the Act violates principles of double jeopardy. Specifically, he asserts that the Act provides for punishment of a prior crime for which he has previously served a prison sentence. The statute provides for civil commitment, and the legislative intent was not punitive but, rather, therapeutic in nature, so the Act is civil. Criminal punishment has retribution or deterrence as its primary objectives and the Act does not implicate either. Intent does not play a role in the Act, unlike a criminal statute, because the focus is on the "mental abnormality" instead of scienter. The threat of confinement would not deter a predator suffering from a "mental abnormality," so the Act is not a deterrent. Accordingly, principles of double jeopardy are not applicable. The Kansas Sexually Violent Predator Act does not violate principles of double jeopardy. Reversed.

ANALYSIS

The Kansas Sexually Violent Predator Act, in effect, supplements criminal penalties of sex offenders. It is imposed only after the criminal sentence is served. In cases where a person is convicted of a sexually violent crime and sentenced to life in prison, the statute is unnecessary. Therefore, it is debatable whether or not, as the dissent argues, Kansas's statute is actually a further criminal penalty in the guise of a civil commitment.

Quicknotes

CERTIORARI A discretionary writ issued by a superior court to an inferior court in order to review the lower court's decisions; the U.S. Supreme Court's writ ordering such review.

DOUBLE JEOPARDY A prohibition against a second prosecution for the same offense after an acquittal or conviction for that offense in a prior proceeding or against multiple punishments for the same offense.

SUBSTANTIVE DUE PROCESS A constitutional safeguard limiting the power of the state, irrespective of how fair its procedures may be; substantive limits placed on the power of the state.

Graham v. Florida

Juvenile convicted of armed burglary (D) v. State (P)

560 U.S. 48 (2010)

NATURE OF CASE: Appeal by a juvenile from the affirmance of the denial of his motion challenging a sentence of life without parole for armed burglary.

FACT SUMMARY: Graham (D), a juvenile, was convicted as an adult of various offenses, including armed burglary. After violating probation and committing new offenses, the trial court imposed a sentence of life without parole.

RULE OF LAW

The Constitution does not permit a juvenile offender to be sentenced to life in prison without parole for a nonhomicide crime.

FACTS: Graham (D), a juvenile, was charged as an adult for various offenses, including armed burglary, which carried a maximum sentence of life imprisonment without parole, and attempted armed robbery, which carried a 15-year term. Graham (D) pleaded guilty and the trial court withheld the adjudication of guilt. The court sentenced Graham (D) to concurrent three-year terms of probation. After spending the first 12 months in jail, he was released and subsequently violated probation within six months by committing new offenses. Graham (D) was then re-arrested and the trial court that adjudicated guilt for his prior crimes sentenced him to life imprisonment without parole for the armed burglary and 15 years for the attempted armed robbery. Graham (D) filed a motion challenging the sentence of life imprisonment without parole, on the grounds that it violated the "proportionality test" under the Eighth Amendment. The motion was denied. The state's intermediate appellate court affirmed and its highest court denied review. The United States Supreme Court granted certiorari.

ISSUE: Does the Constitution permit a juvenile offender to be sentenced to life in prison without parole for a nonhomicide crime?

HOLDING AND DECISION: (Kennedy, J.) No. The Constitution does not permit a juvenile offender to be sentenced to life in prison without parole for a nonhomicide crime. The Eighth Amendment's prohibition against cruel or unusual punishment is measured by "evolving standards of decency that mark the progress of a maturing society." *Estelle v. Gamble*, 429 U.S. 349, 367 (1910). The concept of "proportionality" is central to the Eighth Amendment so that the punishment for a crime is graduated and proportioned to the offense. Addressing the proportionality of sentences falls within two general classifications. The first involves challenges to the length of term-of-years for sentences given consideration to the circumstances in a particular case. The second generally comprises the proportionality standard by certain categorical restrictions on the death penalty. In the first classification, a review of all of the circumstances of the case is necessary to determine whether the sentence is unconstitutionally excessive. Under this approach, if a comparison of a defendant's sentence with the sentences received by other offenders in the same jurisdiction and those imposed for the same crime in other jurisdictions is "grossly disproportionate," then the defendant's sentence is cruel and unusual. For example, a term of life without parole for a defendant's seventh nonviolent felony of passing a worthless check was found to be unconstitutional. Similarly, a sentence of 25 years to life for the theft of a few golf clubs was grossly disproportionate. The second classification uses categorical rules to define Eighth Amendment standards. In previous cases involving the death penalty, two subsets were considered. One subset measured the nature of the offense, and the other subset considered the characteristics of the offender. Capital punishment is impermissible for some nonhomicide crimes against individuals. Where the characteristics of the offender are that the person is below the age of 18 or that their intellectual functioning is in a low range, a life without parole sentence is not allowed. Two considerations are made: first, whether the "objective indicia of society's standards, as expressed in legislative enactments and state practice" determines whether or not there is a national consensus and, second, if the Court's own independent judgment concludes that such a punishment violates the Constitution. *Roper v. Simmons*, 543 U.S. 551, 563-64 (2005).

With regard to Graham (D), sentences of life without parole for a juvenile nonhomicide offender are permitted in some jurisdictions and there is no national consensus against it. However, a comparison of actual sentencing practices suggests that in proportion to the opportunities to impose life without parole, such sentences for juveniles convicted of nonhomicide crimes are rare.

In the judicial exercise of independent judgment, the inquiry focuses on the consideration of the culpability of the offenders in light of the crime and characteristics, along with the severity of the punishment in question and whether the punishment serves legitimate penological goals. Legitimate goals, such as retribution, deterrence, incapacitation, and rehabilitation are justifiable. However, a sentence of life without parole does not

Continued on next page.

serve the desired deterrence for juveniles like Graham (D) who lack maturity and are impulsive. Incapacitation does not apply because a determination that a juvenile is forever incorrigible is questionable. Likewise, a sentence of life imprisonment without parole is inconsistent with the goal of rehabilitation. For someone like Graham (D) the State (P) must give some meaningful opportunity to obtain release based on demonstrated maturity and rehabilitation. A sentence of life without parole for a juvenile convicted of a nonhomicide offense is, therefore, grossly disproportionate, cruel and unusual, and unconstitutional. Reversed and remanded.

ANALYSIS

In *Graham*, the Court continued the trend in treating minors and mentally challenged individuals differently, disavowing life imprisonment for nonhomicide offenses. In reviewing the proportionality test, the Court took note of actual sentencing trends and the goals of sentencing to determine that convicted juvenile offenders should be given an opportunity to gain release at some point in the future.

Quicknotes

CRUEL AND UNUSUAL PUNISHMENT Punishment that is excessive or disproportionate to the offense committed; it is prohibited by the Eighth Amendment to the United States Constitution.

Kennedy v. Louisiana

Convicted child rapist (P) v. State (D)

554 U.S. 407 (2008)

NATURE OF CASE: Appeal of a sentence of death that resulted from a conviction for rape of a child.

FACT SUMMARY: Kennedy (P) was convicted of the aggravated rape of his then eight-year-old stepdaughter, which did not result in her death. Kennedy (P) was sentenced to death under the applicable state law, which was challenged as unconstitutional.

RULE OF LAW

The Constitution bars a convicted offender from being sentenced to death for the rape of a child where the crime did not result, and was not intended to result, in the death of the victim.

FACTS: Petitioner Kennedy was charged with the aggravated rape of his then eight-year-old stepdaughter. The victim's injuries required emergency surgery, but did not result in her death. After a jury trial, Kennedy (P) was convicted and sentenced to death under a state statute authorizing capital punishment for the rape of a child under 12 years of age. The conviction was affirmed by the state's highest court, and the United States Supreme Court granted certiorari.

ISSUE: Does the Constitution bar a convicted offender from being sentenced to death for the rape of a child where the crime did not result, and was not intended to result, in the death of the victim?

HOLDING AND DECISION: (Kennedy, J.) Yes. The Constitution bars a convicted offender from being sentenced to death for the rape of a child where the crime did not result, and was not intended to result, in the death of the victim. A capital punishment must be limited to those offenders who commit a narrow category of the most serious crimes and whose extreme culpability makes them the most deserving of execution. Guidance is taken by "objective indicia of society's standards, as expressed in legislative enactments and state practice with respect to executions." *Roper v. Simmons*, 543 U.S. 551, 563 (2005). Whether the death penalty is disproportionate to the crime committed depends as well upon the standards elaborated by the Court's own understanding and interpretation of the Eighth Amendment. The Eighth Amendment prohibits cruel and unusual punishment. One such standard is whether there is evidence of a national consensus with respect to the death penalty for child rapists. A review shows that there have been no executions for the rape of an adult or child since 1964, and no execution for any other nonhomicide offense has been conducted since 1963. While one state (Louisiana) has sentenced one individual to death for the crime of child rape, there is no national consensus to justify a sentence of death for such a nonhomicide offense. While there are moral grounds to permit the imposition of a death sentence for nonhomicide offenses that result in the victim's fright, the sense of betrayal, and the nature of their injuries that cause prolonged physical and mental suffering, consistent with evolving standards of decency, there is a distinction between intentional first-degree murder on the one hand and nonhomicide crimes against individual persons, even including child rape, on the other hand. Permitting executions for child rape is grossly out of proportion to the crime and does not fulfill the two distinct social purposes, the goals of retribution and deterrence. Forcing such a long-term commitment on child victims to testify in multiple proceedings creates an unfair moral choice and is burdensome. The consequence of a death sentence would increase the risk of the nonreporting of child rape, particularly those committed by family members, and therefore does not serve the goals of deterrence or more effective enforcement. Reversed.

ANALYSIS

The Court found that capital punishment is excessive and focused on the penological goals of retribution and deterrence. While concerned that a sentence of death for a nonhomicide crime was permitted in some instances, the Court noted that the death penalty may not result in more effective enforcement, but may add to the risk of nonreporting of child rape out of fear of negative consequences for the perpetrator, especially if the perpetrator is a family member. Thus, to impose capital punishment in such a case, at least according to the Court, likely would further neither prevention of child rape, nor the child victim's interests.

Quicknotes

CAPITAL PUNISHMENT Punishment by death.

FIRST-DEGREE MURDER The willful killing of a person with deliberation and premeditation; first-degree murder also encompasses those situations in which a person is killed within the perpetration of, or attempt to perpetrate, specified felonies.

Ewing v. California

Convicted felon (D) v. State (P)

538 U.S. 11 (2003)

NATURE OF CASE: Appeal from conviction under a "three strikes" law.

FACT SUMMARY: When Ewing (D) was sentenced to 25 years to life for stealing three golf clubs, under California's "three strikes" law, he argued that such a sentence violated the Eighth Amendment's prohibition against cruel and unusual punishment.

RULE OF LAW

The Eighth Amendment does not prohibit a state from sentencing a repeat felon to a prison term of 25 years to life under the state's "Three Strikes and You're Out" law.

FACTS: On parole from a nine-year prison term, Gary Ewing (D) walked into the pro shop of a golf course and walked out with three golf clubs, priced at $399 apiece, concealed in his pants leg. He was convicted of one count of felony grand theft of personal property in excess of $400. Ewing (D) had been convicted previously of four serious or violent felonies for three prior burglaries and a robbery in an apartment complex. As a newly convicted felon with two or more serious or violent felony convictions in his past, Ewing (D) was convicted under California's newly enacted "three strikes law" to 25 years to life. He appealed, arguing that the sentence violated the Eighth Amendment prohibition against cruel and unusual punishment in that the sentence was grossly disproportionate to his crime.

ISSUE: Does the Eighth Amendment prohibit a state from sentencing a repeat felon to a prison term of 25 years to life under the state's "Three Strikes and You're Out" law?

HOLDING AND DECISION: (O'Connor, J.) No. The Eighth Amendment does not prohibit a state from sentencing a repeat felon to a prison term of 25 years to life under the state's "Three Strikes and You're Out" law. Ewing's (D) sentence is justified by the state's public safety interest in incapacitating and deterring recidivist felons, and amply supported by his own long, serious criminal record. To be sure, his sentence is a long one. However, it reflects a rational legislative judgment, entitled to deference, that offenders who have committed serious or violent felonies and who continue to commit felonies must be incapacitated. This is not the rare case in which the threshold comparison of the crime committed and the sentence imposed leads to an inference of gross disproportionality. In weighing the gravity of Ewing's (D) offense, the Court must place on the scales not only his current felony, but also his long history of felony recidivism. Any other approach would fail to accord proper deference to the policy judgments that find expression in the legislature's choice of sanctions. The Eighth Amendment does not require strict proportionality between crime and sentence. Rather, it forbids only extreme sentences that are grossly disproportionate to the crime. Conviction affirmed.

ANALYSIS

In *Ewing*, the Supreme Court pointed out that although three strikes laws are relatively new, the Court's tradition of deferring to state legislatures in making and implementing such important policy decisions is longstanding. This traditional deference to legislative policy choices finds a corollary in the principle that the Constitution does not mandate adoption of any one penological theory.

Quicknotes

CRUEL AND UNUSUAL PUNISHMENT Punishment that is excessive or disproportionate to the offense committed; it is prohibited by the Eighth Amendment to the United States Constitution.

Miller v. Alabama

Juvenile convicted of murder (D) v. State (P)

567 U.S. 460 (2012)

NATURE OF CASE: Appeal in consolidated cases from judgments affirming the mandatory sentencing of juveniles to life without parole for murder.

FACT SUMMARY: Miller (D) and Jackson (D), 14-year olds convicted of murder and sentenced to a mandatory term of life imprisonment without the possibility of parole, contended that because the sentencing authority was prevented from considering a juvenile's "lessened culpability" and greater "capacity for change," the sentencing scheme violated the Eighth Amendment.

RULE OF LAW

The Eighth Amendment forbids a sentencing scheme that mandates life in prison without possibility of parole for homicide offenders who are under the age of 18.

FACTS: Miller (D) and Jackson (D), 14-year olds each convicted of committing murder after a botched robbery, were each sentenced to a mandatory term of life imprisonment without the possibility of parole. State law mandated that each juvenile die in prison even if a judge or jury would have thought that his youth and its attendant characteristics, along with the nature of his crime, made a lesser sentence (for example, life with the possibility of parole) more appropriate. They contended that because the sentencing authority was prevented from considering a juvenile's "lessened culpability" and greater "capacity for change," the sentencing scheme violated the Eighth Amendment. Their appeals at the state level were denied, and the United States Supreme Court consolidated the cases and granted certiorari.

ISSUE: Does the Eighth Amendment forbid a sentencing scheme that mandates life in prison without possibility of parole for homicide offenders who are under the age of 18?

HOLDING AND DECISION: (Kagan, J.) Yes. The Eighth Amendment forbids a sentencing scheme that mandates life in prison without possibility of parole for homicide offenders who are under the age of 18. *Graham v. Florida,* 560 U.S. 48 (2010), held that the Eighth Amendment prohibits a sentence of life without the possibility of parole for a juvenile convicted of a nonhomicide offense. *Graham* reasoned that juveniles are constitutionally different from adults, both in their mental capacities and their susceptibility to environmental influences. *Graham*'s reasoning as to the nature of juveniles was not crime-specific, however, and that reasoning applies to any life-without-parole sentence for a juvenile, even as *Graham*'s categorical bar relates only to nonhomicide offenses. Most fundamentally, *Graham* insists that youth matters in determining the appropriateness of a lifetime of incarceration without the possibility of parole. The mandatory penalty schemes at issue here, however, prevent the sentencer from considering youth and from assessing whether the law's harshest term of imprisonment proportionately punishes a juvenile offender. This contravenes *Graham*'s foundational principle: that imposition of a state's most severe penalties on juvenile offenders cannot proceed as though they were not children. *Graham* also likened life-without-parole sentences for juveniles to the death penalty. By doing so, *Graham* makes relevant the Court's cases demanding individualized sentencing in capital cases. In particular, those cases have emphasized that sentencers must be able to consider the mitigating qualities of youth. In imposing a state's harshest penalties, a sentencer misses too much if he treats every child as an adult, and by making youth (and all that accompanies it) irrelevant to imposition of that harshest prison sentence, such a scheme poses too great a risk of disproportionate punishment. Reversed.

ANALYSIS

The Court emphasized that because its holding disposed of the cases at bar, it did not need to consider Jackson's (D) and Miller's (D) alternative argument that the Eighth Amendment requires a categorical bar on life without parole for juveniles, or at least, for those age 14 and younger. The Court added that, given its decisions emphasizing children's diminished culpability and heightened capacity for change, it believed that appropriate occasions for sentencing juveniles to this harshest possible penalty would be uncommon, especially given the great difficulty of distinguishing at this early age between the juvenile offender whose crime reflects unfortunate yet transient immaturity, and the rare juvenile offender whose crime reflects irreparable corruption.

Quicknotes

EIGHTH AMENDMENT The Eighth Amendment to the federal constitution prohibits the imposition of excessive bail, fines, and cruel and unusual punishment.

CHAPTER 2

The Criminal Act

Quick Reference Rules of Law

Proctor v. State

Property owner (D) v. State (P)

Okla. Ct. Crim. App., 176 P. 771 (1918)

NATURE OF CASE: Appeal from conviction of violating alcoholic beverage control laws.

FACT SUMMARY: Proctor (D) was convicted of keeping a dwelling with the intent of selling alcoholic beverages there.

RULE OF LAW

A criminal conviction requires an overt illegal act.

FACTS: Proctor (D) was charged with keeping a place with the intent of selling alcoholic beverages there, in contravention of state laws. Neither Proctor (D) nor the state alleged that he actually sold liquor there. Proctor (D) was convicted, and he appealed.

ISSUE: Does a criminal conviction require an overt illegal act?

HOLDING AND DECISION: (Galbraith, J.) Yes. A criminal conviction requires an overt illegal act. It is basic to the criminal justice system that criminal intent alone is insufficient to convict a person. Some sort of illegal act must be performed in furtherance of the intent. Here, all Proctor (D) did was "keep a place." He did not actually perform any illegal activity there. "The keeping of a place" with the unlawful purpose and intent to sell, barter, or give away intoxicating liquors cannot be declared to be a crime for the reason that such an act, although connected with an unlawful intent, still lacks an essential element necessary to constitute a crime under the law, in this, that the statute fails to connect such unlawful intent with any overt act, as a result or consequence, and further fails to charge the possession of the liquors, the very means essential to the consummation of the unlawful purpose to violate the prohibitory law, and therefore the statute under consideration does not define a crime. The information in the instant case did not charge an offense, and the demurrer thereto was well taken and should have been sustained. Since Proctor (D) performed no illegal act, the statute under which he was convicted is invalid, and the conviction must be vacated and the case remanded, with the direction to the trial court to discharge the accused.

ANALYSIS

It is a universal requirement in criminal law that an act is required for a crime to be committed. The reasons for this seem obvious: (1) the difficulty of proving intent without an act, and (2) the fact that criminal law is meant to shape conduct. The problem, of course, is defining exactly what constitutes an act.

Quicknotes

OVERT ACT An open act evidencing an intention to commit a crime.

Jones v. United States

Convicted murderer (D) v. Federal government (P)

308 F.2d 307 (D.C. Cir. 1962)

NATURE OF CASE: Appeal from conviction for involuntary manslaughter.

FACT SUMMARY: Jones (D) was found guilty of the involuntary manslaughter of Green, a 10-month-old baby belonging to Shirley Green, who placed her baby in Jones's (D) care.

RULE OF LAW

Under some circumstances, the omission of a legal duty owed by one individual to another, where such omission results in the death of the one to whom the duty is owed, will make the other chargeable with manslaughter.

FACTS: Anthony Green, the 10-month-old illegitimate child of Shirley Green, was placed in the care of Jones (D), a family friend. The baby died of neglect and malnutrition. Jones (D) was convicted of involuntary manslaughter. There was a conflict in the evidence over whether Jones (D) was paid to take care of the baby. Medical evidence clearly showed the baby to have been shockingly neglected. Jones (D) had ample means to provide food and medical care. Jones (D) took exception to the trial court's failure to instruct the jury that it must find beyond a reasonable doubt that, as an element of the case, she was under a legal duty to provide for the baby.

ISSUE: Under some circumstances, will omission of a legal duty owed by one individual to another, where such omission results in the death of the one to whom the duty is owed, make the other chargeable with manslaughter?

HOLDING AND DECISION: (Wright, J.) Yes. Under some circumstances, the omission of a legal duty owed by one individual to another, where such omission results in the death of the one to whom the duty is owed, will make the other chargeable with manslaughter. The duty must be imposed by law or contract. The omission must be the immediate cause of death. Breach of a legal duty can arise in four situations: (1) where a statute imposes the duty; (2) where one is in a certain status relationship to another; (3) where one has assumed a contractual duty to care for another; and (4) where one has voluntarily assumed the care of another. Whether Jones (D) fits any of those four situations is a question for the jury. Evidence was in conflict particularly on the third and fourth situations. Failure to instruct the jury on a critical element of the crime requires a reversal of the conviction with the matter to be remanded for a new trial.

ANALYSIS

A tentative draft of the Model Penal Code dealing with the issue confronted in the instant case states, "Liability for the commission of an offense may not be based on an omission unaccompanied by action unless: (a) the omission is expressly made sufficient by the law defining the offense; or (b) a duty to perform the omitted act is otherwise imposed by law." M.P.C., Tent. Draft No. 4 (1955), §2.01(3). Here, whether there was a duty was an element of the crime. Failure to find beyond a reasonable doubt on any element of a crime prohibits a conviction. Note that the duty must be legal, not merely moral.

Quicknotes

INVOLUNTARY MANSLAUGHTER The killing of another person without premeditation or deliberation or with the intent to kill or to commit a felony, which may be reasonably expected to result in death or serious bodily injury; involuntary manslaughter is characterized by reckless conduct in the commission of a lawful act, or by the commission of an unlawful act that is not a felony, but which leads to the killing of another.

LEGAL DUTY TO ACT The duty to take some action to assist another in danger; such a duty is only imposed under certain circumstances, such as in accordance with a statute, contract, or relationship between the parties; when the defendant voluntarily assumes responsibility for care of the victim; or if the defendant creates the circumstances placing the victim in danger.

OMISSION The failure to perform an act or obligation that one is required to perform by law.

REASONABLE DOUBT Enough doubt on the part of a fact-finder to acquit a defendant based on the absence of evidence.

United States v. Maldonado

Federal government (P) v. Cocaine distributor (D)

23 F.3d 4 (1st Cir. 1994)

NATURE OF CASE: Appeal from conviction for cocaine possession.

FACT SUMMARY: When cocaine was found in Maldonado's (Zavala's) (D) hotel room, he argued there was insufficient evidence that he "possessed" the cocaine within the meaning of federal drug legislation.

RULE OF LAW

A person with cocaine in the person's room constructively "possesses" the cocaine where the person's knowledge of its existence can reasonably be inferred.

FACTS: Santos, a seaman acting on behalf of federal customs agents, went to a hotel in Puerto Rico with drugs (being tracked by the agents) and asked at the desk for Palestino, the suspected dealer. The desk clerk called the room, and Rafael Angel Zavala Maldonado (Zavala) (D) came to the lobby and took Santos to the hotel room. There, Santos (who had the drugs in a bag with him) told Zavala (D) he had the drugs for Palestino. Zavala (D) told Santos he was a friend of Palestino and would have Palestino come to the hotel. While waiting for Palestino's arrival, Santos placed the bag in the closet of the room, and both Santos and Zavala (D) intended to leave the hotel for a while. However, when they reached the corridor, they were detained by the supervising customs agent and ultimately arrested. Zavala (D) was tried and convicted for possession of cocaine with intent to distribute. He appealed, arguing there was insufficient evidence he was in "possession" of cocaine, within the meaning of the drug statute.

ISSUE: Does a person with cocaine in the person's room constructively "possess" the cocaine where the person's knowledge of its existence can reasonably be inferred?

HOLDING AND DECISION: (Boudin, J.) Yes. A person with cocaine in the person's room constructively "possesses" the cocaine where the person's knowledge of its existence can reasonably be inferred. Constructive possession is the power and intention to exercise control, or dominion and control, over an object not in one's actual possession. One can constructively possess an object while it is hidden at home in a bureau drawer, or while held by an agent, or even while it is secured in a safe deposit box at the bank. Here, although Zavala (D) arguably did not even constructively possess the cocaine while he and Santos were in the hotel room together, once both parties departed from the room leaving the drugs inside, the situation altered. First, Santos surrendered his actual possession of the drugs. Second, with the acquiescence of both parties, the drugs were secured in Zavala's (D) room. In the context of this factual setting, a jury could reasonably have found both requisites of constructive possession: Zavala (D) had sufficient power to control the drugs and an intention to exercise that power. Clearly, the drugs were left in his room with his knowledge and consent while he was awaiting the arrival of an accomplice to pay for them. Zavala's (D) intention to have the drugs stored in his room, incident to their intended transfer to a confederate, is an intention intimately related to his power to control the drugs. Conviction affirmed.

ANALYSIS

The location of drugs or firearms in a defendant's home or car is a common basis for attributing possession to the defendant. As the *Maldonado* case illustrates, this is so even if the residence or room is shared by others. The cases do not, however, say that possession is automatic, but rather that the location of the object in a domain especially accessible to the defendant can (at least where knowledge is admitted or inferred) be enough to permit the jury to find possession.

Quicknotes

POSSESSION The holding of property with the right of disposition.

State v. Barger

State (P) v. Child pornographer (D)

Or. Sup. Ct., 247 P.3d 309 (2011)

NATURE OF CASE: Appeal from conviction for possession of child pornography, based on the trial court's failure to grant the defendant's motion for judgment of acquittal.

FACT SUMMARY: Barger (D) was convicted of possessing child pornography after a search of his computer found images in the temporary Internet cache. These images, which were not saved to his computer, were nevertheless accessible to Barger (D).

RULE OF LAW

A person may not be found guilty of possessing or controlling digital images of sexually explicit conduct involving a child based on evidence showing only that the person searched for and found such images through the Internet on their computer.

FACTS: In the course of investigating a report that Barger (D) had sexually abused a child, the police conducted a search of his computer. Pornographic images of children were discovered on Barger's (D) computer in the temporary Internet cache, which stores web pages from sites visited by the user. These images were not found saved to the computer's hard drive. Barger's (D) motion for judgment of acquittal at the end of State's (P) case was denied, and a jury convicted him. The conviction was affirmed by the Oregon Court of Appeals.

ISSUE: May a person be found guilty of possessing or controlling digital images of sexually explicit conduct involving a child based on evidence showing only that the person searched for and found such images through the Internet on their computer?

HOLDING AND DECISION: (Dyke, J.) No. A person may not be found guilty of possessing or controlling digital images of sexually explicit conduct involving a child based on evidence showing only that the person searched for and found such images through the Internet on their computer. The statute in question requires something more than simply accessing and looking at incorporeal material of the kind involved here to "possess" or "control" that material. While Barger's (D) computer demonstrated that someone had accessed three websites and that all appeared to contain prohibited child pornography, there was no evidence than any such images had been purposefully copied and saved in any user's personal files. Computer users with ordinary skills would not necessarily be aware of the function to recall images or know how to go about accessing information stored in the temporary Internet file cache. The intangible nature of a web image is analogous to seeing something that a visitor has temporarily placed in one's own home. One may be aware of it, may even have asked the visitor to bring it for viewing, but one does not thereby possess the item. There is no support for the idea that a mere unexercised ability to manipulate a thing such as to direct or influence an image constitutes constructive possession. The argument that the mere ability to cause an item to appear on a computer screen is sufficient to constitute "control" or constructive "possession" of the item would improperly imply that any person who uses the Internet (and, indeed, any person who is within physical reach of some tangible item of child pornography) can be deemed to be guilty of violating that statute, at least insofar as the element of possession or control is involved. The statute embodies a considered legislative choice not to criminalize the mere "obtaining" or "viewing" of child pornography without consideration. Thus, the acts at issue here (navigating to a website and bringing the images that the site contains to a computer screen) are not acts that the legislature intended to criminalize. The Defendant's motion for a judgment of acquittal should have been granted. Reversed.

ANALYSIS

The court found that a computer user's act of accessing an Internet web page and intentionally calling digital images of child sexual abuse onto a computer screen did not constitute possession or control of those images within the meaning of that statute. The mere ability to access prohibited child pornography does not equal constructive possession.

Quicknotes

POSSESSION The holding of property with the right of disposition.

Lawrence v. Texas

Homosexual convicted of deviate sexual intercourse (D) v. State (P)

539 U.S. 558 (2003)

NATURE OF CASE: Appeal from conviction of deviate sexual intercourse.

FACT SUMMARY: Lawrence (D) and Garner (D), men who were convicted of engaging in deviate sexual intercourse, argued that the state statute that criminalized sexual intimacy between adult members of the same sex violated their rights to equal protection and due process under the Constitution.

RULE OF LAW

A statute making it a crime for two adult persons of the same sex to engage in certain consensual intimate sexual conduct violates the Due Process Clause.

FACTS: Responding to a reported weapons disturbance in a private residence, police entered Lawrence's (D) apartment and saw him and another adult man, Garner (D), engaging in a private, consensual sexual act (anal sex). They were arrested and convicted of deviate sexual intercourse in violation of a Texas statute forbidding two persons of the same sex to engage in certain intimate sexual conduct involving any contact between any part of the genitals of one person and the mouth or anus of another person, or the penetration of the genitals or the anus of another person with an object. In affirming, the state court of appeals held, inter alia, that the statute was not unconstitutional under the Due Process Clause of the Fourteenth Amendment. The court considered *Bowers v. Hardwick*, 478 U.S. 186 (1986), controlling on that point. The United States Supreme Court granted certiorari.

ISSUE: Does a statute making it a crime for two adult persons of the same sex to engage in certain consensual intimate sexual conduct violate the Due Process Clause?

HOLDING AND DECISION: (Kennedy, J.) Yes. A statute making it a crime for two adult persons of the same sex to engage in certain consensual intimate sexual conduct violates the Due Process Clause. Resolution of this case depends on whether Lawrence (D) and Garner (D) were free as adults to engage in private conduct in the exercise of their liberty under the Due Process Clause. For this inquiry, it is necessary to reconsider the *Bowers* holding. The *Bowers* Court's initial substantive statement—"The issue presented is whether the Federal Constitution confers a fundamental right upon homosexuals to engage in sodomy . . . ," *Bowers*, at 190—discloses the Court's failure to appreciate the extent of the liberty at stake. To say that the issue in *Bowers* was simply the right to engage in certain sexual conduct demeans the claim the individual put forward, just as it would demean a married couple were it said that marriage is only about the right to have sexual intercourse. Although the laws in *Bowers* and here purport to do no more than prohibit a particular sexual act, their penalties and purposes have more far-reaching consequences, involving the most private human conduct, sexual behavior, and in the most private of places, the home. They seek to control a personal relationship that, whether or not entitled to formal recognition in the law, is within the liberty of persons to choose without being punished as criminals. The liberty protected by the Constitution allows homosexual persons the right to choose to enter upon relationships in the confines of their homes and their own private lives and still retain their dignity as free persons.

Having misapprehended the liberty claim presented to it, the Court in *Bowers* stated that proscriptions against sodomy have ancient roots. It should be noted, however, that there is no long-standing history in this country of laws directed at homosexual conduct as a distinct matter. Early American sodomy laws were not directed at homosexuals as such, but instead sought to prohibit nonprocreative sexual activity more generally, whether between men and women or men and men. Moreover, early sodomy laws seem not to have been enforced against consenting adults acting in private. Instead, sodomy prosecutions often involved predatory acts against those who could not or did not consent: relations between men and minor girls or boys, between adults involving force, between adults implicating disparity in status, or between men and animals. The long-standing criminal prohibition of homosexual sodomy upon which *Bowers* placed such reliance is as consistent with a general condemnation of nonprocreative sex as it is with an established tradition of prosecuting acts because of their homosexual character. Far from possessing "ancient roots," American laws targeting same-sex couples did not develop until the last third of the 20th century. Even now, only nine states have singled out same-sex relations for criminal prosecution. Thus, the historical grounds relied upon in *Bowers* are more complex than the majority opinion and the concurring opinion by Chief Justice Burger there indicated. They are not without doubt and, at the very least, are overstated. In *Bowers*, the Court was, of course, making the broader point that for centuries there have been powerful voices to condemn homosexual conduct as immoral, but this Court's obligation is to define the

Continued on next page.

liberty of all, not to mandate its own moral code. The nation's laws and traditions in the past half century are most relevant here. They show an emerging awareness that liberty gives substantial protection to adult persons in deciding how to conduct their private lives in matters pertaining to sex.

Bowers's deficiencies became even more apparent in the years following its announcement. The 25 states with laws prohibiting the conduct referenced in *Bowers* are reduced now to 13, of which four enforce their laws only against homosexual conduct. In those states, including Texas, that still proscribe sodomy (whether for same-sex or heterosexual conduct), there is a pattern of nonenforcement with respect to consenting adults acting in private. One of the cases decided after *Bowers*, *Planned Parenthood of Southeastern Pa. v. Casey*, 505 U.S. 833, confirmed that the Due Process Clause protects personal decisions relating to marriage, procreation, contraception, family relationships, child rearing, and education. The heart of liberty involves a person's autonomy in making those intimate and personal decisions. Here, the petitioners seek a right integral to human freedom in other countries, and this country fails to show a legitimate governmental interest in denying them that right. The private sexual conduct here is not a crime. Reversed and remanded.

ANALYSIS

Only 17 years elapsed between the time *Bowers v. Hardwick*, 478 U.S. 186 (1986), was decided and this case. As Justice Scalia pointed out in his dissent, social perceptions of sexual and other morality change over time. With regard to homosexual intimacy, the change occurred rapidly, rendering the dissenting views in *Bowers* the prevailing view in this case. The dissent in *Bowers* argued for the recognition of an expansive fundamental right that "all individuals have in controlling the nature of their intimate associations with others," and Justice Blackmun in his dissent argued that there is a fundamental right of an individual to conduct intimate relationships in the intimacy of the individual's own home. It seems that it is these rights that the Court implicitly found were "fundamental," not, as Scalia emphasizes, that homosexual sodomy is per se a fundamental right.

Quicknotes

DUE PROCESS CLAUSE Clauses, found in the Fifth and Fourteenth Amendments to the United States Constitution, providing that no person shall be deprived of "life, liberty, or property, without due process of law."

EQUAL PROTECTION CLAUSE A constitutional provision that each person be guaranteed the same protection of the laws enjoyed by other persons in like circumstances.

FOURTEENTH AMENDMENT Declares that no state shall make or enforce any law that shall abridge the privileges and immunities of citizens of the United States. No state shall deny to any person within its jurisdiction the equal protection of the laws.

RATIONAL BASIS REVIEW A test employed by the court to determine the validity of a statute in equal protection actions, whereby the court determines whether the challenged statute is rationally related to the achievement of a legitimate state interest.

STARE DECISIS Doctrine whereby courts follow legal precedent unless there is good cause for departure.

Martin v. State

Public drunk (D) v. State (P)

Ala. Ct. App., 17 So. 2d 427 (1944)

NATURE OF CASE: Appeal from conviction for public drunkenness.

FACT SUMMARY: When Martin (D) was taken from his home by the police and placed onto a public highway, then charged with being drunk in public, he argued he could not be found guilty of the crime since he was involuntarily taken to the public highway.

RULE OF LAW

Under a public drunkenness statute, a voluntary appearance by the accused is presupposed.

FACTS: Police officers arrested Martin (D) at his home and took him onto a public highway where he manifested a drunken condition by using loud and profane language. Martin (D) was convicted for public intoxication and appealed, arguing that the police had involuntarily taken him to the public place.

ISSUE: Under a public drunkenness statute, is a voluntary appearance by the accused presupposed?

HOLDING AND DECISION: (Simpson, J.) Yes. Under a public drunkenness statute, a voluntary appearance by the accused is presupposed. The pertinent provisions of the statute here at issue are that any person who, while intoxicated or drunk, appears in any public place where one or more persons are present and manifests a drunken condition by boisterous or indecent conduct, or loud and profane discourse, shall, on conviction, be fined. Under the plain terms of this statute, a voluntary appearance is presupposed. The sound rule is that an accusation of drunkenness in a designated public place cannot be established by proof that the accused, while in an intoxicated condition, was, as here, involuntarily and forcibly carried to that place by the arresting officer. Conviction reversed.

ANALYSIS

The Model Penal Code §2.01(1) provides that a person is not guilty of an offense unless their liability is based on conduct that includes a voluntary act. The point is that the criminal law cannot hope to deter involuntary behavior thus cannot deter any crime by making an individual liable for actions they cannot control.

People v. Grant

State (P) v. Epileptic (D)

Ill. App. Ct., 360 N.E.2d 809 (1977)

NATURE OF CASE: Appeal of conviction of aggravated battery.

FACT SUMMARY: Grant (D), an epileptic prone to violent episodes, attempted to assault an officer making an arrest.

RULE OF LAW

A person is not criminally responsible for their acts if they have no conscious control over them.

FACTS: Grant (D) suffered from psychomotor epilepsy, which inclined him toward seizures and violent outbursts. While watching an arrest outside a tavern, Grant (D) suddenly threw himself on the officer, attempting to foil the arrest. Grant (D) was himself arrested. He later had a serious seizure and was hospitalized. Grant (D) argued that the whole episode was the result of his illness. The court gave no instruction regarding automatic behavior, although it did instruct the jury regarding insanity. Grant (D) was convicted, and he appealed.

ISSUE: Is a person criminally responsible for their acts if they have no conscious control over them?

HOLDING AND DECISION: (Reardon, J.) No. A person is not criminally responsible for their acts if they have no conscious control over them. Automatic acts must be distinguished from insanity. An insane person may not be able to comprehend the criminal nature of their behavior. One committing automatic acts does but has no control over their behavior. An instruction on insanity was given, but not on automatism. However, an automatic act is not voluntary and will exculpate a defendant. The jury should have been allowed to consider this issue. Reversed and remanded.

ANALYSIS

Insanity relates to the mental aspect of criminal law. Automatism goes to the volitional aspect. The linchpin of this issue concerns conscious control over one's acts. If the conscious mind loses control over the body's acts, then the act in question was not voluntary.

Quicknotes

BATTERY Unlawful contact with the body of another person.

Robinson v. California

Narcotics addict (D) v. State (P)

370 U.S. 660 (1962)

NATURE OF CASE: Appeal from conviction for narcotics addiction.

FACT SUMMARY: Robinson (D) was convicted of being a narcotics addict.

RULE OF LAW

States may not outlaw the condition of narcotics addiction.

FACTS: The police observed track marks on Robinson (D), who also admitted to occasional drug use. Robinson (D) appealed. Robinson (D) was convicted under a California statute that made it a criminal offense for a person to "be addicted to the use of narcotics."

ISSUE: May states outlaw the condition of narcotics addiction?

HOLDING AND DECISION: (Stewart, J.) No. States may not outlaw the condition of narcotics addiction. States may punish a person for use, purchase, or sale of narcotics, or for antisocial behavior resulting from their use. However, the statute under which Robinson (D) was convicted punishes the status of addiction rather than any actual use. Narcotics addiction is an illness, which may be contracted involuntarily. Therefore, the California statute inflicts a cruel and unusual punishment in violation of the Eighth and Fourteenth Amendments by imprisoning a person for their addicted status. Reversed.

CONCURRENCE: (Harlan, J.) Addiction alone does not amount to more than a propensity to use narcotics. Thus, the law authorized criminal punishment for the mere desire to commit a criminal act.

DISSENT: (White, J.) The law should be read as prohibiting the regular, repeated, or habitual use of narcotics immediately prior to one's arrest.

ANALYSIS

Justice Stewart noted that usually a punishment of ninety days in prison would not implicate the Eighth Amendment's ban on cruel and unusual punishment. Justice Harlan's concurrence accurately describes one line of reasoning for striking down the law—there was no criminal act because Robinson's (D) conduct was involuntary. However, another rationale has also been advanced: only past conduct is punishable by law, whereas an addict convicted under the California statute risked being punished for a mere future propensity to violate the statute.

Quicknotes

EIGHTH AMENDMENT Prohibits the imposition of excessive bail, fines, and cruel and unusual punishment.

FOURTEENTH AMENDMENT Declares that no state shall make or enforce any law that shall abridge the privileges and immunities of citizens of the United States. No state shall deny to any person within its jurisdiction the equal protection of the laws.

Grants Pass v. Johnson

Municipality (D) v. Homeless individual (P)

144 S. Ct. 2202 (2024)

NATURE OF CASE: Appeal from affirmance of certification of class action and injunction prohibiting municipality from enforcing public-camping ordinances against homeless individuals.

FACT SUMMARY: The City of Grants Pass (D) had public-camping ordinances that it sought to enforce against homeless individuals. Homeless individuals (P) contended that these ordinances were unconstitutional under the Eighth Amendment's Cruel and Unusual Punishments Clause because the laws effectively punished their status, which required them to sleep outdoors.

RULE OF LAW

The enforcement of generally applicable laws regulating camping on public property does not constitute "cruel and unusual punishment" prohibited by the Eighth Amendment.

FACTS: Grants Pass, Oregon (Grants Pass) (D), like many local governments across the country, has public-camping laws that restrict encampments on public property. The Grants Pass Municipal Code prohibits activities such as camping on public property or parking overnight in the city's parks. Initial violations can trigger a fine, whereas multiple violations can result in punishment including imprisonment. In a prior decision, *Martin v. Boise*, 920 F.3d 584 (2019), the Ninth Circuit held that the Eighth Amendment's Cruel and Unusual Punishments Clause bars cities from enforcing public-camping ordinances like these against homeless individuals whenever the number of homeless individuals in a jurisdiction exceeds the number of "practically available" shelter beds, on the grounds that the homeless were effectively being punished for their "status" and not for any crime. After *Martin*, suits against western cities like Grants Pass (D) proliferated. Homeless individuals (P) filed a putative class action on behalf of homeless people living in Grants Pass (D), claiming that the city's ordinances against public camping violated the Eighth Amendment because the laws punished the "status" of being homeless. The district court certified the class and entered a *Martin* injunction prohibiting Grants Pass (D) from enforcing its laws against homeless individuals in the city. Applying *Martin's* reasoning, the district court found everyone without shelter in Grants Pass (D) was "involuntarily homeless" because the city's total homeless population outnumbered its "practically available" shelter beds. A divided panel of the Ninth Circuit affirmed in relevant part, concluding that the homeless in Grants Pass (D) cannot be punished for camping with rudimentary forms of protection from the elements. The United States Supreme Court granted certiorari.

ISSUE: Does the enforcement of generally applicable laws regulating camping on public property constitute "cruel and unusual punishment" prohibited by the Eighth Amendment?

HOLDING AND DECISION: (Gorsuch, J.) No. The enforcement of generally applicable laws regulating camping on public property does not constitute "cruel and unusual punishment" prohibited by the Eighth Amendment. The Eighth Amendment's Cruel and Unusual Punishments Clause was adopted to ensure that the new Nation would never resort to certain barbaric punishments that had been tolerated in England. The Clause focuses on the question regarding what method or kind of punishment a government may impose after a criminal conviction, not on the question whether a government may criminalize particular behavior in the first place. Thus, it is a poor foundation on which to rest the kind of decree the plaintiffs (P) seek in this case. In *Robinson v. California*, 370 U.S. 660 (1962), the Court addressed a challenge to a criminal conviction under a California statute providing that "'[n]o person shall . . . be addicted to the use of narcotics.'" In response to that challenge, the Court invoked the Cruel and Unusual Punishments Clause to hold that California could not enforce its law making the "status" of narcotic addiction a criminal offense, recognizing that imprisonment for 90 days is not, in the abstract, a punishment that is either cruel or unusual, but that when punishing "status," even one day in prison would be cruel and unusual. However, Grants Pass's (D) public-camping ordinances do not criminalize status. The public-camping laws prohibit actions undertaken by any person, regardless of status. It makes no difference whether the charged defendant is currently a person experiencing homelessness or not; it could be a backpacker on vacation, or a student camping out in protest on the lawn of a municipal building. Because the public-camping laws in this case do not criminalize status, *Robinson* is not implicated. Moreover, there is no need to extend *Robinson* here because the Court already rejected its application to a law like the one at issue; in *Powell v. Texas*, 392 U.S. 514 (1968), the Court confronted a defendant who had been convicted under a Texas statute making it a crime to "get drunk or be found in a state of intoxication in any public place." Like the plaintiffs (P) here, Powell argued that his drunkenness

Continued on next page.

was an "involuntary" byproduct of his status as an alcoholic. The Court, however, did not agree that Texas's law effectively criminalized Powell's status as an alcoholic. Writing for a plurality, Justice Marshall observed that *Robinson* does not curtail a state's authority to secure a conviction when the accused has committed some act society has an interest in preventing, notwithstanding that the defendant's conduct might in some sense be described as involuntary or occasioned by a particular status. That is because there is nothing in the Cruel and Unusual Punishments Clause that limits government's ability to criminalize certain actions. Instead, a variety of other legal doctrines and constitutional provisions work to protect those in the criminal justice system from a conviction. Further, the danger of extending *Robinson* to "involuntary" acts is that the Court would become the ultimate arbiter of the standards of criminal responsibility, in diverse areas of the criminal law, throughout the country. *Martin v. Boise*, 920 F.3d 584 (2019), exemplifies much of what can go wrong when courts try to set such standards unmoored from the Constitution. Under *Martin*, cities must allow public camping by those who are "involuntarily" homeless. How are city officials and law enforcement officers to know what it means to be "involuntarily" homeless, or whether any particular person meets that standard? Is it enough that a homeless person has turned down an offer of shelter? Or does it matter why? Cities routinely confront individuals who decline offers of shelter for any number of reasons, ranging from safety concerns to individual preferences. How are cities and their law enforcement officers on the ground to know which of these reasons are sufficiently weighty to qualify a person as "involuntarily" homeless? The answers to such questions, in any event, are not to be found in the Cruel and Unusual Punishments Clause, nor are federal judges specially equipped to provide them. Because the Eighth Amendment does not grant federal judges primary responsibility for assessing the causes of homelessness and devising responses thereto, the Ninth Circuit's judgment is reversed.

DISSENT: (Sotomayor, J.) Sleep is a biological necessity, not a crime, and, for some people, sleeping outside is their only option. Grants Pass (D) jails and fines those people for sleeping anywhere in public at any time, including in their cars, if they use as little as a blanket to keep warm or a rolled-up shirt as a pillow. For people with no access to shelter, that punishes them for being homeless, for their status. *Robinson* instructs that punishing people for their status is "cruel and unusual" under the Eighth Amendment. The majority ignores these realities, focusing not on the plight of the homeless, but instead focusing on the plight of municipalities that are unable to adequately respond to the homelessness epidemic experienced by municipalities all across the country. However, the case is only about whether the Constitution permits criminalizing sleeping outside when there is nowhere else to go. Although the myriad reasons for homelessness are complex, criminalizing homelessness does not improve the situation, but causes instead a destabilizing cascade of harm that may, in fact, aggravate the situation. For people with nowhere else to go, fines and jail time do not deter behavior, reduce homelessness, or increase public safety. Shelter beds that are available in theory may be practically unavailable because of "restrictions based on gender, age, income, sexuality, religious practice, curfews that conflict with employment obligations, and time limits on stays." Grants Pass's (D) ordinances criminalize being homeless: The status of being homeless (lacking available shelter) is defined by the very behavior singled out for punishment (sleeping outside). This conclusion is borne out by the ordinances' purpose, text, and enforcement, as for someone with no available shelter, the only way to comply with the ordinances is to leave Grants Pass (D) altogether—which was Grants Pass's (D) intent. The legislative record of Grants Pass's (D) city council shows that the idea behind the ordinances was deterrence. One member said, "[m]aybe they aren't hungry enough or cold enough . . . to make a change in their behavior." And, the council's president said, "[t]he point is to make it uncomfortable enough for [homeless people] in our city so they will want to move on down the road." The ordinances' text also singles out homeless people by defining "campsite" as "any place where bedding, sleeping bag, or other material used for bedding purposes" is placed "for the purpose of maintaining a temporary place to live." Finally, the ordinances are enforced as intended, by targeting the homeless. Officers testified that someone violates the ordinances only if they do not "have another home to go to." That is the definition of being homeless. The majority does not contest any of this. So much for the ordinances applying to backpackers and students. *Robinson* should squarely resolve this case, and, indeed, the majority seems to agree that an ordinance that fined and jailed "homeless" people would be unconstitutional. However, the majority's resort to, and use of, *Powell* is wrong. The Court in *Powell* considered the distinction between status and conduct but could not agree on a controlling rationale. Four Justices concluded that Robinson covered any "condition [the defendant] is powerless to change," and four Justices rejected that view. Justice White, casting the decisive fifth vote, left the question open because the defendant had "made no showing that he was unable to stay off the streets on the night in question." The *Powell* Court considered a statute that criminalized voluntary conduct (getting drunk) that could be rendered involuntary by a status (alcoholism); here, the ordinances criminalize conduct (sleeping outside) that defines a particular status (homelessness), so are unconstitutional under any of the opinions in *Powell*. By turning a blind eye to the

Continued on next page.

factual and legal realities presented, and seeing only what it wants, the majority has abdicated its role in safeguarding constitutional liberties for the most vulnerable among us.

ANALYSIS

It seems that the majority and dissent share very little common ground as to what, precisely, the principal issue of the case is, as well as to what the Cruel and Unusual Punishments Clause prohibits. The majority emphasizes that the key issue is whether the Eighth Amendment grants federal judges primary responsibility for assessing the causes of homelessness and devising responses for how to best handle such a pressing social question. The dissent, however, says that the only question for the Court is whether the Constitution permits punishing homeless people with no access to shelter for sleeping in public with as little as a blanket to keep warm. As to the Cruel and Unusual Punishments Clause, the majority asserts that the Clause focuses on the question what method or kind of punishment a government may impose after a criminal conviction, rather than what conduct government may criminalize in the first place. Justice Sotomayor, however, observes that the Court has repeatedly cited *Robinson v. California,* 370 U.S. 660 (1962), for the proposition that the Eighth Amendment imposes a substantive limit on what can be made criminal and punished, and that the Clause not only limits the kinds of punishment that can be imposed on those convicted of crimes, but also proscribes punishment grossly disproportionate to the severity of the crime and also imposes substantive limits on what can be made criminal and punished as such. *Ingraham v. Wright,* 430 U.S. 651 (1977). Given how far apart the Justices are on these, as well as other, legal issues raised by the case, it is surprising that at least they seem to agree that inflicting "unnecessary suffering" that is grossly disproportionate to the severity of a crime, or that serves no penological purpose, violates the Clause, with neither the majority nor the dissent casting any doubt on this long-standing principle that is firmly rooted in the Court's precedents.

Quicknotes

CRUEL AND UNUSUAL PUNISHMENT Punishment that is excessive or disproportionate to the offense committed, or a law that punishes a person's "status"; such punishment or law is prohibited by the Eighth Amendment to the U.S. Constitution.

EIGHTH AMENDMENT Prohibits the imposition of excessive bail, fines, and cruel and unusual punishment.

ORDINANCE Law or statute usually enacted by a municipal government.

Keeler v. Superior Court

Ex-husband (D) v. State (P)

Cal. Sup. Ct., 2 Cal. 3d 619, 87 Cal. Rptr. 481 (1970)

NATURE OF CASE: Petition for a writ of prohibition in murder prosecution.

FACT SUMMARY: Keeler (D) was charged with murder after causing the death of an unborn viable fetus by kicking the mother in her abdomen.

RULE OF LAW
Causing the death of a viable fetus is not a homicide.

FACTS: Upon learning that his ex-wife was pregnant with another man's child, Keeler (D) kicked her in the abdomen. The fetus was delivered stillborn via a caesarian section. Medical evidence proved that Keeler's (D) assault had killed the fetus. He was charged with murder. He moved to dismiss, contending that a fetus was not a "human being" within the meaning of the statute defining murder. The motion was denied.

ISSUE: Is causing the death of a viable fetus a homicide?

HOLDING AND DECISION: (Mosk, J.) No. Causing the death of a viable fetus is not a homicide. California's murder statute, Penal Code § 187, defines murder as "the unlawful killing of a human being, with malice aforethought." This law, adopted in 1872, has never been modified. The original codification of California law was meant to be based on common-law principles. Under common law existing since at least 1797, an unborn child was not considered a person for purposes of supporting a murder charge. Under rules of statutory construction, it is to be assumed that the legislature was aware of the common-law meanings of the terms it incorporated into the law it enacted. This being so, § 187's term "human being" does not include a viable fetus. Writ of prohibition granted.

ANALYSIS

The present decision was very unpopular. Within months, the California legislature amended § 187 to include "fetus" within the statute. The law now reads as follows: "(a) Murder is the unlawful killing of a human being, or a fetus, with malice aforethought. (b) This section shall not apply [if] (1) the act complied with Therapeutic Abortion Act, (2) . . . [t]he result of childbirth would be death to the mother . . . , and (3) the act was . . . consented to by the mother." Note that the amendment to § 187 does not mention viability of the fetus as a criterion.

Quicknotes

VIABLE FETUS The point at which a child is capable of living outside of its mother's womb.

United States v. Hudson and Goodwin

Federal government (P) v. Publishers of a libel (D)

11 U.S. (7 Cranch) 32 (1812)

NATURE OF CASE: Appeal from a demurrer to an indictment for a libel on the President and Congress.

FACT SUMMARY: When Hudson (D) and Goodwin (D) were indicted for a newspaper libel against the President and Congress of the United States, they argued that the circuit courts of the United States had no common-law jurisdiction in cases of libel.

RULE OF LAW

United States courts may not exercise common-law jurisdiction in criminal cases.

FACTS: Hudson (D) and Goodwin (D) were indicted for a libel against the President and Congress of the United States that appeared in a newspaper. They both filed a general demurrer in the federal Circuit Court, which was divided as to whether the circuit courts of the United States had a common-law jurisdiction in cases of libel. The case was certified to the United States Supreme Court.

ISSUE: May United States courts exercise common-law jurisdiction in criminal cases?

HOLDING AND DECISION: (Johnson, J.) No. United States courts may not exercise common-law jurisdiction in criminal cases. The powers of the general government are made up of concessions from the several states. Whatever is not expressly given to the former the latter reserves. The judicial power of the United States is a constituent part of those concessions, namely, that power is to be exercised by courts organized for the purpose and brought into existence by an effect of the legislative power of the Union. Of all the courts that the United States may, under their general powers, constitute, one only, the Supreme Court, possesses jurisdiction derived immediately from the Constitution, and of which the legislative power cannot deprive it. All other courts created by the general government possess no jurisdiction except what is given them by the power that creates them, and can be vested with none but what the power ceded to the general government will authorize them to confer. The legislative authority of the Union must first make an act a crime, affix a punishment to it, and declare the court that shall have jurisdiction of the offense.

ANALYSIS

In *Hudson and Goodwin*, the Supreme Court established that the federal courts could impose liability only for crimes defined by statute.

Quicknotes

INDICTMENT A formal written accusation made by the prosecution to the grand jury under oath, charging an individual with a criminal offense.

LIBEL A false or malicious publication subjecting a person to scorn, hatred, or ridicule, or injuring the person in relation to the person's occupation or business.

Rogers v. Tennessee

Murderer (D) v. State (P)

532 U.S. 451 (2001)

NATURE OF CASE: Appeal from a murder conviction.

FACT SUMMARY: When Rogers (D) was convicted of murder after the Tennessee Supreme Court abolished the common-law year and a day rule, he argued that his conviction violated ex post facto principles.

RULE OF LAW

A judicial alteration of a common-law doctrine of criminal law violates ex post facto principles only where it is unexpected and indefensible by reference to the law that had been expressed prior to the conduct in issue.

FACTS: Wilbert Rogers (D) was convicted in a Tennessee state court of second-degree murder. Rogers (D) had stabbed the victim in the heart, causing cardiac arrest and a coma. The victim died of a kidney infection, a common complication of comas, after 15 months. At common law, the year and a day rule provided that no defendant could be convicted of murder unless the victim died by the defendant's act within a year and a day of the act. The Tennessee Supreme Court abolished the rule as it had existed at common law in Tennessee and applied its decision to Rogers (D) to uphold the conviction. The state murder statute made no mention of the year and a day rule. Rogers (D) appealed, arguing that, despite its absence from the murder statute, the year and a day rule persisted as part of the common law of Tennessee and, as such, precluded his conviction.

ISSUE: Does a judicial alteration of a common-law doctrine of criminal law violate ex post facto principles only where it is unexpected and indefensible by reference to the law that had been expressed prior to the conduct in issue?

HOLDING AND DECISION: (O'Connor, J.) Yes. A judicial alteration of a common-law doctrine of criminal law violates ex post facto principles only where it is unexpected and indefensible by reference to the law that had been expressed prior to the conduct in issue. The Tennessee court's abolition of the year and a day rule was not unexpected and indefensible. The rule is widely viewed as an "outdated relic" of the common law. Since no good reasons exist for retaining the rule, the rule has been legislatively and judicially abolished in the vast majority of jurisdictions recently to have addressed the issue. Common-law courts frequently look to the decisions of other jurisdictions in determining whether to alter or modify a common-law rule in light of changed circumstances, increased knowledge, and general logic and experience. Due process does not require a person to apprise themselves of the common law of all 50 states in order to guarantee that their actions will not subject them to punishment in light of a developing trend in the law that has not yet made its way to their own state. At the same time, however, the fact that a vast number of jurisdictions have abolished a rule that has so clearly outlived its purpose is surely relevant to whether the abolition of the rule in a particular case can be said to be unexpected and indefensible by reference to the law as it then existed. Affirmed.

DISSENT: (Scalia, J.) The Court has approved the conviction of a man for a murder that was not murder (but only manslaughter) when the offense was committed. It thus violates the principle of no penalty without law, dating from the ancient Greeks and described as one of the most widely held principles in the entire history of human thought.

ANALYSIS

In the *Rogers* case, the Supreme Court noted that, at the time of the crime, the year and a day rule had only "the most tenuous foothold" as part of the criminal law of Tennessee. The rule did not exist as part of the state's statutory criminal code and had never once served as a ground of decision in any prosecution for murder in the state.

Quicknotes

COMMON LAW A body of law developed through the judicial decisions of the courts as opposed to the legislative process.

EX POST FACTO After the fact; a law that makes subsequent activity criminal or increases the punishment for a crime that occurred, or eliminates a defense that was available to the defendant prior to its passage.

MANSLAUGHTER The killing of a person without premeditation or deliberation, or with the intent to kill or to commit a felony that may be reasonably expected to result in death or serious bodily injury; manslaughter is characterized by reckless conduct or by some adequate provocation on the part of the actor, as determined by a subjective standard.

SECOND-DEGREE MURDER The unlawful killing of a person, without premeditation, and characterized by either intent to kill or by a reckless disregard for human life.

Chicago v. Morales

Municipality (P) v. Accused gang member (D)

527 U.S. 41 (1999)

NATURE OF CASE: Review of state court ruling on constitutionality of city ordinance.

FACT SUMMARY: Morales (D) challenged an anti-gang ordinance passed by the City of Chicago (P) on the basis that the wording of the statute defining "loitering" was so vague as to make the statute unconstitutional.

RULE OF LAW

A statute providing penalties for criminal conduct is unconstitutionally vague if it fails to give sufficient notice regarding the type of conduct prohibited.

FACTS: Morales (D) and others were accused as "criminal street gang members" under a new ordinance passed by the City of Chicago (P) prohibiting persons from "loitering" with one another in public places. A City of Chicago (P) commission solicited witness testimony and made a series of findings suggesting that an increase in street activity was a primary cause of the escalation in violent and drug-related crimes, and that a common function of loitering was to enable a street gang to establish control over particular areas. In addition, the commission discovered that loitering by street gang members in public places intimidated law-abiding citizens and limited access to these areas by creating a "justifiable fear for the safety of persons and property" in the areas where loitering took place. In response, the City of Chicago (P) passed the Gang Congregation Ordinance, which created a criminal offense punishable by a fine of up to $500, as well as imprisonment and community service, for "loitering" by suspected street gang members in public places. The statute defined four elements of the crime of "loitering": first, a police officer must reasonably believe that at least two or more persons present in a public place are gang members; second, these persons must be "loitering" by remaining in one place with no apparent purpose; third, the officer must order these persons to disperse; and finally, the order to disperse must be disobeyed by the suspected gang members. Morales (D) challenged the ordinance on the basis that it broadly covered a significant amount of additional activity beyond what should be interpreted as "loitering" and was therefore unconstitutionally vague. The Supreme Court of Illinois concluded the ordinance was unconstitutionally vague because it did not provide specific limits on the discretion of police officers to determine what conduct constituted "loitering" and the City of Chicago (P) filed for review of that determination.

ISSUE: Is a statute providing penalties for criminal conduct unconstitutionally vague if it fails to give sufficient notice regarding the type of conduct prohibited?

HOLDING AND DECISION: (Stevens, J.) Yes. A statute providing penalties for criminal conduct is unconstitutionally vague if it fails to give sufficient notice regarding the type of conduct prohibited. Clearly, a law directly prohibiting intimidating conduct similar to that described by the City of Chicago (P) commission is constitutional on its face. However, such a law may still be found unconstitutionally vague for two reasons: first, the law fails to provide the type of notice that permits ordinary persons to understand the conduct prohibited; and second, the wording of the law encourages arbitrary and discriminatory enforcement. Citizens should not have to speculate as to the meaning of a law. The requirement of notice is not met here because the order to disperse takes place before an officer knows whether the prohibited conduct has occurred, and is therefore an unjustifiable impairment of liberty if the loiterer is harmless and innocent. In addition, the statute establishes only minimal guidelines for law enforcement to follow. Police officers may exercise absolute discretion when assessing a group of bystanders for dispersal. The City of Chicago (P) asserts that the statute provides limitations on a police officer's discretion, because it does not permit a dispersal order to issue if a person has an apparent purpose, or until the officer reasonably believes that "loitering" is taking place. However, these limitations are insufficient because they do not directly address the degree of discretion an officer may exercise. The ability to assess a "loitering" situation is only subjectively limited by the officer's own evaluation of the circumstances. The Illinois Supreme Court's ruling that the statute in question is unconstitutional was correctly concluded and is therefore affirmed.

ANALYSIS

Justice Stevens's opinion suggests that the Gang Congregation Ordinance could have been worded optimally to include conduct that was apparent, such as the effort by gang members to publicize the gang's dominance over a certain area. Use of this phrasing explicitly would have satisfied constitutional concerns of specificity; however, the Court ironically noted that

Continued on next page.

the absence of this descriptive language not only expanded the statute's inclusion of harmless behavior but excluded those exact circumstances where the statute would have played a critical role in addressing the intended problem.

Quicknotes

FOURTEENTH AMENDMENT Declares that no state shall make or enforce any law that shall abridge the privileges and immunities of citizens of the United States. No state shall deny to any person within its jurisdiction the equal protection of the laws.

VAGUENESS AND OVERBREADTH Characteristics of a statute that make it difficult to identify the limits of the conduct being regulated.

CHAPTER 3

The Guilty Mind

Quick Reference Rules of Law

Commonwealth v. Mixer

State (P) v. Driver for common carrier (D)

Mass. Sup. Ct., 207 Mass. 141 (1910)

NATURE OF CASE: Appeal in prosecution for committing a strict liability offense.

FACT SUMMARY: A statute made it a crime to illegally transport intoxicating liquor but did not include knowledge or willfulness as an element. Mixer (D), a driver for a common carrier, contended he could not be convicted under the statute after he transported a barrel containing liquor because he did not know and had no reason to suspect that there was intoxicating liquor in the barrel. A seller or consignor had delivered the barrel for transportation and had violated the law by failing to mark the barrel to indicate it contained liquor, so that Mixer (D) did not have a culpable mind, which, Mixer (D) contended, was necessary to sustain any criminal conviction.

RULE OF LAW

A common carrier or its employee can be convicted under a statute that makes it a crime to illegally transport intoxicating liquor but that does not include knowledge or willfulness as an element, notwithstanding that the employee does not know and has no reason to suspect that there is intoxicating liquor in a package delivered for transportation by a seller or consignor who has violated the law by failing to mark such package plainly and legibly with the kind and amount of liquor it contains.

FACTS: A statute made it a crime to illegally transport intoxicating liquor without license or permission into dry towns but did not include knowledge or willfulness as an element. Punishment for violating the statute included fines and imprisonment. Mixer (D), a driver for a common carrier, had in the cargo for transportation a sugar barrel, not marked by the seller or consignor as required by law for packages containing intoxicating liquor. There was nothing about the appearance of the barrel to cause suspicion as to its contents, and Mixer (D) was ignorant that it contained intoxicating liquor. Mixer (D) was prosecuted under the statute. The trial court refused to instruct the jury that unless Mixer (D) knew that the barrel contained intoxicating liquor or from its appearance and all the circumstances ought reasonably to have been put on inquiry as to its contents, he should be acquitted. Mixer (D) argued that this refusal was error, contending he could not be convicted under the statute because he did not know and had no reason to suspect that there was intoxicating liquor in the barrel, so that he did not have a culpable mind, which, Mixer (D) contended, was necessary to sustain any criminal conviction. Mixer (D) appealed [by bringing exceptions] to the state's highest court, which granted review.

ISSUE: Can a common carrier or its employee be convicted under a statute that makes it a crime to illegally transport intoxicating liquor but that does not include knowledge or willfulness as an element, notwithstanding that the employee does not know and has no reason to suspect that there is intoxicating liquor in a package delivered for transportation by a seller or consignor who has violated the law by failing to mark such package plainly and legibly with the kind and amount of liquor it contains?

HOLDING AND DECISION: (Rugg, J.) Yes. A common carrier or its employee can be convicted under a statute that makes it a crime to illegally transport intoxicating liquor but that does not include knowledge or willfulness as an element, notwithstanding that the employee does not know and has no reason to suspect that there is intoxicating liquor in a package delivered for transportation by a seller or consignor who has violated the law by failing to mark such package plainly and legibly with the kind and amount of liquor it contains. In the prosecution of crimes under the common law apart from statute, it ordinarily is necessary to allege and prove a guilty intent, and, as a general principle, a crime is not committed if the mind of the person doing the act is innocent. For there to be a crime, there must be a confluence of evil intent and an unlawful action. Nevertheless, in recent times, the legislature in the exercise of the police power has prohibited under criminal penalty the performance of a specific act. The only fact to be determined in these cases is whether the defendant did the act. Thus, in the public's interest, the burden is placed upon the actor of ascertaining at their peril whether their act is within the prohibition of any criminal statute. There are many examples of such exercise of legislative power, which frequently has been applied to statutes respecting intoxicating liquor. Thus, it is necessary to examine the terms and history of the statute upon which the complaint against Mixer (D) was founded, and the antecedent enactments of the legislature touching the general subject, to determine whether the statute at bar is such a statute. A predecessor statute included a willfulness element. However, after the consolidation of pre-existing enactments, the word "willfully" was omitted, and has not since appeared in any statute touching the transportation of intoxicating

Continued on next page.

liquor, including the statute under which Mixer (D) was charged. It is obvious from these successive enactments that the legislature was struggling to make it more and more difficult to transport liquor secretly into cities and towns where licenses were not granted. For these reasons, the statute at bar is within the class of statutes that does not require a culpable mind for an act to be criminalized. Although not requiring a guilty mind to criminalize an act may seem harsh, this raises not a question of judicial construction, but of legislative policy, with which the courts cannot interfere so long as no constitutional guaranty is infringed. Here, the language of the statute under consideration is plain and unequivocal. It contains no words, such as "willfully" or "knowingly," indicating a vicious intent as a part of the crime created. There is nothing about it to suggest an exception for the benefit of one who inadvertently violates its terms. Its phraseology discloses a legislative determination that society can best be protected against the evil aimed at by a rigorous application of an inflexible rule. Exceptions overruled. [Affirmed.]

ANALYSIS

The type of statute challenged in this case creates what is known as a strict liability offense, meaning an offense that does not have guilty intent as one of its elements. The doing of the proscribed act constitutes the offense, and any considerations of mens rea are immaterial to the question of guilt. The court provides numerous examples of such strict liability offenses that were in effect when the case was decided in 1910 and explains that these offenses were defined and justified pursuant to government's police power to address conduct considered inimical to the public's welfare. Such strict liability offenses also were enacted to address conduct for which proving mens rea is deemed impractical or too costly. Although many strict liability offenses are for relatively minor offenses, such as many traffic infractions, strict liability offenses can also be enacted to address more serious crimes, such as statutory rape, or tax evasion. Strict liability offenses are also used in the regulatory context to protect the public's health and safety. The United States Supreme Court held in *United States v. Balint*, 258 U.S. 250 (1922), that strict liability offenses, such as the one at issue in *Mixer*, were constitutional and did not offend due process rights. However, depending on the severity and nature of a strict liability offense, some courts have read a mens rea requirement into the statute that defines the offense, notwithstanding that the statute is silent as to mens rea. See, e.g., *Morissette v. United States*, 342 U.S. 246 (1952).

Quicknotes

CRIMINAL INTENT An intention to carry out a criminal offense.

DUE PROCESS RIGHTS The constitutional mandate requiring the courts to protect and enforce individuals' rights and liberties consistent with prevailing principles of fairness and justice and prohibiting the federal and state governments from such activities that deprive citizens of a life, liberty, or property interest.

MENS REA Criminal intent.

STRICT LIABILITY OFFENSE Criminal offense that does not have a mens rea element, so that only proof of the commission or omission of a specified act is sufficient to impose liability for the act, regardless of intent, motive, or mental state at the time of the act.

United States v. Wulff

Federal government (P) v. Alleged violator of federal act (D)

758 F.2d 1121 (6th Cir. 1985)

NATURE OF CASE: Government's appeal from dismissal of an indictment charging violation of the Migratory Bird Treaty Act.

FACT SUMMARY: When Wulff (D) was indicted for selling migratory bird parts in violation of the Migratory Bird Treaty Act, he argued that since the statute does not require guilty knowledge, imposition of a felony conviction would violate his due process.

RULE OF LAW

Absence of a requirement that the government must prove some degree of scienter for a felony conviction violates due process.

FACTS: A federal grand jury returned a one-count indictment charging Robert Wulff (D) with selling migratory bird parts in violation of the Migratory Bird Treaty Act (MBTA), which makes it a felony to sell any migratory bird. The indictment was based on a sale made by Wulff (D) to a government agent of a necklace made of a red-tailed hawk and great-horned owl talons. Both birds are protected species under the MBTA. Wulff (D) moved to dismiss on the grounds that the statute does not require guilty knowledge and that therefore imposition of a felony conviction would be a violation of due process. The federal district court agreed and dismissed the indictment. The Government (P) appealed.

ISSUE: Does absence of a requirement that the government must prove some degree of scienter for a felony conviction violate due process?

HOLDING AND DECISION: (Milburn, J.) Yes. Absence of a requirement that the government must prove some degree of scienter for a felony conviction violates due process. The question here is not whether scienter is an element of the offense or whether Congress made a rational choice in legislating a felony conviction for the commercialization of protected birds. Rather, the issue is whether the absence of a requirement that the government must prove some degree of scienter for a felony conviction violated Wulff's (D) right to due process. Here, it does. The elimination of the element of criminal intent does not violate the due process clause only (1) where the penalty is relatively small and (2) conviction would not irreparably damage one's reputation. The Migratory Bird Treaty Act (MBTA) fails to meet this criteria. The felony penalty carries a maximum sentence of two years' imprisonment or two thousand dollars fine, or both. This is not a relatively small penalty. Furthermore, a felony conviction irreparably damages one's reputation. To wit, a convicted felon loses, among other civil rights, the right to sit on a jury and the right to possess a gun. Affirmed.

ANALYSIS

As the *Wulff* case illustrates, in order for one to be convicted of a felony under the Migratory Bird Treaty Act (MBTA), a crime unknown to the common law that carries a substantial penalty, Congress must require the prosecution to prove the defendant acted with some degree of scienter. Otherwise, a person acting with a completely innocent state of mind could be subjected to a severe penalty and experience grave damage to their reputation. This, notes the court in *Wulff*, "the Constitution does not allow."

Quicknotes

DUE PROCESS RIGHTS The constitutional mandate requiring the courts to protect and enforce individuals' rights and liberties consistent with prevailing principles of fairness and justice and prohibiting the federal and state governments from such activities that deprive citizens of a life, liberty, or property interest.

FELONY A criminal offense of greater seriousness than a misdemeanor; felonies are generally defined pursuant to statute as any crime that is punishable by death or by a term of imprisonment exceeding one year.

SCIENTER Knowledge of certain facts; often refers to "guilty knowledge" that implicates liability.

Lambert v. California

Convicted forger (D) v. State (P)

355 U.S. 225 (1957)

NATURE OF CASE: Appeal from conviction for failure to register under a California law that requires registration of convicted felons.

FACT SUMMARY: Lambert (D), a convicted forger who was living in Los Angeles, did not register with the authorities as a convicted felon and was charged with failing to do so (in violation of Los Angeles Municipal Code § 52.39).

RULE OF LAW

One may not be punished for failure to register as a convicted felon (consistent with the requirements of due process) unless the state can show (1) circumstances that might move one to inquire as to the necessity of registration or (2) actual knowledge of the duty to register.

FACTS: Lambert (D) was a convicted forger who had been living in Los Angeles for seven years. Los Angeles Municipal Code § 52.39 made it unlawful for any convicted felon to be, or remain, in Los Angeles for a period of more than five days without registering. Lambert (D), who claimed to have no actual knowledge of the duty to register, had not registered, was arrested, and was convicted. The appeal raised the issue of whether or not some mens rea was required in this circumstance by the Due Process Clause of the Fourteenth Amendment.

ISSUE: May one be punished for failure to register as a convicted felon (consistent with the requirements of due process) if the state cannot show (1) circumstances that might move one to inquire as to the necessity of registration or (2) actual knowledge of the duty to register?

HOLDING AND DECISION: (Douglas, J.) No. One may not be punished for failure to register as a convicted felon (consistent with the requirement of due process) unless the state can show (1) circumstances that might move one to inquire as to the necessity of registration or (2) actual knowledge of the duty to register. The circumstances of this case show absolutely nothing that should have alerted Lambert (D) to the need for registration, effectively denying her the opportunity to avoid the consequences of the law or to defend any prosecution brought under it. Unless Lambert (D) can be shown to have had actual knowledge of the duty to register, this result would conflict with the requirements of notice that are found in the Due Process Clause of the Fourteenth Amendment. Reversed.

ANALYSIS

The student should be careful to keep the holding of this case appropriately narrow. The Supreme Court held that ignorance of the law covering the conduct in question will be a defense only when (1) we are dealing with an omission to act or (2) the omission to act is under circumstances that would not move one to inquire as to the need to act. Therefore, if the state made a law that criminalized failure to aid a choking or drowning person, a defendant would not be able to claim that the defendant was unaware of the law because there were circumstances that should have alerted the defendant. In general, a defendant will not be able to use this ignorance of the law defense whenever the omission runs counter to established notions of morality or common sense.

Quicknotes

PROCEDURAL DUE PROCESS The constitutional mandate that, if the state or federal government acts so as to deny a citizen of a life, liberty, or property interest, the individual is first entitled to notice and the right to be heard.

Regina v. Faulkner

Government (P) v. Thief (D)

Ct. of Crown Cases Reserved, Ireland, 13 Cox C.C. 550 (1877)

NATURE OF CASE: Appeal of arson conviction.

FACT SUMMARY: Faulkner (D), trying to steal rum from a ship, accidently started a fire, destroying the entire ship.

RULE OF LAW
One is criminally liable for a crime collateral to an intended crime only when it is a natural and probable consequence of the intended crime.

FACTS: Faulkner (D) boarded a ship to steal rum. During the course thereof he accidentally started a fire that destroyed the ship. Faulkner (D) was tried and convicted of both the attempted theft and the fire. Faulkner (D) appealed the arson conviction.

ISSUE: Is one criminally liable for a crime collateral to an intended crime only when it is a natural and probable consequence of the intended crime?

HOLDING AND DECISION: [Judge not stated in casebook excerpt.] Yes. One is criminally liable for a crime collateral to an intended crime only when it is a natural and probable consequence of the intended crime. Reversed.

CONCURRENCE: (Barry, J.) To hold one criminally liable for all consequences of their criminal acts is too broad a proposition.

CONCURRENCE: (Fitzgerald, J.) Only those consequences that are natural and probable from a crime should be chargeable to a defendant.

CONCURRENCE: (O'Brien, J.) Had Faulkner (D) acted recklessly, a conviction might be proper, but no such instruction was presented to the jury.

DISSENT: (Keogh, J.) The jury properly ruled on intention and malice.

ANALYSIS

The statute under which Faulkner (D) was prosecuted required malice for a conviction. This was probably the element lacking, yet the Court and the concurrences did not discuss it. The concurrence of Justice O'Brien might be read to equate malice with recklessness, but the opinion is silent as to whether that was what he was thinking.

Quicknotes

ARSON The unlawful burning of a building or structure.

MALICE The intention to commit an unlawful act without justification or excuse.

People v. Gory

State (P) v. Convicted possessor of marijuana (D)

Cal. Sup. Ct., 28 Cal.2d 450 (1946)

NATURE OF CASE: Appeal from order denying defendant's motion for a new trial in prosecution for a strict liability possession offense.

FACT SUMMARY: Gory (D), who was convicted for possessing marijuana, contended that it was error for the trial judge not to give the jury an instruction that a guilty verdict had to be predicated on Gory's (D) "knowingly" having in his possession the marijuana charged in the information.

RULE OF LAW

(1) Where a defendant is charged with a strict liability possession offense, and the evidence puts into issue whether the defendant had knowledge of the presence of the contraband object that the defendant is charged with possessing, it is error for a trial court not to give to the jury an instruction that the defendant's guilt is predicated on the defendant knowingly having such objects in the defendant's possession, where the meaning of the word "possession" includes the exercise of dominion and control over the thing possessed.

(2) Where a defendant is charged with a strict liability possession offense, and the evidence puts into issue whether the defendant had knowledge of the presence of the contraband object that the defendant is charged with possessing, it is not error for a trial court not to give to the jury an instruction that the defendant's guilt is predicated on the defendant's guilty knowledge of the character of the contraband, and guilty intent to possess it.

FACTS: Gory (D) was a prisoner at a county farm where he shared living quarters with around 30 other prisoners in a bunkhouse. As part of the equipment issued to each prisoner, he received a metal box—18 inches long, 12 inches wide, 8 inches deep—in which he kept his toilet articles and small personal effects. There was no way of locking these boxes, each of which bore a number corresponding to the bed number of the space occupied by the particular prisoner. Each prisoner's box was placed on the floor near the head of his bed. During the day when the prisoners were away from the living quarters, one man was left in charge to "keep the inmates from monkeying with other people's property." One day, Officer Gunderson and several accompanying officers entered the bunkhouse. While his associates searched the boxes of other prisoners in the bunkhouse, Officer Gunderson went to Gory's (D) bed—on which Gory (D) was lying—picked up the metal box, opened it, and found marijuana scattered from the top down to the bottom just loose in the box. However, Officer Gunderson did not find any marijuana on Gory's (D) person or in his clothes. When asked what he knew about the marijuana and where he obtained it, and in the face of an accusation that the marijuana belonged to Gory (D), Gory (D) did not answer. Gory (D) was charged with the strict liability offense of possessing marijuana. At trial, Gory (D) admitted that the material that the officers identified as marijuana was taken from his box, but he stated that he had never seen it before the officers removed it from the box. The trial judge gave the jury the following instructions, among others, but then withdrew them:

> Instruction 12: In order for defendant to have in his possession the objects charged in the information, you must be convinced by the evidence and beyond a reasonable doubt that he knowingly had such objects in his possession. The meaning of the word "possession" includes the exercise of dominion and control over the thing possessed.

> Instruction 13: Even if you find from the evidence beyond a reasonable doubt that the defendant had in his possession, flowering tops of Indian Hemp or loco-weed [marijuana], before you can find the defendant guilty of possessing the same, you must also be convinced beyond a reasonable doubt that the defendant had a guilty knowledge of the character of said flowering tops of Indian Hemp and possessed a guilty intent. If you find that the defendant was innocent of the knowledge of the character of the flowering tops of Indian Hemp or did not have a guilty knowledge of possessing said flowering tops of Indian Hemp, then you will find the defendant not guilty and must acquit him.

Gory (D) was convicted. On appeal, he contended that it was prejudicial error for the trial judge to have withdrawn these instructions from the jury. The state's highest court granted review.

ISSUE:

(1) Where a defendant is charged with a strict liability possession offense, and the evidence puts into issue

Continued on next page.

whether the defendant had knowledge of the presence of the contraband object that the defendant is charged with possessing, is it error for a trial court not to give to the jury an instruction that the defendant's guilt is predicated on the defendant knowingly having such objects in the defendant's possession, where the meaning of the word "possession" includes the exercise of dominion and control over the thing possessed?

(2) Where a defendant is charged with a strict liability possession offense, and the evidence puts into issue whether the defendant had knowledge of the presence of the contraband object that the defendant is charged with possessing, is it error for a trial court to not give to the jury an instruction that the defendant's guilt is predicated on the defendant's guilty knowledge of the character of the contraband, and guilty intent to possess it?

HOLDING AND DECISION: (Spence, J.)

(1) Yes. Where a defendant is charged with a strict-liability possession offense, and the evidence puts into issue whether the defendant had knowledge of the presence of the contraband object that the defendant is charged with possessing, it is error for a trial court not to give to the jury an instruction that the defendant's guilt is predicated on the defendant knowingly having such objects in the defendant's possession, where the meaning of the word "possession" includes the exercise of dominion and control over the thing possessed. The law makes the matter of knowledge in relation to Gory's (D) awareness of the presence of the object a basic element of the offense of possession, which, as used in the context of statute under which Gory (D) was charged, means an "immediate and exclusive possession and one under the dominion and control of defendant." Knowledge of the existence of the object is essential to "physical control thereof with the intent to exercise such control" and such knowledge must necessarily precede the intent to exercise, or the exercise of, such control. Thus, Instruction 12 should have been given to the jury, as the use of the word "knowingly" in that instruction imports only a knowledge that the facts exist that bring the act or omission within the provisions of the statute under which Gory (D) was charged. It does not encompass any knowledge of the unlawfulness of such act or omission. In other words, Instruction 12 invoked the element of knowledge in the sense of Gory's (D) awareness of the presence of the marijuana in the box given him for the storage of his personal effects at the prison farm and so presented to the jury an issue of fact determinative of his guilt or innocence of the possession prohibited by statute. Because the principal fact relied on by the prosecution was the finding of marijuana in Gory's (D) unlocked box, and because of the denial by Gory (D) of knowledge of its presence there, it was the trial court's duty, on proper instructions, to submit to the jury the question as to whether he had knowledge of the presence of the marijuana. [Reversed as to this issue.]

(2) No. Where a defendant is charged with a strict-liability possession offense, and the evidence puts into issue whether the defendant had knowledge of the presence of the contraband object that the defendant is charged with possessing, it is not error for a trial court not to give to the jury an instruction that the defendant's guilt is predicated on the defendant's guilty knowledge of the character of the contraband, and guilty intent to possess it. The "mere possession, except as authorized" of marijuana is sufficient to constitute the statutory offense in question, without regard for scienter or specific intent to violate the law as would follow from evidence establishing defendant's knowledge of the contraband character of the property. This kind of "knowledge" is immaterial to a strict liability possession offense. Accordingly, it was not error for the trial judge to withdraw Instruction 13 from the jury. [Affirmed as to this issue.]

The judgment and the order denying defendant's motion for a new trial are reversed.

ANALYSIS

The importance of proper instructions on the question of Gory's (D) possession of the contraband is readily apparent from the fact record. Matters tending to establish his guilt were that the marijuana was found in his box and the circumstance of his silence in the face of accusations that it belonged to him. Matters tending to establish his innocence were the box being unlocked, showing that the marijuana conceivably could have been placed there by someone other than Gory (D), and his denial at the trial that he had ever seen the contraband prior to its discovery by the officers. Thus, this may be said to be a close case on the record. It is distinguishable from cases where the evidence includes express admissions and statements made by defendant with respect to the possession of narcotics, which supplied the final link in the chain of circumstances connecting the defendant with the offense charged against them. It also is distinguishable from cases where the required possession of drugs was shown by testimony that the defendant threw the drug out of the window, or otherwise disposed of it upon the approach of the arresting officers, and that it was later returned and identified as having been in the custody and under the control of the defendant prior to the defendant's arrest.

Continued on next page.

Quicknotes

INFORMATION A formal sworn charging document filed by a prosecutor or other duly authorized public official that initiates formal court proceedings against a criminal defendant, and that contains the charges against the defendant and the factual basis for the charges; as distinguished from an "indictment," which in other respects is like an "information," but instead of being filed by a prosecutor or public official, is issued by a grand jury.

JURY INSTRUCTIONS A communication made by the court to a jury regarding the applicable law involved in a proceeding.

KNOWINGLY Intentionally; willfully; committing an act with knowledge as to its probable consequences.

PREJUDICIAL ERROR An error that affects the outcome of a trial, the judgment of which may be reversed, establishing a basis for a new trial.

STRICT LIABILITY OFFENSE Criminal offense that does not have a mens rea element, so that only proof of the commission or omission of a specified act is sufficient to impose liability for the act, regardless of intent, motive, or mental state at the time of the act.

Simms v. District of Columbia

Convicted vehicle tamperer (D) v. Municipality (P)

D.C. Ct. App., 612 A. 2d 215 (1992)

NATURE OF CASE: Appeal from affirmance of conviction for vehicle tampering.

FACT SUMMARY: Simms (D), who had been convicted by a hearing commissioner of tampering with a vehicle—a general intent crime—contended that it was error for the commissioner to have refused Simms's (D) mistake of fact defense that Simms (D) honestly and reasonably believed the vehicle at issue, a Volkswagen Jetta, had been abandoned. The Government (P) countered that even if the commissioner had committed error as asserted by Simms (D), such error was harmless because the evidence showed that Simms (D) was not certain the Jetta had been abandoned but alternatively believed it might have been stolen.

RULE OF LAW

A defendant who has been charged with a general intent property offense must be allowed to plead a mistake of fact defense based on the defendant's belief that the property at issue was abandoned by its owner.

FACTS: A police officer observed a group of people attempting to raise a parked Volkswagen Jetta automobile onto the crane of a tow truck in a location from which the police previously had recovered numerous stolen cars. Simms (D) was standing near a jack, and he was placing boards underneath the car. The officer observed that the Jetta did not appear to have been there long. After a computerized check identified the Jetta as a stolen vehicle, the officer charged Simms (D) with the regulatory offense of tampering with a vehicle. At a bench trial before a hearing commissioner, defense witnesses testified that the Jetta seemed abandoned to them, as it had been in the bushes for around a month. Simms (D) testified that he had noticed "a Jetta abandoned" in the same place for "approximately three weeks to a month, [and that] the windows are all busted out and the car is totally destroyed." He also acknowledged telling a person looking for Jetta parts that, "I don't know if it's been stolen or abandoned, as far as I know it's abandoned. . . ." On cross-examination, when asked if he had said he did not know if the Jetta was stolen or abandoned, Simms (D) explained that he knew the Jetta did not belong to him and that he had seen the Jetta five or six times over the three-weeks-to-a-month period. The hearing commissioner rejected Simms's (D) defense that he believed the Jetta had been abandoned by its owner, ruling that, in general, abandonment has to be proved by unequivocal, clear and decisive evidence but that since Simms (D) was not a member of any statutory class permitted to touch a vehicle (i.e., the vehicle's owner, the vehicle owner's representative or a government official), abandonment in the nature of a mistake of fact was not a defense. Alternatively, the commissioner ruled that even under a mistake of fact defense, the evidence and the facts did not support such a defense, and that the commissioner found beyond a reasonable doubt that Simms (D) was guilty. The state's trial court affirmed. Simms (D) appealed to the state's intermediate appellate court, contending that the hearing commissioner had erred in rejecting Simms's (D) mistake of fact defense based on abandonment.

ISSUE: Must a defendant who has been charged with a general intent offense be allowed to plead a mistake of fact defense based on the defendant's belief that property was abandoned by its owner?

HOLDING AND DECISION: (Rogers, C.J.) Yes. A defendant who has been charged with a general intent property offense must be allowed to plead a mistake of fact defense based on the defendant's belief that the property at issue was abandoned by its owner. In general intent crimes, such as tampering with another's vehicle, a defendant may interpose a mistake of fact defense if the defendant proves to the satisfaction of the fact finder that the mistake was both (1) honest and (2) reasonable. Thus, Simms's (D) mistake of fact defense is a proper defense to tampering with an automobile because it can negate the general intent to commit the crime, thereby demonstrating that Simms (D) did not physically make contact with the stolen Jetta with an "unlawful purpose." Accordingly, the commissioner erred by not allowing Simms (D) to present this defense. However, where the mistake of fact is based on a claim that the defendant mistakenly believed property had been abandoned by its owner, an abandonment must be made to appear affirmatively by the party relying on it, and an intention to abandon will not ordinarily be presumed, and this is particularly true if the conduct of the owner can be explained consistently with a continued claim. Thus, proof of abandonment must be made by the one asserting it by clear, unequivocal, and decisive evidence. Here, the evidence supports the commissioner's findings that Simms (D) was not certain the Jetta had been abandoned, so that the commissioner's error was harmless. Specifically, Simms (D) had stated that he did not know whether the car was abandoned or stolen; the Jetta was only about two years old, and had a current registration tag on the rear; the Jetta was in an

Continued on next page.

area where numerous stolen vehicles had previously been recovered; and there was no testimony of any structural damage to the body of the car that would suggest that the Jetta's damage resulted from an automobile accident. Thus, there was sufficient evidence for the commissioner to find that Simms (D) realized that the car might not be abandoned. Affirmed.

ANALYSIS

As the court in this case observed, proof of general intent, as an element of a general intent offense, requires the absence of an exculpatory state of mind such as mistake of fact. The court ruled that Simms (D) did not carry the burden of proving that his belief that the Jetta was abandoned was honest and reasonable, noting that due process requires the prosecution to prove every element of a crime by proof beyond a reasonable doubt. The court explained that a mistake of fact defense based on a defendant's belief that property was abandoned by its owner necessarily turns on the defendant's reasonable belief and not on the lawful owner's actual intention to abandon the owner's property, so that as with any other mistake of fact defense to a general intent crime, the defense of abandonment rests on whether the defendant's belief was honest and reasonable, and is not a special kind of mistake of fact defense placing a heavier burden on the defendant. However, in other jurisdictions, mistake of fact is treated as an affirmative defense, as to which the defendant not only must produce evidence that supports the defense (burden of production) but also must prove the defense (burden of proof).

Quicknotes

BENCH TRIAL A non-jury trial where the judge determines the facts, applies the law, and renders judgment.

GENERAL INTENT The intent to conduct an act but without the intent to commit an unlawful act.

HARMLESS ERROR An error committed during trial that does not require the reviewing court to overturn or modify the trial court's judgment in that it did not affect the appellant's substantial rights or the disposition of the action.

MISTAKE OF FACT An unintentional mistake in knowing or recalling a fact without the will to deceive.

STRICT LIABILITY OFFENSE Criminal offense that does not have a mens rea element, so that only proof of the commission or omission of a specified act is sufficient to impose liability for the act, regardless of intent, motive, or mental state at the time of the act.

People v. Ryan

State (P) v. Drug possessor (D)

N.Y. Ct. App.*, 626 N.E.2d 51 (1993)

NATURE OF CASE: Appeal from conviction for drug possession.

FACT SUMMARY: Ryan (D) claimed that he was convicted of felony drug possession even though he did not know how much weight of the drug he had.

RULE OF LAW

Laws against drug possession include a mens rea element for the weight of the drugs.

FACTS: Ryan (D) asked his friend Hopkins to order and receive a shipment of hallucinogenic mushrooms on his behalf. The police were tipped off to Hopkins's receipt of the drugs, and an investigator delivered the drugs to Hopkins. After Hopkins was arrested, he informed on Ryan (D) and taped a conversation in which he told Ryan (D) that there were two pounds of mushrooms. Ryan (D) was convicted of felony drug possession for having more than 625 milligrams of a hallucinogen after evidence showed that the package delivered to Hopkins contained well over that amount. Ryan (D) appealed, claiming that he did not knowingly possess that amount of drugs.

ISSUE: Do laws against drug possession include a mens rea element for the weight of the drugs?

HOLDING AND DECISION: (Kaye, C.J.) Yes. Laws against drug possession include a mens rea element for the weight of the drugs. The statute at issue provides that a person is guilty for knowingly and unlawfully possessing a certain amount of drugs. The language of the law demonstrates that "knowingly" applies to the weight element as well as to the possession element. This reading is supported by the rule that statutes defining crimes include a mens rea requirement for all material elements unless there is a clear intent to create a strict liability crime. Therefore, if a single mens rea is set forth in a criminal law, it presumptively applies to all elements of the offense unless there is a contrary legislative intent. In the present case, the purpose of the knowledge requirement is partially to avoid over-penalizing a person who unwittingly possesses a larger amount of a controlled substance than anticipated. Since Ryan (D) knew only that he possessed two pounds of mushrooms, he did not knowingly possess the requisite amount of hallucinogens, in absence of evidence that two pounds of mushrooms usually contain that amount of hallucinogen. Reversed.

*The New York Court of Appeals is New York State's highest court.

ANALYSIS

The court's decision allows the use of inferences to prove the knowledge requirement. Thus, knowledge of the weight of substances can be inferred from the defendant's handling of the material. The court also noted that many drugs are measured by aggregate weight, which includes cutting agents.

Quicknotes

KNOWINGLY Intentionally; willfully; committing an act with knowledge as to its probable consequences.

MATERIAL ELEMENT OF CRIME A part of a crime that must be demonstrated by the prosecution in order to convict a defendant.

MENS REA Criminal intent.

STRICT LIABILITY OFFENSE Criminal offense that does not have a mens rea element, so that only proof of the commission or omission of a specified act is sufficient to impose liability for the act, regardless of intent, motive, or mental state at the time of the act.

Elonis v. United States

Individual convicted of making threatening communications online (D) v. Federal government (P)

575 U.S. 723 (2015)

NATURE OF CASE: Appeal from affirmance of conviction of crime under 18 U.S.C. § 875(c) of making threatening communications in interstate commerce.

FACT SUMMARY: Elonis (D), who was convicted of making threatening communications on social media, contended that to be convicted under 18 U.S.C. § 875(c), which criminalizes the making of threatening communications in interstate commerce, the Government (P) had to show that he intended to communicate a true threat.

RULE OF LAW

To obtain a conviction under 18 U.S.C. § 875(c), which makes it a crime to transmit in interstate commerce "any communication containing any threat . . . to injure the person of another," the government must prove that the defendant intended to communicate a true threat.

FACTS: Federal law, in 18 U.S.C. § 875(c), makes it a crime to transmit in interstate commerce "any communication containing any threat . . . to injure the person of another." After his wife left him and took their children with her, Elonis (D) started posting on the social networking website Facebook self-styled rap lyrics containing graphically violent language and imagery concerning his wife, co-workers, a kindergarten class, and police officers. These posts were often interspersed with disclaimers that the lyrics were "fictitious" and not intended to depict real persons. Nevertheless, his soon-to-be ex-wife felt threatened by these posts and, claiming she was afraid for her life, obtained a restraining order against Elonis (D). Elonis (D) was eventually arrested based on his posts and charged with five counts of violating § 875(c). At trial, Elonis (D) requested a jury instruction that the Government (P) was required to prove that he intended to communicate a "true threat." Instead, the district court told the jury that Elonis (D) could be found guilty if a reasonable person would foresee that his statements would be interpreted as a threat. Elonis (D) was convicted on four of the five counts and renewed his jury instruction challenge on appeal. The court of appeals affirmed, holding that § 875(c) requires only the intent to communicate words that a defendant understands, and that a reasonable person would view, as a threat. The United States Supreme Court granted certiorari.

ISSUE: To obtain a conviction under 18 U.S.C. § 875(c), which makes it a crime to transmit in interstate commerce "any communication containing any threat . . . to injure the person of another," must the government prove that the defendant intended to communicate a true threat?

HOLDING AND DECISION: (Roberts, C.J.) Yes. To obtain a conviction under 18 U.S.C. § 875(c), which makes it a crime to transmit in interstate commerce "any communication containing any threat . . . to injure the person of another," the government must prove that the defendant intended to communicate a true threat. Section 875(c) does not indicate whether the defendant must intend that the communication contain a threat, and the parties can show no indication of a particular mental state requirement in the statute's text. Elonis (D) claims that the word "threat," by definition, conveys the intent to inflict harm. However, common definitions of "threat" speak to what the statement conveys—not to the author's mental state. Nonetheless, mere omission from a criminal statute of any mention of criminal intent does not dispense with such a requirement. Federal criminal statutes that are silent on the required mental state should be read to include only that mens rea is necessary to separate wrongful from innocent conduct. In some cases, a general requirement that a defendant act knowingly is sufficient, but where such a requirement would fail to protect the innocent actor, the statute would need to be read to require specific intent. The presumption in favor of a scienter requirement should apply to each of the statutory elements that criminalize otherwise innocent conduct. In the context of § 875(c), such a presumption requires proof that a communication was transmitted and that it contained a threat. Because the crucial element separating legal innocence from wrongful conduct in this context is the threatening nature of the communication, the mental state requirement must apply to the fact that the communication contains a threat. Elonis's (D) conviction was premised solely on how his posts would be viewed by a reasonable person, a standard feature of civil liability in tort law inconsistent with the conventional criminal conduct requirement of "awareness of some wrongdoing." Thus, Elonis (D) was convicted under a negligence standard, rather than a criminal standard. Because Elonis's (D) mental state was not considered by the jury, his conviction cannot stand. Reversed and remanded.

Continued on next page.

ANALYSIS

To show that Elonis (D) intended to communicate a true threat, the Government (P) could show that Elonis (D) transmitted a communication for the purpose of issuing a threat or with knowledge that the communication would be viewed as a threat. The Court declined to address whether a mental state of recklessness would also suffice.

Quicknotes

CRIMINAL INTENT An intention to carry out a criminal offense.

MENS REA Criminal intent.

NEGLIGENCE Conduct falling below the standard of care that a reasonable person would demonstrate under similar conditions.

People v. Bray

State (P) v. Felon (D)

Cal. Ct. App., 52 Cal. App. 3d 494 (1975)

NATURE OF CASE: Appeal of conviction for illegal possession of firearm.

FACT SUMMARY: Not certain whether a previous conviction constituted a felony, Bray (D) purchased a gun, stating he had no felony convictions.

RULE OF LAW

In a non-strict liability crime, lack of knowledge of facts necessary for criminal intent exculpates the defendant.

FACTS: Bray (D) was convicted of being an accessory to a crime. He was given probation. Years later, having obtained a job as a security officer, Bray (D) purchased a firearm. Prior to purchasing a gun, Bray (D) was required to affirm that he had no prior felony convictions. Bray (D) stated he had none, not believing his prior conviction to be a felony. Bray (D) was charged and convicted of falsifying his record by not listing the conviction. Bray (D) appealed.

ISSUE: In a non-strict liability crime, does lack of knowledge of facts necessary for criminal intent exculpate a defendant?

HOLDING AND DECISION: (Brown, P.J.) Yes. In a non-strict liability crime, lack of knowledge of facts necessary for criminal intent exculpates a defendant. One cannot form intent without knowledge of the underlying relevant facts. Here, Bray (D) in fact did not know that he was a felon, and the fact that he was given no jail time makes this lack of knowledge quite reasonable. Reversed.

ANALYSIS

It is an old axiom of the law that "ignorance of the law is no excuse." However, as this case demonstrates, ignorance of the facts sometimes is. Nonetheless, it can sometimes be a problem figuring out whether a certain lack of knowledge was of law or facts.

Quicknotes

FELONY A criminal offense of greater seriousness than a misdemeanor; felonies are generally defined pursuant to statute as any crime that is punishable by death or by a term of imprisonment exceeding one year.

STRICT LIABILITY Liability for all injuries proximately caused by a party's conducting of certain inherently dangerous activities without regard to negligence or fault.

United States v. Baker

Federal government (P) v. Watch dealer (D)

807 F.2d 427 (5th Cir. 1986)

NATURE OF CASE: Appeal from conviction for trafficking in counterfeit goods.

FACT SUMMARY: Baker (D) claimed that he was not guilty of trafficking in counterfeit watches because he did not know that Congress had enacted a new law criminalizing his conduct.

RULE OF LAW
Ignorance of the law is not an excuse.

FACTS: In 1984 Congress enacted the Trademark Counterfeiting Act, which criminalized conduct that had formerly been subject to civil penalties only. It penalized anyone who intentionally trafficked in goods and knowingly used a counterfeit mark. Baker (D) intentionally and knowingly dealt in counterfeit Rolex watches and was convicted. Baker (D) appealed, claiming that he did not know that trafficking in counterfeiting goods was a crime.

ISSUE: Is ignorance of the law an excuse?

HOLDING AND DECISION: (Reavley, J.) No. Ignorance of the law is not an excuse. While this principle is often overstated, it remains true that criminal law does not require knowledge that an act is illegal. A defendant may not avoid prosecution by simply claiming that they had not brushed up on the law. In the present case, Baker's (D) conduct met the required mental state because he admittedly had knowledge of dealing in counterfeiting goods. His knowledge of the new law is irrelevant. Affirmed.

ANALYSIS

Professors LaFave and Scott's criminal law treatise points out that it is important to distinguish between the defendant's mental state required for the commission of a crime and a claim of ignorance that certain conduct was proscribed by law. In other words, ignorance of certain factual conditions specified by the governing law may lead to acquittal, but ignorance of which conditions are actually contained in that law will not. This principle dates back to the beginning of English common law.

Quicknotes

MISTAKE OF LAW An error involving a misunderstanding or incorrect application of law.

Cheek v. United States

Tax evader (D) v. Federal government (P)

498 U.S. 192 (1991)

NATURE OF CASE: Appeal from conviction for income tax evasion.

FACT SUMMARY: Cheek (D) claimed that he was not guilty of willful tax evasion because he believed that income taxes were unconstitutional, that wages were not income, and that he was not a taxpayer within the meaning of the Internal Revenue Code.

RULE OF LAW

A subjective misunderstanding about the law is a defense to willful evasion of taxes.

FACTS: Cheek (D) failed to file federal income tax returns between 1980 and 1986. The federal Government (P) charged Cheek (D) with willfully attempting to evade his tax obligations. These offenses were specific intent crimes that require the defendant to have acted willfully. During the period in question, Cheek (D) was active in anti-tax movements and testified that he believed that the federal income tax was unconstitutional. Cheek (D) argued that since this belief was sincere, he lacked the willfulness required for conviction. At trial, the court instructed the jury that an honest but unreasonable belief was not a defense that negates willfulness. Cheek (D) was convicted and subsequently appealed.

ISSUE: Is a subjective misunderstanding about the law a defense to willful evasion of taxes?

HOLDING AND DECISION: (White, J.) Yes. A subjective misunderstanding about the law is a defense to willful evasion of taxes. Willfulness requires that the government prove that the defendant voluntarily and intentionally violated a duty imposed by law. The government cannot prove knowledge of the duty if the defendant was ignorant of it, misunderstood it, or believed it did not exist. This belief must be held in good faith but does not need to be objectively reasonable. Since the tax system is complex, proof of knowledge of the law is required to show willfulness. However, claims that the tax laws are unconstitutional do not arise from innocent mistakes caused by the complexity of the Internal Revenue Code. Instead, these claims reveal full knowledge and a conclusion, however wrong, that the provisions are invalid. Thus, a defendant's view about the validity of the law is irrelevant. Accordingly, Cheek's (D) claims about his view that the law was unconstitutional were properly excluded from consideration by the jury. However, it was error for the trial court to instruct the jury that Cheek's (D) subjective beliefs that wages were not income and that he was not a taxpayer within the meaning of the Code and should not be considered by the jury in determining willfulness. Remanded.

ANALYSIS

This decision has not been extended by other courts outside the tax law context. However, the Supreme Court reached a similar decision in *Ratzlaf v. United States*, 501 U.S. 135 (1994), interpreting a banking law. Congress immediately revised the law by removing the willful requirement.

Quicknotes

SPECIFIC INTENT The intent to commit a specific unlawful act for which one is later charged. Specific intent is a required element for criminal liability for certain crimes.

SUBJECTIVE A belief that is personal to an individual.

WILLFULLY An act that is undertaken intentionally, knowingly, and with the intent to commit an unlawful act without a justifiable excuse.

Commonwealth v. Twitchell

State (P) v. Parents (D)

Mass. Sup. Jud. Ct., 617 N.E.2d 609 (1993)

NATURE OF CASE: Appeal from convictions for involuntary manslaughter.

FACT SUMMARY: Christian Scientist parents (D) did not seek medical treatment for their child's illness and the child died.

RULE OF LAW

Mistake of law can be a defense when the government official charged with enforcing that law has issued a mistaken or misleading ruling about the law upon which the defendants relied.

FACTS: Christian Scientist parents (D) did not seek medical treatment for their child for an illness that is usually successfully treated by surgery. The parents did obtain official religious counseling about their responsibilities as parents and relied on documents prepared by their denomination. These religious papers had relied on a misleading interpretation of the law written by the Attorney General of Massachusetts. Following their convictions for involuntary manslaughter, the parents (D) appealed, claiming their mistake of law should excuse their conduct.

ISSUE: Can mistake of law be a defense when the government official charged with enforcing that law has issued a mistaken or misleading ruling about the law upon which the defendants relied?

HOLDING AND DECISION: (Wilkins, J.) Yes. Mistake of law can be a defense when the government official charged with enforcing that law has issued a mistaken or misleading ruling about the law upon which the defendants relied. In very narrow circumstances, mistake of law can be a defense to charges of involuntary manslaughter. These circumstances include instances where the mistake of law grows out of the misleading or false opinion provided by the government official charged with interpreting the law. In the instant case, the parents (D) based their conduct in part on the misleading opinion of the Attorney General. Reversed and remanded for new trial if the Attorney General concludes that prosecution is necessary.

ANALYSIS

The defense of entrapment by estoppel rests on the principles of fairness and the Due Process Clause of the Fifth Amendment. The theory is that if a person tried to determine the law and consulted the official interpretation of the law, they should not be liable for false official government pronouncement. The person must be actually misinformed or misled by the interpretation given by the government official charged with interpreting the law.

Quicknotes

INVOLUNTARY MANSLAUGHTER The killing of another person without premeditation or deliberation or with the intent to kill or to commit a felony, which may be reasonably expected to result in death or serious bodily injury; involuntary manslaughter is characterized by reckless conduct in the commission of a lawful act, or by the commission of an unlawful act that is not a felony, but which leads to the killing of another.

MISTAKE OF LAW An error involving a misunderstanding or incorrect application of law.

State v. Cameron

State (P) v. Assailant (D)

N.J. Sup. Ct., 514 A.2d 1302 (1986)

NATURE OF CASE: Appeal of reversal of conviction of assault, illegal weapon possession, and resisting arrest.

FACT SUMMARY: Cameron (D) wished to invoke voluntary intoxication as a defense to a charge of assault, illegal weapon possession, and resisting arrest.

RULE OF LAW

Voluntary intoxication may be a defense to a charge of assault, illegal weapon possession, and resisting arrest.

FACTS: Cameron (D) became involved in an altercation with several individuals, which resulted in charges of assault, illegal weapon possession, and resisting arrest. At trial, the court refused to permit her to raise the defense of voluntary intoxication, and Cameron (D) was convicted. A state court of appeals reversed, ruling that the defense should have been permitted. The state supreme court granted review.

ISSUE: May voluntary intoxication be a defense to a charge of assault, illegal weapon possession, and resisting arrest?

HOLDING AND DECISION: (Clifford, J.) Yes. Voluntary intoxication may be a defense to a charge of assault, illegal weapon possession, and resisting arrest. At common law, voluntary intoxication could be a defense to a "specific intent" crime but not a "general intent" crime. New Jersey has statutorily changed the culpability element of criminal law, so that mens rea now has four categories: "knowing," "purposeful," "reckless," and "criminally negligent." By statute, voluntary intoxication may be raised as a defense to crimes involving the first two mental states. Here, the assault, illegal weapon possession, and resisting arrest all fall within the first two categories, so the defense would be applicable. Reversed.

ANALYSIS

Voluntary intoxication used to be both a complete and an incomplete defense. In the latter situation, it could reduce a charge, such as the diminished capacity defense might. The trend in recent years has been to permit it to be a complete defense only, to be used when it negates an element of the offense in question.

Quicknotes

GENERAL INTENT The intent to conduct an act but without the intent to commit an unlawful act.

MENS REA Criminal intent.

SPECIFIC INTENT The intent to commit a specific unlawful act for which one is later charged. Specific intent is a required element for criminal liability for certain crimes.

VOLUNTARY INTOXICATION The voluntary consumption of substances that the defendant knows or should know will obscure their judgment; voluntary intoxication may be considered when determining whether the defendant possessed the requisite intent.

State v. Joseph

State (P) v. Convicted first-degree murderer (D)

W.V. Sup. Ct., 590 S.E.2d 718 (2023)

NATURE OF CASE: Appeal from first-degree murder conviction on grounds of diminished capacity.

FACT SUMMARY: Robert Joseph (D) contended that at his trial for first-degree murder, the court erred in excluding as insufficient the testimony of Joseph's (D) treating physicians and an expert witness regarding Joseph's (D) diminished capacity at the time of the murder. The State (P) contended that the testimony failed to establish that Joseph (D) suffered from diminished capacity.

RULE OF LAW

(1) When an offense charged is a crime for which there is a lesser included offense, the diminished capacity defense is available to permit the defendant to introduce expert testimony regarding a mental disease or defect that rendered the defendant incapable, at the time the crime was committed, of forming a mental state that is an element of the crime charged, so that the defendant is not guilty of the particular crime charged, but may be convicted for a lesser included offense.

(2) Where, pursuant to the diminished capacity rule, an expert directly addresses a defendant's mental capacity at the time of the charged criminal offense, and the expert opines that the defendant was, as a consequence of the defendant's mental defect, unable to formulate intent or malice or to premeditate under the circumstances at that time, the expert has presented sufficient evidence for the expert to be allowed to testify before the jury.

FACTS: Robert Joseph (D) was in his truck in Scott Light's driveway. Joseph (D) had been looking for a mutual friend, Jessica Martin. When Joseph (D) learned that Light had driven Martin and another friend to a certain location, Joseph (D) spun his tires in the driveway, and Light yelled at him to stop the truck. Light then walked over to Joseph's (D) truck, pulled the driver's door open, and the two men argued. During the argument, Light pointed his finger at Joseph (D), who slapped Light's hand away. According to Joseph (D), Light then struck or slapped him on the left side of the head. Joseph (D) testified that, upon being slapped, he saw a "blue flash," and his hand landed on a .22 caliber pistol that was lying on the seat of his truck. Joseph (D) grabbed the pistol and fired five shots into Light, who died. Several years before this incident, Joseph (D) had been involved in a motorcycle accident, and, among the serious injuries he sustained was a crush injury to his left frontal skull. Joseph (D) was charged with first-degree murder and sought to assert the defense of diminished capacity resulting from the brain injury he had sustained in his motorcycle accident. He offered the testimony of three doctors in support of this defense. One doctor had treated Joseph (D) 11 years after the accident, after Joseph (D) had been hospitalized for treatment of threatening behavior and substance abuse following a DUI arrest. The second doctor, a board-certified psychiatrist, had also seen Joseph (D) professionally on a number of occasions. The third doctor, and expert, was Dr. Robert Solomon, a forensic psychologist. The trial court heard testimony from each of these doctors *in camera.* Dr. Solomon testified that under the circumstances that existed at the time Joseph (D) shot Light, Joseph's (D) ability to plan, organize, and carry out decision-making processes were extremely flawed as a result of his brain injury, but that in other circumstances the situation might be different. Dr. Solomon also testified that within a scientific certainty Joseph's (D) capacity was diminished during that particular time frame. The trial court interpreted Dr. Solomon's testimony as indicating that although Joseph (D) was capable of formulating an intent to kill, malice and premeditation, that he believed under the circumstance of this particular case, the rapidity of the situation prevented Joseph (D) from formulating malice or premeditation. The trial court went on to state that whether Joseph (D) acted with malice or premeditated on a particular occasion were issues for jury determination. The trial court ruled that, although the state had recognized the defense of diminished capacity, the testimony of the three doctors was insufficient upon which to base the defense. Therefore, the court excluded the testimony of these three witnesses. At the close of all the evidence, Joseph (D) was convicted of first-degree murder. On appeal to the state's highest court, Joseph (D) contended that the trial court had committed error in excluding the expert testimony.

ISSUE:

(1) When an offense charged is a crime for which there is a lesser included offense, is the diminished capacity defense available to permit the defendant to introduce expert testimony regarding a mental disease or defect that rendered the defendant incapable, at the

Continued on next page.

time the crime was committed, of forming a mental state that is an element of the crime charged, so that the defendant is not guilty of the particular crime charged, but may be convicted for a lesser included offense?

(2) Where, pursuant to the diminished capacity rule, an expert directly addresses a defendant's mental capacity at the time of the charged criminal offense, and the expert opines that the defendant was, as a consequence of the defendant's mental defect, unable to formulate intent or malice or to premeditate under the circumstances at that time, has the expert presented sufficient evidence for the expert to be allowed to testify before the jury?

HOLDING AND DECISION: [Judge not stated in casebook extract.]

(1) Yes. When an offense charged is a crime for which there is a lesser included offense, the diminished capacity defense is available to permit the defendant to introduce expert testimony regarding a mental disease or defect that rendered the defendant incapable, at the time the crime was committed, of forming a mental state that is an element of the crime charged, so that the defendant is not guilty of the particular crime charged, but may be convicted for a lesser included offense. Generally, what is sometimes referred to as the "diminished capacity defense" allows a defendant to offer evidence of the defendant's mental condition with respect to the defendant's capacity to achieve the mens rea or intent required for commission of the offense charged. However, it is not accurate to refer to this rule as a "defense," as it does not provide any ground for acquittal not provided in the definition of the offense, and it does not establish a complete defense. Moreover, it is not considered a justification or excuse for a crime. Thus, some courts believe it is more like a rule of evidence that permits the defendant to present evidence of the defendant's inability to form the mens rea for the crime charged at the time of the crime, but also leaves open the possibility that the defendant may be charged with a lesser included offense for which the defendant did have the requisite mens rea. Although this rule has been applied in criminal prosecutions in this state, it has never been formally and expressly adopted. For example, evidence of voluntary intoxication has been allowed to show that a defendant was incapable of forming the required mental state for first-degree murder, with the caveat that although it is true that voluntary drunkenness does not ordinarily excuse a crime, it may reduce the degree of the crime or negate a specific intent. It would be inequitable to allow evidence of a diminished capacity where voluntary intoxication is involved yet deny such evidence where an organic brain injury or other brain injury or disease is involved. Accordingly, the diminished capacity rule is adopted in this state to permit a defendant to introduce expert testimony regarding a mental disease or defect that rendered the defendant incapable, at the time the crime was committed, of forming a mental state that is an element of the crime charged. This defense is asserted ordinarily when the offense charged is a crime for which there is a lesser included offense. This is so because the successful use of this defense renders the defendant not guilty of the particular crime charged but does not preclude a conviction for a lesser included offense.

(2) Yes. Where, pursuant to the diminished capacity rule, an expert directly addresses a defendant's mental capacity at the time of the charged criminal offense, and the expert opines that the defendant was, as a consequence of the defendant's mental defect, unable to formulate intent or malice or to premeditate under the circumstances at that time, the expert has presented sufficient evidence for the expert to be allowed to testify before the jury. It seems that the trial court interpreted the diminished capacity defense as requiring a complete inability to form the necessary mental elements of a crime. On the contrary, a defendant who raises a diminished capacity defense challenges their capacity to premeditate and deliberate at the time of the criminal act. Here, Dr. Solomon's testimony was addressed directly to Joseph's (D) mental capacity at the time he shot Light, and Dr. Solomon opined that at that time, Joseph (D) was, as a consequence of his mental defect, unable to formulate intent or malice or to premeditate under the circumstances. Thus, in the instant case, there plainly was sufficient evidence to allow Dr. Solomon to testify before the jury. Accordingly, the trial court was clearly wrong in excluding this evidence and prohibiting Joseph (D) from presenting his defense attacking the State's (P) case in chief. Therefore, Joseph's (D) conviction is overturned and the case remanded for a new trial.

ANALYSIS

As this case illustrates, the diminished capacity doctrine is designed to permit a defendant to introduce expert testimony regarding the defendant's impaired mental condition to show that the defendant was incapable of forming a specific criminal intent. As the court notes, the doctrine customarily is utilized to negate the elements of premeditation and deliberate intent in first-degree murder or malice aforethought in second degree murder. The reason for allowing a defendant to assert the defense of diminished capacity is to permit the jury to determine if the defendant should be convicted of

Continued on next page.

some lesser degree of homicide because the requisite mental intent to commit first-degree or second-degree murder is not present by virtue of the defendant's mental disease or defect. However, the existence of a mental illness is not alone sufficient to trigger a diminished capacity defense, and it must be shown by psychiatric or psychological testimony that some type of mental illness rendered the defendant incapable of forming the specific intent elements of the charged crime.

Quicknotes

DIMINISHED CAPACITY A defense to criminal liability that the perpetrator suffered from a mental incapacity at the time the crime was committed so that the defendant did not possess the requisite mental state for that crime, but may have had the requisite mental state for a lesser included crime.

FIRST-DEGREE MURDER The willful killing of a person with deliberation and premeditation; first-degree murder also encompasses those situations in which a person is killed within the perpetration of, or attempt to perpetrate, specified felonies.

IN CAMERA In the judge's private chambers.

MENS REA Criminal intent.

MENTAL CAPACITY The ability to comprehend the nature, terms, and effect of the act in which one is engaged.

CHAPTER 4

Causation

Quick Reference Rules of Law

Regina v. Martin Dyos

Government (P) v. Alleged murderer (D)

Cent. Crim. Ct., Crim. L. Rev. 660-62 (1979)

NATURE OF CASE: Criminal proceeding for murder.

FACT SUMMARY: Martin Dyos (D) had caused an injury to the right forehead of RM, but no evidence could be offered as to the cause of a second injury to RM or which injury was the cause of death.

RULE OF LAW

One's act cannot be held to be the cause of death of another if the death would, or could, have occurred without the act.

FACTS: A number of persons, including Martin Dyos (D), faced criminal charges as the result of a fight that occurred between two groups of youths after a dance. Martin Dyos (D) was charged with murder and grievous bodily harm. Evidence was offered that he had caused injury to the right forehead of RM by means of a brick and that RM, who died nine days later from his injuries, had also received an injury behind his right ear. There was no evidence as to the cause of this later injury. The pathologist concluded that both wounds were potentially fatal and either could "very probably" cause death, and that there was a "reasonable and sensible" possibility that RM might have recovered from the first injury, whichever that was.

ISSUE: Can one's act be held to be the cause of death of another if the death would, or could, have occurred without the act?

HOLDING AND DECISION: (Cantley, J.) No. One's act cannot be held to be the cause of death of another if the death would, or could, have occurred without the act. One is not the cause of another's death in the legal sense unless the death was a natural and probable consequence of one's act. In this case, the Crown had to exclude the possibility that death was caused by an injury other than the one caused by Martin Dyos (D). Since another injury did occur that may reasonably have been the cause of death of RM and for which Martin Dyos (D) has not been shown to be responsible, the count of murder cannot go to the jury. After the ruling, Dyos pled guilty to two of the lesser counts.

ANALYSIS

Commentators have dubbed the causation requirement highlighted in this case the "but for" causation principle. It is also often referred to as the factual cause, the de facto cause, or the scientific cause, and should be distinguished from "cause" in another sense, i.e., "proximate" cause or "legal" cause. When looking at the notion of "but for" causation, it should be remembered that an omission can be a "but for" cause of a result.

Quicknotes

"BUT FOR" TEST A necessary cause. If the cause had not happened, then the result would not have followed.

PROXIMATE CAUSE The natural sequence of events without which an injury would not have been sustained.

Hubbard v. Commonwealth

Manslaughter defendant (D) v. State (P)

Ky. Ct. App., 202 S.W.2d 634 (1947)

NATURE OF CASE: Appeal from a voluntary manslaughter conviction.

FACT SUMMARY: When Hubbard (D) was convicted for the voluntary manslaughter of a jailor who suffered a fatal heart attack while attempting to subdue Hubbard (D), the latter argued that his actions were not the legally proximate cause of the death.

RULE OF LAW

Criminal liability for death arises only where death or serious bodily harm was the probable and natural consequence of the accused's act.

FACTS: Robert Hubbard (D) was arrested for being drunk in a public place and was taken before the county judge. Being too drunk to be tried, Hubbard (D) was ordered to jail but refused to go peaceably. Dyche, the jailor, tried to subdue Hubbard (D) in a scuffle. Hubbard (D) was finally persuaded to get off the floor, and he, a deputy, and Dyche left the courthouse for jail. Dyche suffered a fatal heart attack as he left the courthouse. Hubbard (D) had never struck Dyche, and Dyche never received a physical injury from the scuffle. Hubbard (D) was charged with, and convicted of, voluntary manslaughter. Hubbard (D) appealed, arguing that his act of initially resisting being taken from the courthouse was not the legally proximate cause of Dyche's heart attack and subsequent death.

ISSUE: Does criminal liability for death arise only where death or serious bodily harm was the probable and natural consequence of the accused's act?

HOLDING AND DECISION: (Stanley, Commr.) Yes. Criminal liability for death arises only where death or serious bodily harm was the probable and natural consequence of the accused's act. Where the cause of death was not due to a corporal blow or injury (essential under the early common law) or to some hostile demonstration or overt act directed toward the person of the decedent, there is no criminal liability unless the death was the natural and probable consequence of an indirect, unlawful act of the accused. If there is reasonable doubt as to this point, as here, it would be unjust to punish the accused. Here, Hubbard's (D) misdemeanor must be regarded as too remote—not in time, but as to cause. The deceased, knowing he had a serious heart condition, undertook a task which he knew would excite him or create an emotional state of mind, which he also well knew he should have avoided. His intervening act in rolling and tumbling in pain on the courthouse yard, instead of lying quiet and still, was probably as much responsible for his ensuing death as was the initial excitement caused by Hubbard's (D) conduct. It would be too speculative to say that Hubbard's (D) misdemeanor act of resisting arrest was sufficiently proximate to impose criminal homicide liability upon him in this factual setting. Reversed.

ANALYSIS

One cannot escape culpability simply because factors other than their act contributed to the death of another or hastened it. Under most modern decisions, death caused or accomplished through fright, fear, or nervous shock may form a basis for criminal responsibility. On the other hand, it is held that to warrant a conviction for homicide, the act of the accused must be the proximate cause of death; that if there was an intervening cause for which the accused was not responsible and but for which death would not have occurred, the accused is blameless.

Quicknotes

INTERVENING ACT An event whose occurrence breaks the causal chain between the tortfeasor's acts and the resulting injury.

MISDEMEANOR A crime that does not constitute a felony. A misdemeanor is generally less severe and results in a lesser punishment.

VOLUNTARY MANSLAUGHTER The killing of another person without premeditation, deliberation, or malice aforethought, but committed while in the "heat of passion" or upon some adequate provocation, thereby reducing the charge from murder to manslaughter.

Commonwealth v. Rhoades

State (P) v. Arsonist (D)

Mass. Sup. Jud. Ct., 401 N.E.2d 342 (1980)

NATURE OF CASE: Appeal from conviction for murder.

FACT SUMMARY: Rhoades (D) was found guilty of second-degree murder after the judge charged the jury that Rhoades (D) was liable for second-degree murder if the victim died "as a result" of his act, or if his act "in any way contributed to hasten or was part of the proximate cause of the death."

RULE OF LAW

One is criminally liable for the death of another only if one's action was the proximate cause of death, i.e., a cause which, in the natural and continuous sequence, produced the death, and without which the death would not have occurred.

FACTS: Captain Trainor was among the firefighters responding to the fire that Rhoades (D) set. Captain Trainor went inside the burning building to rescue persons thought to be trapped inside. Captain Trainor encountered intense heat and experienced difficulty in getting air through his face mask. Captain Trainor collapsed on the roof of the building. A medical expert found that Captain Trainor died as the result of a coronary thrombosis precipitated by the combination of cold weather, stress, and smoke inhalation. Rhoades (D) was found guilty of second-degree murder after the judge instructed the jury that he was liable for second-degree murder if Captain Trainor died "as a result" of his act, or if his act "in any way contributed to hasten, or was part of the proximate cause of," Captain Trainor's death. Rhoades (D) appealed, claiming the instruction was in error.

ISSUE: Is one criminally liable for the death of another only if one's action was the proximate cause of death, i.e., a cause which, in the natural and continuous sequence, produced the death, and without which the death would not have occurred?

HOLDING AND DECISION: [Judge not stated in casebook excerpt.] Yes. One is criminally liable for the death of another only if one's action was the proximate cause of death, i.e., a cause which, in the natural and continuous sequence, produced the death, and without which the death would not have occurred. The jury instruction at issue in this case exposed Rhoades (D) to potential liability for events not proximately caused by his felonious act in setting the fire. It left the jury with the impression that if his act in setting the fire in any way constituted a link, no matter how remote, in the chain of events leading to Captain Trainor's death, Rhoades (D) should be convicted. It failed to explain the need to find that his action was the proximate cause of death, i.e., a cause which, in the natural and continuous sequence, produced the death, and without which the death would not have occurred. Reversed and remanded.

ANALYSIS

Section 2.03 of the Model Penal Code addresses the issue of the causal relationship between conduct and result. It provides, in pertinent part, conduct that "is the cause of a result when: (a) it is an antecedent but for which the result in question would not have occurred; and (b) the relationship between the conduct and result satisfies any additional causal requirements plainly imposed by law."

Quicknotes

PROXIMATE CAUSE The natural sequence of events without which an injury would not have been sustained.

SECOND-DEGREE MURDER The unlawful killing of another person, without premeditation, and characterized by either intent to kill or by a reckless disregard for human life.

Commonwealth v. Root

State (P) v. Driver (D)

Pa. Sup. Ct., 403 Pa. 571, 170 A.2d 310 (1961)

NATURE OF CASE: Appeal from conviction for involuntary manslaughter.

FACT SUMMARY: Root's (D) conviction for involuntary manslaughter was reviewed to determine if his unlawful and reckless conduct in participating in an automobile race on a highway was a sufficiently direct cause of the death of the competing driver to warrant his being charged with criminal homicide.

RULE OF LAW

The tort liability concept of proximate cause has no proper place in prosecutions for criminal homicide and more direct causal connection is required for conviction.

FACTS: Root (D) and another person were participants in an automobile race on a rural three-lane highway one night. Root (D) was in the lead. The other party attempted to pass him when a truck was closely approaching from the opposite direction. In so doing, he swerved to the wrong side of the road and slammed head-on into the oncoming truck. He died as a result, and Root (D) was convicted of involuntary manslaughter. The conviction was affirmed on appeal, but the Supreme Court of Pennsylvania reviewed the important question whether Root's (D) unlawful and reckless conduct was a sufficiently direct cause of the death to warrant his being charged with criminal homicide.

ISSUE: Does the tort liability concept of proximate cause have no proper place in prosecutions for criminal homicide and is more direct causal connection required for conviction?

HOLDING AND DECISION: (Jones, C.J.) Yes. The tort liability concept of proximate cause has no proper place in prosecutions for criminal homicide and more direct causal connection is required for conviction. One essential element of the crime of involuntary manslaughter is that the unlawful or reckless conduct charged to the defendant was the direct cause of the death in issue. Although precedent is to be found for application of the tort law concept of "proximate cause" in fixing responsibility for criminal homicide, the want of any rational basis for its use in determining criminal liability can no longer be disregarded. Thus, utilizing that concept in this case was improper. Reversed.

DISSENT: (Eagen, J.) Root's (D) conduct was a direct cause of the death. The victim was responding to a situation Root (D) helped create, his reaction should have been expected, and it was clearly foreseeable.

ANALYSIS

Since only the other participating racer was killed, the question comes to mind whether the court's view would be different if the innocent truck driver had been killed. A Florida case involving just such a scenario suggests that the result would indeed be different. *Jacob v. State*, 184 So. 2d 711, 716, 717 (Fla. 1966).

Quicknotes

INVOLUNTARY MANSLAUGHTER The killing of another person without premeditation or deliberation or with the intent to kill or to commit a felony, which may be reasonably expected to result in death or serious bodily injury; involuntary manslaughter is characterized by reckless conduct in the commission of a lawful act, or by the commission of an unlawful act that is not a felony, but which leads to the killing of another.

PROXIMATE CAUSE The natural sequence of events without which an injury would not have been sustained.

RECKLESSNESS The conscious disregard of substantial and justifiable risk.

United States v. Hamilton

Federal government (P) v. Assailant (D)

182 F. Supp. 548 (D.D.C. 1960)

NATURE OF CASE: Trial on a charge of murder in the second degree.

FACT SUMMARY: Victim, who was recuperating in hospital after being severely beaten by Hamilton (D), died of asphyxiation when he had a convulsion and pulled out life support tubes attached to his throat.

RULE OF LAW

A person is guilty of homicide where, even though a wound that person inflicts on another is not in and of itself fatal, they thereby set in action a chain of causation that results in the victim's death.

FACTS: Hamilton (D) severely beat the victim during a quarrel. The victim fell to the ground, but Hamilton (D), in an uncontrollable rage, continued to pummel him about the head and face. While in a semi-comatose, violent condition and shock, the victim was rushed to the hospital where tubes were attached to his throat to keep his airways clear of blood. Three days later, the victim fell into convulsions after restraints were removed from his hands, immediately pulled out the tubes with his own hands, and died of asphyxiation. Hamilton (D) was charged with second-degree murder.

ISSUE: Is a person guilty of homicide where, even though a wound that person inflicts on another is not in and of itself fatal, they thereby set in action a chain of causation that results in the victim's death?

HOLDING AND DECISION: (Holtzoff, J.) Yes. A person is guilty of homicide where, even though a wound that person inflicts on another is not in and of itself fatal, they thereby set in action a chain of causation that results in the victim's death. Here, the victim pulled out the life support tubing, which was affirmative action that contributed to his own death. That action, however, is immaterial. It has no effect on Hamilton's (D) liability if it could be shown that, but for pulling out the tubes, which may have been a conscious, deliberate act, the victim would have lived. In other decisions, liability for a homicide has been imposed on the assailant where the victim, who has been dealt a serious but not mortal blow, takes their own life shortly thereafter. The victim's death was a natural and probable consequence of Hamilton's (D) unlawful and criminal treatment. The court must determine whether Hamilton (D) is guilty of homicide or assault with a dangerous weapon. Based on the injuries inflicted and the applicable law, Hamilton (D) is guilty of homicide.

ANALYSIS

Liability for a homicide is clearest when the victim's reaction is instinctive, as where B, in order to escape A's murderous approach, hurls themself out a window, and falls to B's death. Less clear cut are those cases, as here, where the victim's intervening act is more voluntary. However, even in apparently extreme situations, courts have imposed liability for a homicide. In one such case, the victim could have saved himself if he had submitted to an operation for the amputation of his leg; he refused, and gangrene was the listed medical cause of death. Nonetheless, the original act of assault was held to be the legal cause of death. The court reasoned that, although the victim's response—his refusal to undergo the amputation—was unreasonable, it was not abnormal.

Quicknotes

INTERVENING CAUSE A cause, not anticipated by the initial actor, which is sufficient to break the chain of causation and relieve the initial actor of liability.

MANSLAUGHTER The killing of a person without premeditation or deliberation, or with the intent to kill or to commit a felony that may be reasonably expected to result in death or serious bodily injury; manslaughter is characterized by reckless conduct or by some adequate provocation on the part of the actor, as determined by a subjective standard.

SECOND-DEGREE MURDER The unlawful killing of another person, without premeditation, and characterized by either intent to kill or by a reckless disregard for human life.

People v. Kevorkian

State (P) v. Doctor (D)

Mich. Sup. Ct., 447 Mich. 436, 527 N.W.2d 714 (1994)

NATURE OF CASE: Appeal to quash information and dismiss murder charges.

FACT SUMMARY: Dr. Jack Kevorkian (D) was charged with murder for assisting in two suicides.

RULE OF LAW

Providing the means for another's suicide is not murder.

FACTS: Dr. Kevorkian (D) assisted with the suicides of two women in Michigan prior to the enactment of the state's assisted suicide statute. One of the women was successfully connected to Dr. Kevorkian's (D) "suicide machine" and used it as instructed by Dr. Kevorkian (D). The machine first releases barbiturates, then poison, after being activated by the patient. The other woman was fitted with a mask by Dr. Kevorkian (D). The mask was connected to a carbon monoxide cylinder, which the woman opened. The State (P) charged Dr. Kevorkian (D) with murder. The trial court granted Dr. Kevorkian's (D) motion to quash the information and dismiss the charges. The Michigan Court of Appeals reversed and remanded and Dr. Kevorkian (D) appealed to the Michigan Supreme Court.

ISSUE: Is providing the means for another's suicide murder?

HOLDING AND DECISION: (Cavanagh, C.J.) No. Providing the means for another's suicide is not murder. Under the common law, murder is the unlawful killing of a person with malice aforethought. Previous decisions in Michigan have held that providing the means by which another commits suicide is sufficient for a murder conviction. However, recent decisions draw a distinction between active participation in a suicide and mere involvement in the events leading up to the suicide. Courts have generally held that a person may be prosecuted for murder if that person's conduct goes beyond the conduct the assisted suicide statutes were intended to cover. Furthermore, other newer decisions have held that a closer nexus between an act and a death is required to meet the causation requirement. It should be noted that if a person recklessly or negligently provides the means for suicide, that person can be guilty of involuntary manslaughter. Therefore, Kevorkian (D) may not be charged with murder. Reversed and remanded.

ANALYSIS

The ruling follows cases in other states that do not hold persons liable for murder for providing the means to commit suicide or by being involved in the events leading up to the suicide. However, participation in the final overt act that leads to death, such as firing a gun, is murder and not assisted suicide. Conviction for murder requires that death occur as a direct and natural result of a defendant's act. Providing the tools or instructions on how to commit suicide, but without participating in the final overt act is now generally viewed under assisted suicide statutes rather than murder.

Quicknotes

INVOLUNTARY MANSLAUGHTER The killing of another person without premeditation or deliberation or with the intent to kill or to commit a felony, which may be reasonably expected to result in death or serious bodily injury; involuntary manslaughter is characterized by reckless conduct in the commission of a lawful act, or by the commission of an unlawful act that is not a felony, but which leads to the killing of another.

MURDER Unlawful killing of another person either with deliberation and premeditation, or by conduct demonstrating a reckless disregard for human life.

Commonwealth v. Carter

State (P) v. Youth convicted of involuntary manslaughter (D)

Mass. Sup. Ct., 115 N.E.3d 559 (2019)

NATURE OF CASE: Appeal from conviction for involuntary manslaughter for encouraging a suicide.

FACT SUMMARY: Michellle Carter (D) contended that her conviction for involuntary manslaughter for encouraging her boyfriend, Conrad Roy, purely by phone conversation and texts, to follow through on his latest suicide attempt, was unsupported by the evidence, and violated her constitutional due process and free speech rights. The Commonwealth (P) asserted that her speech constituted conduct that was wanton and reckless and resulted in Roy's death.

RULE OF LAW

(1) A person can be convicted of involuntary manslaughter where the evidence shows beyond a reasonable doubt that their words, whether verbal or written, were wanton or reckless, overcame the will of another, and caused the other person to commit suicide.

(2) A state law is not unconstitutionally vague where a person can be charged under the law with involuntary manslaughter for reckless or wanton conduct, including verbal or written conduct, causing another person to commit suicide.

(3) A First Amendment free speech violation does not result from convicting a defendant of involuntary manslaughter for reckless and wanton use of words, whether verbal or written, to overcome the will of another and cause the other person to commit suicide.

FACTS: Michellle Carter (D), when she was 17, had a depressed, suicidal 18-year-old boyfriend, Conrad Roy III. They did not live close to each other, so they primarily communicated by cellphone, either by text or call. Roy had expressed to Carter (D) the desire to end his life by suicide many times, and he even made several attempts that were unsuccessful, usually because he stopped short of the final act, or sought help in some way. Carter (D) initially advised him to seek counseling, which advice Roy rejected. Roy continued to obsess about committing suicide, which was a constant topic of their communications. At some point, Carter (D) had a change of heart, and sought to help Roy achieve his goal. Carter (D) helped Roy plan how, where, and when he would kill himself and downplayed his fears about how his suicide would affect his family. She also repeatedly chastised him for his indecision and delay, texting, for example, that he "better not be bullshitting me and saying you're gonna do this and then purposely get caught" and made him "promise" to kill himself. The plan was for Roy to end his life by carbon monoxide poisoning, so Roy got a water pump that he would use to generate carbon monoxide in his closed truck. On the planned day, Roy drove his truck to a local store's parking lot and started the pump. While the pump was operating, filling the truck with carbon monoxide, Carter (D) and Roy were in contact by cell phone. Carter (D) sent a text to a friend that read, "he just called me and there was a loud noise like a motor and I heard moaning like someone was in pain, and he wouldn't answer when I said his name. I stayed on the phone for like 20 minutes and that's all I heard." A few minutes later, she again texted that friend: "I think he just killed himself." Not long after, she sent a similar text to another friend, stating: "He called me, and I heard like muffled sounds and some type of motor running, and it was like that for 20 minutes, and he wouldn't answer. I think he killed himself." Weeks later, she texted the first friend again, saying in part: "I failed [Roy] I wasn't supposed to let that happen and now I'm realizing I failed him. [H]is death is my fault like honestly I could have stopped him I was on the phone with him and he got out of the car because it was working and he got scared and I fucking told him to get back in . . . because I knew he would do it all over again the next day and I couldn't have him live the way he was living anymore I couldn't do it I wouldn't let him." Carter (D) did not call anyone for help notwithstanding that she knew Roy was dying. Roy's body was found in his truck the next day. Carter (D) was charged as a youthful offender with, and convicted of, involuntary manslaughter for what she said to Roy, and for failing to seek help. Carter (D) appealed her conviction on the grounds that it was unsupported by the evidence and violated her constitutional due process and free speech rights. The Commonwealth (P) asserted that her speech constituted conduct that was wanton and reckless and resulted in Roy's death. The state's highest court affirmed the Juvenile Court judge's denial of the motion to dismiss the youthful offender indictment, concluding that there was probable cause to show that the coercive quality of Carter's (D) verbal conduct overwhelmed whatever willpower Roy had to cope with his depression, and that, but for her admonishments, pressure, and instructions, Roy would not have gotten back into his truck and poisoned himself to death. Carter

Continued on next page.

(D) waived her right to a jury trial, and the case was tried to a judge in the Juvenile Court. Carter (D) was convicted as charged and appealed. The state's highest court granted review.

ISSUE:

(1) Can a person be convicted of involuntary manslaughter where the evidence shows beyond a reasonable doubt that their words, whether verbal or written, were wanton or reckless and overcame the will of another and caused the other person to commit suicide?

(2) Is a state law unconstitutionally vague where a person can be charged under the law with involuntary manslaughter for reckless or wanton conduct, including verbal or written conduct, causing another person to commit suicide?

(3) Does a First Amendment free speech violation result from convicting a defendant of involuntary manslaughter for reckless and wanton use of words, whether verbal or written, to overcome the will of another and cause the other person to commit suicide?

HOLDING AND DECISION: (Kafker, J.)

(1) Yes. A person can be convicted of involuntary manslaughter where the evidence shows beyond a reasonable doubt that their words, whether verbal or written, were wanton or reckless, overcame the will of another, and caused the other person to commit suicide. Carter (D) points out that the judge's remarks on the record, explaining the guilty verdict, contain no express finding that her words had a "coercive quality" that caused Roy to follow through with his suicide. However, the trial judge's finding of causation in this context, at that precise moment in time, includes the concept of coercion, in the sense of overpowering Roy's will. The evidence, in the light most favorable to the Commonwealth (P), shows that notwithstanding that Roy took numerous steps toward his suicide, he broke that chain of self-causation by exiting his truck and taking himself out of the toxic environment that it had become, which was completely consistent with his earlier attempts at suicide. The judge found that, once Roy left the truck, Carter (D) overpowered Roy's will and thus caused his death. As Carter (D) explained a few months after the suicide, in a text to her friend, "[The victim's] death is my fault like honestly I could have stopped him I was on the phone with him and he got out of the [truck] because it was working and he got scared and I fucking told him to get back in . . . because I knew he would do it all over again the next day and I couldn't have him live the way he was living anymore I couldn't do it I wouldn't let him." From this evidence, the trial judge could have properly found that Roy, who was mentally ill and vulnerable, had managed to reconsider his latest suicide attempt by removing himself from the truck as it filled with carbon monoxide, but that in his weakened state he was badgered back into the gas-infused truck by Carter (D), his girlfriend and closest, if not only, confidant in this suicidal planning, the person who had been constantly pressuring him to complete their often discussed plan, fulfill his promise to her, and finally commit suicide. Then after she convinced him to get back into the carbon monoxide filled truck, she did absolutely nothing to help him: She did not call for help or tell him to get out of the truck as she listened to him choke and die. In sum, the evidence at trial, in the light most favorable to the Commonwealth (P), was sufficient to establish Carter's (D) guilt beyond a reasonable doubt.

(2) No. A state law is not unconstitutionally vague where a person can be charged under the law with involuntary manslaughter for reckless or wanton conduct, including verbal or written conduct, causing another person to commit suicide. Carter (D) maintains that her due process rights were violated because she lacked fair notice that she could be convicted of involuntary manslaughter for her role in Roy's suicide, on the grounds that the law of involuntary manslaughter is unconstitutionally vague as applied to her conduct. Carter's (P) argument is unpersuasive. Involuntary manslaughter is a common-law offense, and conduct similar to that of Carter (D) has been ruled unlawful in this state for over 100 years. Thus, Carter (D) had notice from the common law that her conduct could be the basis for an involuntary manslaughter charge. Accordingly, the law is not unconstitutionally vague as applied to her conduct.

(3) No. A First Amendment free speech violation does not result from convicting a defendant of involuntary manslaughter for reckless and wanton use of words, whether verbal or written, to overcome the will of another and cause the other person to commit suicide. There is no free speech violation where a defendant is convicted of involuntary manslaughter for reckless and wanton, pressuring text messages and phone calls, preying upon well-known weaknesses, fears, anxieties, and promises, that finally overcome the willpower to live of a mentally ill, vulnerable, young person, thereby coercing the person to commit suicide. Carter (D) cannot escape liability just because she carried out her reckless and wonton conduct by using only words. The crime is directed at a course of conduct, rather than speech, and the proscribed conduct is not necessarily associated with speech. Therefore, no free speech concerns are

Continued on next page.

implicated by Carter's (D) conviction for involuntary manslaughter, which was carried out only by words.

Affirmed.

ANALYSIS

Carter is a landmark case, as no other case previously held that verbal encouragement of suicide alone is sufficient to support an involuntary manslaughter charge. Not only is homicide liability for another person's suicide rare, such liability ordinarily requires a tangible contribution to the suicide in addition to the verbal encouragement. *Carter* was criticized on the grounds that it greatly stretched the boundaries of criminal law as well as narrowing the free-speech protections of the First Amendment by characterizing speech as an overt act, notwithstanding that the United States Supreme Court has never included assisting suicide as a category of speech, such as obscenity or fighting words, that does not enjoy First Amendment protection. *Carter* could end up being merely a one-off decision, or it could encourage other courts, and legislatures, to criminalize speech alone under circumstances like those at issue in *Carter*.

Quicknotes

DUE PROCESS The mandate in the Fifth and Fourteenth Amendments to the U.S. Constitution requiring the courts to protect and enforce individuals' rights and liberties consistent with prevailing principles of fairness and justice and prohibiting the federal and state governments from such activities that deprive its citizens of a life, liberty, or property interest.

FIRST AMENDMENT Prohibits Congress from enacting any law respecting an establishment of religion or prohibiting the free exercise of religion; or abridging the freedom of speech or of the press, the right of peaceful assembly, and the right to petition for a redress of grievances.

INVOLUNTARY MANSLAUGHTER The killing of a person without premeditation, deliberation, malice aforethought, or the intent to kill or to commit a felony that may be reasonably expected to result in death or serious bodily injury; involuntary manslaughter is characterized by reckless conduct in the commission of a lawful act, or by the commission of an unlawful act that is not a felony, but that leads to the killing of another.

RIGHT OF FREE SPEECH Right guaranteed by the First Amendment to the U.S. Constitution prohibiting Congress from enacting any law abridging freedom of speech or of the press. The U.S. Supreme Court has interpreted this right as applying to the entire federal government, and the Due Process Clause of the Fourteenth Amendment has been interpreted as preventing the states from abridging this right.

Commonwealth v. Levesque

State (P) v. Homeless person who accidently started a fire (D)

Mass. Sup. Jud. Ct., 436 Mass. 443, 766 N.E.2d 50 (2002)

NATURE OF CASE: Appeal of trial court's granting of defendants' motion to dismiss charges for lack of evidence to support involuntary manslaughter based on wanton and reckless conduct for failure to report a fire.

FACT SUMMARY: Levesque (D) and Julie Ann Barnes (D), were homeless and living in a vacant factory building. After accidentally starting a fire, Levesque (D) failed to report the incident and six firefighters died battling the blaze. Having been charged with involuntary manslaughter, the trial court granted the defendants' motion to dismiss based on insufficient evidence.

RULE OF LAW

A duty of reasonable care is imposed on a criminal defendant who creates a life-threatening risk to another.

FACTS: Levesque (D) and Julie Ann Barnes (D) were homeless and living in a vacant factory building. A candle they were using accidentally tipped over and caused a fire. Unable to put out the blaze, the defendants left the warehouse and did not report the fire to the authorities, despite having time and passing several occupied locations where public telephones were available. The fire was not reported until later that evening. Upon arriving on the scene, fire fighters were advised that there might be homeless persons inside the warehouse. The firefighters entered the warehouse to locate any persons that might have been inside and to evaluate their tactics to combat the fire. During these efforts six firefighters died. The trial court granted the defendants' motion to dismiss, finding that there was no legal duty to report the fire and the failure to act did not satisfy the standard of wanton and reckless conduct required for manslaughter charges. The Commonwealth (P) appealed, and the Supreme Judicial Court of Massachusetts granted the application for direct appellate review.

ISSUE: Is a duty of reasonable care imposed on a criminal defendant who creates a life-threatening risk to another?

HOLDING AND DECISION: (Cowin, J.) Yes. A duty of reasonable care is imposed on a defendant who creates a life-threatening risk to another. A conviction will be based on any failure to act or omission. Wanton or reckless conduct usually consists of an affirmative act "like driving an automobile or discharging a firearm," *Commonwealth v. Welansky*, 316 Mass. 383, 397, 55 N.E.2d 902 (1944). An omission, however, may form the basis of a manslaughter conviction where the defendant has a duty to act. It is true that, in general, one does not have a duty to take affirmative action; however, a duty to prevent harm to others arises when one creates a dangerous situation, whether that situation was created intentionally or negligently. Both civil and criminal law imposes on people a duty to act reasonably. It is consistent with society's general understanding that certain acts need to be accompanied by some kind of warning by the actor. In applying this principle to the present case: (1) where one's actions create a life-threatening risk to another, there is a duty to take reasonable steps to alleviate the risk; and (2) where a defendant's failure to exercise reasonable care to prevent the risk he created is reckless and results in death, the defendant can be convicted of involuntary manslaughter. Levesque (D) and his co-defendant started the fire and then increased the risk of harm from that fire by allowing it to burn without taking adequate steps either to control it or to report it to the proper authorities. Whether a defendant has satisfied this duty will depend on the circumstances of the particular case and the steps that the defendant can reasonably be expected to take to minimize the risk. Although, in this case, the defendants apparently could not have successfully put out the fire, they could have given reasonable notice of the danger they created. Reversed and remanded.

ANALYSIS

Involuntary manslaughter requires evidence of wanton or reckless conduct. The motion's judge reasoned that because the Commonwealth (P) conceded the fire was started accidentally, and because Massachusetts courts have not found a duty to report or extinguish a fire, the defendant's failure to do so was merely negligent. The Massachusetts Supreme Judicial Court, however, rejected this finding by stating that individuals have a duty to prevent harm to others when they create a dangerous situation, whether that situation was created intentionally or negligently. Because the defendants' failure to exercise reasonable care to prevent the risk they created was reckless and resulted in death, they could ultimately be convicted of involuntary manslaughter.

Continued on next page.

Quicknotes

INVOLUNTARY MANSLAUGHTER The killing of another person without premeditation or deliberation or with the intent to kill or to commit a felony, which may be reasonably expected to result in death or serious bodily injury; involuntary manslaughter is characterized by reckless conduct in the commission of a lawful act, or by the commission of an unlawful act that is not a felony, but which leads to the killing of another.

MANSLAUGHTER The killing of a person without premeditation or deliberation, or with the intent to kill or to commit a felony that may be reasonably expected to result in death or serious bodily injury; manslaughter is characterized by reckless conduct or by some adequate provocation on the part of the actor, as determined by a subjective standard.

RECKLESS CONDUCT Conduct that is conscious and creates a substantial and unjustifiable risk of harm to others.

WILLFUL AND WANTON CONDUCT Unlawful intentional or reckless conduct without regard to the consequences.

PART 3

Crimes Against the Person

Quick Reference Rules of Law

PAGE

1. *Perez Hernandez v. United States.* A nonviolent offensive touching that causes no physical injury, and that is not a sexual touching, may constitute a simple assault where the defendant acts knowing that the touching will cause offense. 64

Perez Hernandez v. United States

Individual convicted of assault (D) v. Federal government (P)

D.C. Ct. App., 286 A.3d 990 (2022) (en banc)

NATURE OF CASE: Rehearing en banc, after reversal by intermediate appellate court panel, of conviction in action for simple assault.

FACT SUMMARY: Winston Perez Hernandez (D) contended that he could not be convicted of simple assault for simply touching his acquaintance, Alimamy Tarawallie, notwithstanding that Tarawallie made it clear to Perez Hernandez (D) that he did not want to be touched, because he did not have the subjective intent to injure Tarawallie, so that the touching was not objectively and intentionally offensive. The Government (P) countered that a touching can be offensive where the defendant has special reason to believe that more or less will be permitted by the individual the defendant touches.

RULE OF LAW

A nonviolent offensive touching that causes no physical injury, and that is not a sexual touching, may constitute a simple assault where the defendant acts knowing that the touching will cause offense.

FACTS: A group of men got together to watch a World Cup soccer game at the home of Alimamy Tarawallie. After the game, Tarawallie was upset by the game's outcome. Perez Hernandez (D), one of the men at the gathering, approached Tarawallie, started speaking with Tarawallie, and poked him. Tarawallie admonished Perez Hernandez (D) to not touch him again. However, Perez Hernandez (D) did touch Tarawallie again, and Tarawallie reacted violently and punched Perez Hernandez (D). Perez Hernandez (D) was charged with simple assault and found guilty after a bench trial. On appeal, a panel of the jurisdiction's intermediate appellate court held that the evidence was legally insufficient to sustain Perez Hernandez's (D) conviction for simple assault because the Government (P) had proven no more than an unwanted touching. The panel stated that there must be proof that a defendant acted with force or violence, and that a touch is inherently neither "forceful" nor "violent" within the common understanding (or even legal understanding) of those terms. The jurisdiction's intermediate appellate court decided to rehear the appeal en banc.

ISSUE: May a nonviolent, offensive touching that causes no physical injury, and that is not a sexual touching, constitute a simple assault where the defendant acts knowing that the touching will cause offense?

HOLDING AND DECISION: (Fisher, J.) Yes. A nonviolent offensive touching that causes no physical injury, and that is not a sexual touching, may constitute a simple assault where the defendant acts knowing that the touching will cause offense. In this jurisdiction, common-law assault is prohibited. The definition and elements of assault have evolved over time. Foundational case law defined common-law assault as an attempt with force or violence to do a corporal injury to another. Later cases held that "violence" in its ordinary meaning is not a necessary element of assault, nor is physical injury, and the parties here agreed that common-law simple assault encompasses even the slightest offensive touching, even though it causes or threatens no actual physical harm to the victim. However, the Government (P) asserted that assault, historically described as a "general intent" crime, is properly proved by showing that a defendant engaged in assaultive conduct purposely, knowingly, or recklessly, whereas Perez Hernandez (D) argued that a subjective intent to injure is an essential element of assault, meaning that it is necessary to have an intent to harm or offend, and not merely an intent to do the touching. Thus, he asserted that to constitute a simple assault, an unwanted touching must be both objectively and intentionally offensive. Although the Government (P) agreed that, as a general matter, the test is what would be offensive to an ordinary person not unduly sensitive as to personal dignity, it argued that a touching is also offensive where the defendant has special reason to believe that more or less will be permitted by the individual being touched. Historically in this jurisdiction, assault was categorized as a "general intent" crime requiring no "specific intent" to cause injury. This distinction has been criticized significantly, and, because there is no statutory scheme in the jurisdiction setting forth such categorizations, the court looks to the Model Penal Code (MPC) to supply those. Under the MPC's "purposely" definition, in a case like this, making contact with a victim (the "touching" portion of an offensive touching) cannot be inadvertent, or, in MPC terms, it must be the defendant's "conscious object to engage in conduct of that nature." Model Penal Code § 2.02(2)(a)(i). Because the United States Supreme Court has held that a presumption of a knowledge (scienter) requirement should apply to each of the statutory elements that criminalize otherwise innocent conduct, what makes the contact an assault is the offensive nature of the touch. Accordingly, the court holds that the mens rea requirement for the offensiveness of a touch may be satisfied by applying the MPC concepts of purpose and knowledge, and that the defendant takes actions with the knowledge that the touching will be offensive. Additionally, in

Continued on next page.

assessing the offensive nature of the contact, the finder of fact must consider the totality of the circumstances; a touching is offensive if it offends a person's reasonable sense of personal dignity. Under the circumstances, a reasonable fact finder could conclude that the touching was offensive because Perez Hernandez (D) knew that Tarawallie would find the contact offensive but nevertheless touched him. Although the findings of fact permit such a conclusion, the trial court did not expressly state that Perez Hernandez (D) actually knew that Tarawallie would be offended, and it is not clear that such a finding is implicit in what the trial court said. Therefore, the case is remanded to the trial court for further findings on whether Perez Hernandez (D) knew when he acted that the touching would offend Tarawallie.

ANALYSIS

The court indicated that when the charge of assault is based on an offensive touching, as it was in this case, it is fruitless to think of the crime as "an attempt with force or violence to do a corporal injury to another." Instead, the court stated that it should be recognized that the conduct is an assault because it is a completed battery. Thus, for an assault based on an offensive touching, the government must prove that the defendant (1) touched another; (2) that the defendant did so purposely, not by accident; (3) that the touching offended the other person; (4) that the touching would offend a person's reasonable sense of personal dignity; and (5) that the defendant either acted with the purpose of causing offense or acted knowing that the touching would cause offense.

Quicknotes

ASSAULT The intentional placing of another in fear of immediate bodily injury.

ASSAULT AND BATTERY Any unlawful touching of another person without justification or excuse.

BATTERY Unlawful contact with the body of another person.

BENCH TRIAL A non-jury trial where the judge determines the facts, applies the law, and renders judgment.

EN BANC The hearing of a matter by all the judges of the court, rather than by the necessary quorum or small panel of the judges.

GENERAL INTENT The intent to conduct an act but without the intent to commit an unlawful act.

KNOWINGLY Intentionally; willfully; committing an act with knowledge as to its probable consequences.

MENS REA Criminal intent.

PURPOSELY Intentionally; a person's conscious object to engage in conduct of a certain nature.

SPECIFIC INTENT The intent to commit a specific unlawful act for which one is later charged; specific intent is a required element for criminal liability for certain crimes.

SPECIFIC-INTENT CRIME A crime that requires the intent to commit a specific unlawful act in order for criminal liability to be imposed.

CHAPTER 5

Intentional Homicide

Quick Reference Rules of Law

Francis v. Franklin

[Party not identified] (P) v. Convicted murder (D)

471 U.S. 307 (1985)

NATURE OF CASE: Appeal of murder conviction.

FACT SUMMARY: Franklin (D), a convict, apparently accidentally shot an individual while escaping from prison.

RULE OF LAW

A jury instruction may not imply that a defendant must disprove intent to kill.

FACTS: Franklin (D) escaped from custody during a routine dental visit, seizing the gun of a guard. He entered the house of the decedent, demanding a vehicle. The decedent stated he had no vehicle and slammed the door. The door hit Franklin's (D) gun, and it discharged. The bullet went through the door, killing the decedent. At Franklin's (D) murder trial, the jury was instructed that the law presumes that a person intends the natural consequences of his acts. Franklin (D) was convicted, and he appealed.

ISSUE: May a jury instruction imply that a defendant must disprove intent to kill?

HOLDING AND DECISION: (Brennan, J.) No. A jury instruction may not imply that a defendant must disprove intent to kill. The prosecution has the burden of proving this essential element of a murder charge, and any jury instruction that implies the contrary is prejudicial. Here, the instruction could reasonably have implied to the jury that it was presumed that Franklin (D) intended to kill, and for that reason the conviction must be reversed.

ANALYSIS

Basic to a murder conviction is the requirement of intent to kill. This is what separates murder from manslaughter. Intent can be either an actual desire to kill (usually classified as murder one) or extremely reckless behavior (usually classified as murder two).

Quicknotes

MANSLAUGHTER The killing of a person without premeditation or deliberation, or with the intent to kill or to commit a felony that may be reasonably expected to result in death or serious bodily injury; manslaughter is characterized by reckless conduct or by some adequate provocation on the part of the actor, as determined by a subjective standard.

MURDER Unlawful killing of a person either with deliberation and premeditation or by conduct demonstrating a reckless disregard for human life.

United States v. Watson

Federal government (P) v. Convicted murderer (D)

D.C. Ct. App., 501 A.2d 791 (1985)

NATURE OF CASE: Appeal of conviction of murder.

FACT SUMMARY: Watson (D) was convicted of murder even though no one witnessed the few moments prior to Watson's (D) firing a gun at the victim.

RULE OF LAW

Murder may be proved absent evidence of what occurred in the few moments prior to the fatal assault.

FACTS: A police officer chased Watson (D) into his home, having seen him driving a stolen car. In the home were three girls. The officer demanded that Watson (D) surrender. He responded by fighting back. Watson (D) was able to knock away the officer's gun. Watson (D) grabbed the gun and having the officer pinned down, pointed the gun at his chest. At this point the girls ran to the other rooms. A few words were exchanged between Watson (D) and the officer, and a shot was fired. The officer later died. Watson (D) was charged with murder. The jury rejected his manslaughter defense and found him guilty of murder. Watson (D) appealed.

ISSUE: May murder be proved absent evidence of what occurred in the few moments prior to the fatal assault?

HOLDING AND DECISION: (Rogers, J.) Yes. Murder may be proved absent evidence of what occurred in the few moments prior to the fatal assault. Murder requires premeditation, which, in the context of a homicide arising out of an altercation, requires deliberation. The homicide must not arise out of the heat of the fight but must be a conscious choice. To prove such deliberation, however, no direct evidence of the fatal moment is necessary. A jury may find, from all the circumstances, deliberation did occur. Here, the jury was given evidence of a fight in which Watson (D) had trained the gun on the officer for a significant period of time prior to the pulling of the trigger. While time does not necessarily prove deliberation, it is probative thereof. The jury could reasonably find Watson (D) to have deliberated. Affirmed.

ANALYSIS

Some have criticized the legal definition of premeditation. It is argued that the definition permits both scenarios in the same category of crime, although most would agree the latter crime to be much more morally reprehensible. In some states, a difference between the situations is drawn so that only certain aggravated examples of first-degree murder can give rise to the death penalty.

Quicknotes

DELIBERATION Reflection; the pondering and weighing of the consequences of an action.

FIRST-DEGREE MURDER The willful killing of a person with deliberation and premeditation; first-degree murder also encompasses those situations in which a person is killed within the perpetration of, or attempt to perpetrate, specified felonies.

MANSLAUGHTER The killing of a person without premeditation or deliberation, or with the intent to kill or to commit a felony, that may be reasonably expected to result in death or serious bodily injury; manslaughter is characterized by reckless conduct or by some adequate provocation on the part of the actor, as determined by a subjective standard.

PREMEDITATION The contemplation of undertaking an activity prior to action.

People v. Walker

State (P) v. Convicted murderer (D)

Ill. App. Ct., 204 N.E.2d 594 (1965)

NATURE OF CASE: Appeal of conviction for murder.

FACT SUMMARY: Walker (D), having killed a man during an altercation, contended that it was done in the heat of passion and therefore was, at most, manslaughter.

RULE OF LAW

A homicide occurring while the killer is in an excited, irrational state is properly charged as manslaughter.

FACTS: Walker (D) was with some acquaintances when Stenneth, a stranger, came up to them and demanded that they gamble. When the group refused, Stenneth pulled a knife. He made several lunges at Walker (D), to little effect. Stenneth then succeeded in lacerating Walker (D). Walker (D) responded by hurling a brick at Stenneth, which knocked him down. Walker (D) then grabbed the knife, still in Stenneth's hand, and cut his throat. The entire episode lasted five to ten minutes, with no pauses. Walker (D) was charged with murder. He was convicted, and he appealed.

ISSUE: Is a homicide occurring while the killer is in an excited, irrational state properly charged as manslaughter?

HOLDING AND DECISION: (Drucker, J.) Yes. A homicide occurring while the killer is in an excited, irrational state is properly charged as manslaughter. When a killing occurs without deliberation, the law provides that the malice aforethought necessary to sustain a murder charge has not arisen. A serious and highly provoking injury is considered sufficient to produce the excited state necessary for manslaughter to exist. Here, Stenneth did inflict a knife injury on Walker (D). Walker's (D) subsequent killing of Stenneth, while not occurring immediately thereafter, occurred in the same sequence of events. In view of this, as a matter of law, Walker's (D) killing of Stenneth was an act of manslaughter. Reversed and remanded.

ANALYSIS

The crucial aspect of manslaughter is lack of deliberation. Time is necessarily an important factor in this analysis, but it is not determinative. A brief pause between provocation and homicide may be sufficient to negate heat of passion. Reflection takes only a moment.

Quicknotes

HEAT OF PASSION DEFENSE A defense utilized in order to reduce a charge of murder to manslaughter, it is based on the theory that the perpetrator was under adequate provocation so that they were incapable of forming the premeditation necessary for first-degree murder.

HOMICIDE The killing of one person by another person.

MANSLAUGHTER The killing of a person without premeditation or deliberation, or with the intent to kill or to commit a felony that may be reasonably expected to result in death or serious bodily injury; manslaughter is characterized by reckless conduct or by some adequate provocation on the part of the actor, as determined by a subjective standard.

Ex parte Fraley

State (P) v. Father (D)

Okla. Ct. Crim. App., 109 P. 295 (1910)

NATURE OF CASE: Application for habeas corpus based on denial of bail.

FACT SUMMARY: Fraley (D) shot and killed a man who he believed had killed his son nine or ten months before.

RULE OF LAW

An objective standard will be used in gauging the "cooling down" period for murder versus manslaughter.

FACTS: Fraley (D) shot and killed a man. Testimony demonstrated that Fraley (D) walked up to the decedent, shot him, and then said, "I told you I'd kill you." The man had apparently killed Fraley's (D) son nine or ten months before and had been acquitted of wrongdoing. Fraley (D) argued that he killed in the heat of passion, and that therefore he could only be guilty of manslaughter. When the court denied bail, Fraley (D) applied for habeas corpus.

ISSUE: Will an objective standard be used in gauging the "cooling down" period for murder versus manslaughter?

HOLDING AND DECISION: (Richardson, J.) Yes. An objective standard will be used for gauging the "cooling down" period for murder versus manslaughter. A killing in the heat of passion is manslaughter, not murder. However, there must be a point at which the law will not give a defendant the benefit of this rule, even if he has in fact not "cooled down." Here, we are talking about nine or ten months, a period far longer than the law can possibly allow. Bail denied.

ANALYSIS

As stated in the opinion, a "reasonable person" standard is used in determining a "cooling down" period. A subjective standard is also used, but if the actor's subjective state of mind remains agitated too long, the "reasonable person" standard takes over. One actually has to question the validity of this in that the argument can be made that reasonable people don't lose their heads to the point of killing.

Quicknotes

COOLING PERIOD A sufficient period after provocation for an individual to regain composure and after which the individual is presumed to understand the consequences of their actions.

HABEAS CORPUS A proceeding in which a defendant brings a writ to compel a judicial determination of whether the defendant is lawfully being held in custody.

HEAT OF PASSION DEFENSE A defense utilized in order to reduce a charge of murder to manslaughter, it is based on the theory that the perpetrator was under adequate provocation so that they were incapable of forming the premeditation necessary for first-degree murder.

MANSLAUGHTER The killing of a person without premeditation or deliberation, or with the intent to kill or to commit a felony that may be reasonably expected to result in death or serious bodily injury; manslaughter is characterized by reckless conduct or by some adequate provocation on the part of the actor, as determined by a subjective standard.

MURDER Unlawful killing of a person, either with deliberation and premeditation or by conduct demonstrating a reckless disregard for human life.

OBJECTIVE STANDARD A standard that is not personal to an individual but is dependent on some external source.

SUBJECTIVE STANDARD A standard that is based on the personal belief of an individual.

Rowland v. State

Husband convicted of murder of wife (D) v. State (P)

Miss. Sup. Ct., 35 So. 826 (1904)

NATURE OF CASE: Appeal of conviction for murder.

FACT SUMMARY: Rowland (D) killed his wife immediately after seeing her commit adultery.

RULE OF LAW

The proper charge against one killing a spouse in reaction to witnessing adultery is manslaughter, not murder.

FACTS: Rowland (D) witnessed his wife getting out of bed with another man. Rowland (D), in a fit of rage, shot at the man, but hit his wife instead, killing her. Rowland (D) was indicted for murder. He was convicted, and he appealed.

ISSUE: Is the proper charge against one killing a spouse in reaction to witnessing adultery manslaughter, not murder?

HOLDING AND DECISION: (Truly, J.) Yes. The proper charge against one killing a spouse in reaction to witnessing adultery is manslaughter, not murder. Because of the inherently provocative nature of adultery, the law presumes that any homicide committed in such a situation would be manslaughter rather than murder. Here, Rowland (D) was charged with murder, and this was improper. Reversed.

ANALYSIS

Jurisdictions vary as to how proximate to the "act" an observation of adultery must be for a homicide not to be chargeable as murder. A few jurisdictions at common law required actually viewing intercourse. The more prevalent view was that any observation that would leave one to conclude with reasonable certainty adultery had occurred was sufficient.

Quicknotes

ADULTERY Sexual intercourse between a married person and another who is not that person's spouse, or between a person and another who is married.

HEAT OF PASSION DEFENSE A defense utilized in order to reduce a charge of murder to manslaughter, it is based on the theory that the perpetrator was under adequate provocation so that they were incapable of forming the premeditation necessary for first-degree murder.

MANSLAUGHTER The killing of a person without premeditation or deliberation, or with the intent to kill or to commit a felony that may be reasonably expected to result in death or serious bodily injury; manslaughter is characterized by reckless conduct or by some adequate provocation on the part of the actor, as determined by a subjective standard.

MURDER Unlawful killing of a person, either with deliberation and premeditation or by conduct demonstrating a reckless disregard for human life.

People v. Berry

State (P) v. Husband convicted of first-degree murder of wife (D)

Cal. Sup. Ct., 18 Cal. 3d 509, 134 Cal. Rptr. 415 (1976)

NATURE OF CASE: Appeal from a first-degree murder conviction.

FACT SUMMARY: Berry (D) strangled his wife after she had repeatedly frustrated him sexually and tormented him with tales of her involvement with another man.

RULE OF LAW

A party who kills a victim in the heat of passion induced by a prolonged period of taunting and provocation can be guilty only of voluntary manslaughter.

FACTS: Berry (D), a 46-year-old cook, married a 20-year-old woman named Rachel. Three days after their marriage, Rachel returned to her native Israel for a period of about two weeks. When she came back, she told Berry (D) that she had fallen in love with a man named Yako, with whom she had been involved sexually. About ten days later, Berry (D) choked Rachel. She went to a hospital and also notified the police, who caused a warrant to be issued for Berry's (D) arrest. He had, in the interim, left the couple's apartment and spent a short time with a friend. Two days after the original choking incident, Berry (D) returned to the couple's apartment, but Rachel did not appear until the following morning. He told Rachel that he wanted to talk with her, but she began screaming and when he was unable to stop her, Berry (D) strangled her to death with a telephone cord. At his murder and assault trial, Berry (D) did not deny the killing. Instead, he testified to a two-week period of torment during which his wife had sometimes demanded immediate sexual gratification and other times refused to have relations at all, constantly taunting Berry (D) with threats of leaving to live with Yako, and regaling him with stories of her affair. Berry (D) claimed that the killing had occurred in the heat of passion. A psychiatrist corroborated this testimony, adding that Rachel had been suicidal and had deliberately driven Berry (D) to kill her. Despite this testimony, the trial judge refused to charge the jury concerning voluntary manslaughter. Berry (D) was convicted of first-degree murder, but he appealed.

ISSUE: May a party who kills a victim in the heat of passion induced by a prolonged period of taunting and provocation be guilty only of voluntary manslaughter??

HOLDING AND DECISION: (Sullivan, J.) Yes. A party who kills a victim in the heat of passion induced by a prolonged period of taunting and provocation can be guilty only of voluntary manslaughter. According to the oft-cited case of *People v. Logan*, 175 Cal. 45 (1917), the issue of whether or not a killing occurred in the heat of passion should at least be submitted to the jury. It is up to the jurors to decide whether or not the circumstances were such as would naturally have aroused an ordinary and reasonable person to a passionate state. "Heat of passion" defies precise definition, but verbal taunts and admissions of infidelity have been held sufficient to justify the finding of such a condition. The State (P) argues that Berry's (D) night alone was a sufficient cooling-off period to diminish his rage, but this overlooks the fact that the killing was but the culmination of a protracted period of continual torment and passion. The testimony of Berry (D) and the psychiatrist amply establishes that Berry's (D) state of mind at the time of the killing was such that he should have been convicted only of voluntary manslaughter. Reversed.

ANALYSIS

As *People v. Berry* illustrates, a party's state of mind may be a sufficient mitigating factor to reduce the extent of their liability even though it may not justify an outright acquittal. Certain familiar fact patterns are traditionally deemed sufficient to reduce a charge from first-degree murder to voluntary manslaughter. Circumstances that typically provoke one sufficiently to reduce one's culpability include being threatened with unlawful arrest, finding one's wife (but not necessarily husband) engaged in an adulterous act, or being assaulted viciously. In most jurisdictions, words are usually not adequate to provide the necessary provocation. Enlightened jurisdictions are gradually accepting the proposition that circumstances justifying provocation are not limited to fixed fact patterns, but may encompass virtually an infinite number of situations.

Quicknotes

FIRST-DEGREE MURDER The willful killing of a person with deliberation and premeditation; first-degree murder also encompasses those situations in which a person is killed within the perpetration of, or attempt to perpetrate, specified felonies.

HEAT OF PASSION DEFENSE A defense utilized in order to reduce a charge of murder to manslaughter, it is based on the theory that the perpetrator was under adequate

Continued on next page.

provocation so that they were incapable of forming the premeditation necessary for first-degree murder.

VOLUNTARY MANSLAUGHTER The killing of a person without premeditation, deliberation, or malice aforethought, but committed while in the "heat of passion" or upon some adequate provocation, thereby reducing the charge from murder to manslaughter.

People v. Wu

State (P) v. Mother convicted of murder of son (D)

Cal. Ct. App., 235 Cal. App. 3d 614 (1991)

NATURE OF CASE: Appeal from conviction for murder.

FACT SUMMARY: Wu (D) sought to introduce evidence of her cultural background to explain her mental state when she killed her son.

RULE OF LAW

Evidence of a defendant's cultural background is relevant on the issue of the mental state required for murder.

FACTS: Helen Wu (D), an immigrant from China, had a difficult on-and-off-again relationship with Gary Wu. The two had a son, Sidney, who became a pawn in their battles. Helen (D) strangled Sidney and then attempted to kill herself so she could care for him in the afterlife. She claimed that she was unconscious during the killing. Helen (D) was charged and convicted of second-degree murder after the prosecution (P) argued that she killed her son to take revenge on Gary. Helen (D) attempted to argue to the jury that she was in an intense emotional upheaval because she believed that Sidney would be mistreated by Gary's family because he had been born out of wedlock. The trial court rejected a proposed jury instruction that noted to the jury that they could consider Helen's (D) cultural background in deciding on her mental state. Helen Wu (D) appealed.

ISSUE: Is evidence of a defendant's cultural background relevant on the issue of the mental state required for murder?

HOLDING AND DECISION: (Timlin, J.) Yes. Evidence of a defendant's cultural background is relevant on the issue of the mental state required for murder. The essential mental states at issue for murder are (1) premeditation, (2) malice aforethought, and (3) specific intent to kill. Generally, all relevant evidence is admissible. Evidence of a defendant's cultural background is relevant on the issue of premeditation. In the present case, the prosecution (P) argued that Wu's (D) statements in the days before the killing indicated planning. However, the evidence of Wu's (D) Chinese background provided an alternative theory—that Wu (D) intended to kill herself and that when Wu (D) discovered that Sidney was being mistreated, it triggered an emotional response. Thus, Wu's (D) cultural background could have shown the existence of heat of passion at the time of the killing. Since the requested jury instruction was a correct statement of law and was the basis of the defense, the conviction is reversed.

ANALYSIS

The court also ruled that the trial court should have given an instruction on unconsciousness. Helen Wu (D) had presented evidence that the act of strangulation was committed while she was in an unconscious state. Generally, acting while unconscious negates the mental state required for crimes.

Quicknotes

HEAT OF PASSION DEFENSE A defense utilized in order to reduce a charge of murder to manslaughter, it is based on the theory that the perpetrator was under adequate provocation so that they were incapable of forming the premeditation necessary for first-degree murder.

PREMEDITATION The contemplation of undertaking an activity prior to action.

SECOND-DEGREE MURDER The unlawful killing of a person, without premeditation, and characterized by either intent to kill or by a reckless disregard for human life.

SPECIFIC INTENT The intent to commit a specific unlawful act for which one is later charged. Specific intent is a required element for criminal liability for certain crimes.

CHAPTER 6

Unintentional Homicide

Quick Reference Rules of Law

Commonwealth v. Welansky

State (P) v. Nightclub owner convicted of manslaughter (D)

Mass. Sup. Jud. Ct., 55 N.E.2d 902 (1944)

NATURE OF CASE: Appeal of manslaughter conviction.

FACT SUMMARY: A fire erupted at a nightclub belonging to Welansky (D), and many patrons were killed because emergency exits were blocked.

RULE OF LAW

Considered disregard for the safety of others is sufficient for the sort of recklessness that may support a manslaughter conviction.

FACTS: Welansky (D) operated a Boston nightclub. The club consisted of several different lounges over two stories. The club had five exits, which were ostensibly to be used for emergency purposes. These had, however, either been hidden for aesthetic purposes or otherwise did not work properly. On a crowded evening a fire swept through the club, and many patrons were killed when the exits proved unpassable. Welansky (D) was charged with manslaughter and convicted. He appealed.

ISSUE: Is considered disregard for the safety of others sufficient for the sort of recklessness that may support a manslaughter conviction?

HOLDING AND DECISION: (Lummus, J.) Yes. Considered disregard for the safety of others is sufficient for the sort of recklessness that may support a manslaughter conviction. While recklessness usually consists of an affirmative act, it need not be. When one is charged with the safety of others and makes a conscious decision to do the unsafe thing, inaction may constitute negligence. Here, Welansky (D) intentionally failed to make the emergency exits passable, and this certainly could be called reckless. Affirmed.

ANALYSIS

The critical issue here was not the acts of Welansky (D), but rather his state of mind. The court rejected the idea that mere carelessness on Welansky's part could have supported a conviction. The determinative fact was that Welansky (D) weighed the alternatives before acting (or failing to act). As the court said, negligence is usually not a crime.

Quicknotes

MANSLAUGHTER The killing of a person without premeditation or deliberation, or with the intent to kill or to commit a felony that may be reasonably expected to result in death or serious bodily injury; manslaughter is characterized by reckless conduct or by some adequate provocation on the part of the actor, as determined by a subjective standard.

NEGLIGENCE Conduct falling below the standard of care that a reasonable person would demonstrate under similar conditions.

RECKLESSNESS The conscious disregard of substantial and justifiable risk.

State v. Williams

State (P) v. Parents convicted of manslaugher of son (D)

Wash. Ct. App., 484 P.2d 1167 (1971)

NATURE OF CASE: Appeal of manslaughter conviction.

FACT SUMMARY: Mr. and Mrs. Williams (D) failed to obtain medical aid for their 17-month-old child and he died as a result.

RULE OF LAW

Where the failure of a person to act while under a duty to do so is the proximate cause of the death of another, that person may be convicted of involuntary manslaughter, notwithstanding that their conduct was no more than ordinary negligence.

FACTS: Mrs. Williams (D) had a son by a previous marriage before she married Mr. Williams (D). When the lad, only 17 months old, developed a toothache, neither she nor her husband considered it serious enough to seek out medical help. As the tooth became worse and abscessed, however, the Williamses (D) became apprehensive but did not seek medical or dental care for the boy, fearing that the welfare department might take him away if they saw how bad he looked. Eventually, the boy developed gangrene from which the smell was clearly noticeable, and pneumonia, from which he died about ten days later. The Williamses (D) were convicted of manslaughter on these facts. They appealed.

ISSUE: Where the failure of a person to act while under a duty to do so is the proximate cause of the death of another, may that person be convicted of involuntary manslaughter, notwithstanding that their conduct was no more than ordinary negligence?

HOLDING AND DECISION: (Horowitz, C.J.) Yes. Where the failure of a person to act while under a duty to do so is the proximate cause of the death of another, that person may be convicted of involuntary manslaughter, notwithstanding that their conduct was no more than ordinary negligence. There is no question but that the Williamses (D) were under a duty to obtain medical care for their seriously ill son, and their fear of the welfare department does not excuse this duty. The tough question here is whether the seriousness of the child's illness became sufficiently apparent to them early enough for their failure to do anything about it to be declared the proximate cause of the boy's death. Medical experts, however, testified that the gangrenous condition of the boy's cheek must have been apparent both by sight and smell to his parents for some ten days before he died. Clearly they were on notice as to the seriousness of their son's illness in time to prevent him from dying of it. Conviction affirmed.

ANALYSIS

This case points up a modern departure from the common-law rule that involuntary manslaughter required an act of gross negligence (i.e., criminal negligence). Ordinary negligence may arise either by act or, as above, by omission while under a duty to act. As in tort, its general formulation is the "failure of a man of reasonable prudence to exercise due care under the circumstances." Note, however, that this "objective" standard (i.e., what a reasonable man would do) runs the risk of undermining individualized justice by sanctioning punishment regardless of the subjective knowledge of the wrongdoer. In *Williams*, for example, it appeared that the parents were illiterate—wholly ignorant of the most rudimentary principles of health care—and honestly did not know their son was in trouble.

Quicknotes

GROSS NEGLIGENCE The intentional failure to perform a duty with reckless disregard of the consequences.

INVOLUNTARY MANSLAUGHTER The killing of a person without premeditation or deliberation or with the intent to kill or to commit a felony, which may be reasonably expected to result in death or serious bodily injury; involuntary manslaughter is characterized by reckless conduct in the commission of a lawful act, or by the commission of an unlawful act that is not a felony, but which leads to the killing of another.

OBJECTIVE STANDARD A standard that is not personal to an individual but is dependent on some external source.

PROXIMATE CAUSE The natural sequence of events without which an injury would not have been sustained.

Mayes v. The People

Husband convicted for murder of wife (D) v. State (P)

Ill. Sup. Ct., 106 Ill. 306, 46 Am. Rep. 698 (1883)

NATURE OF CASE: Appeal of conviction for murder.

FACT SUMMARY: Mayes (D) was convicted of murder following a charge to the jury that said, in effect, that an act done with an abandoned and malignant heart causing death may be murder, even if death was not intended.

RULE OF LAW

An act done with an abandoned and malignant heart causing death may be murder, even if death is not intended.

FACTS: Mayes (D) came home after an evening at a saloon. Unfriendly words were exchanged between Mayes (D) and his wife. His wife then told him that she and their daughter were retiring for the night. At this point, Mayes (D) threw a glass as his wife. It struck an ignited oil lamp she was carrying, splattering burning oil all over her. Her burns proved fatal. Mayes (D) was charged with murder. The court instructed the jury that an act done with an abandoned and malignant heart causing death to occur may be murder, even if death was not intended. Mayes (D) was convicted, and he appealed.

ISSUE: May an act done with an abandoned and malignant heart causing death be murder, even if death is not intended?

HOLDING AND DECISION: (Scholfield, J.) Yes. An act done with an abandoned and malignant heart causing death may be murder, even if death is not intended. Murder requires malice, but malice does not require intent to kill. When an unlawful action is committed with deliberation in a situation such that great bodily harm is likely to result, such malice may be inferred. Hence, Mayes (D) unlawfully threw an object at his wife under circumstances likely to cause great bodily harm. That he may not have intended death is of no import. He is responsible for the consequences at his acts. Affirmed.

ANALYSIS

The type of conduct that gives rise to murder of this type might be described as aggravated recklessness or extreme recklessness. "Recklessness," in itself, is synonymous with "foolhardiness," and this is not sufficient for murder (involuntary manslaughter is the more proper charge). The standard might be best described as a "conscious disregard for human life."

Quicknotes

INVOLUNTARY MANSLAUGHTER The killing of a person without premeditation or deliberation or with the intent to kill or to commit a felony, which may be reasonably expected to result in death or serious bodily injury; involuntary manslaughter is characterized by reckless conduct in the commission of a lawful act, or by the commission of an unlawful act that is not a felony, but which leads to the killing of another.

MALICE The intention to commit an unlawful act without justification or excuse.

MURDER Unlawful killing of a person either with deliberation and premeditation or by conduct demonstrating a reckless disregard for human life.

RECKLESSNESS The conscious disregard of substantial and justifiable risk.

State v. Martin

State (P) v. Murderer (D)

N.J. Sup. Ct., 573 A.2d 1359 (1990)

NATURE OF CASE: Appeal from murder conviction based on felony-murder doctrine.

FACT SUMMARY: When Martin (D) was convicted of felony murder, he argued that the trial court erred in instructing the jury that it did not matter whether the act that caused the death was committed recklessly or unintentionally or accidently.

RULE OF LAW

A defendant is liable for felony murder only if the death is not too remote, accidental in its occurrence, or too dependent on another's volitional act to have a just bearing on the defendant's culpability.

FACTS: Daniel Martin (D) and four other persons attended a late-night party at which all participants were intoxicated and using marijuana. An altercation arose and all participants left the building except one woman. Shortly thereafter, the building was on fire. The woman who remained had passed out in the apartment from intoxication and died from smoke inhalation from the fire. As Martin (D) had left the apartment, he set the fire by lighting a paper bag containing trash, saying that he intended only to "make a mess of things," but that he "didn't mean to hurt nobody." Martin (D) was convicted of felony murder resulting from his arson. He appealed, arguing that the trial court erred in instructing the jury that it did not matter whether the act that caused the death was committed recklessly or unintentionally or accidently.

ISSUE: Is a defendant liable for felony murder only if the death is not too remote, accidental in its occurrence, or too dependent on another's volitional act to have a just bearing on the defendant's culpability?

HOLDING AND DECISION: (Pollock, J.) Yes. A defendant is liable for felony murder only if the death is not too remote, accidental in its occurrence, or too dependent on another's volitional act to have a just bearing on the defendant's culpability. To the extent that the felony-murder rule holds an actor liable for a death irrespective of the actor's mental state, the rule cuts across the grain of criminal law. Generally, people are not criminally culpable for the consequences of their acts unless those consequences were intended, contemplated, or foreseeable. Because the felony-murder rule runs counter to normal rules of criminal culpability, it received careful attention from the drafters of the Model Penal Code who objected to the rule as "a form of strict liability to which we are opposed." The New Jersey statute, on the other hand, while rejecting the Model Penal Code approach and keeping the felony-murder rule, provides that when causing a particular result is a material element of an offense for which absolute liability is imposed by law, the element is not established unless the actual result is a "probable consequence" of the actor's conduct. In effect, the New Jersey statute provides that the actual result—death, in the case of felony murder—is not established unless it is the probable consequence of the commission of the felony. The term "probable consequence" manifests legislative intent that some deaths are simply too remotely related to the commission of the felony to justify holding the actor responsible not only for the death but also for commission of the felony. Accordingly, here the trial court erred in instructing the jury that under the felony-murder rule it did not matter whether the act which caused death is committed recklessly or unintentionally or accidently. Reversed and remanded.

ANALYSIS

Instead of treating felony murder as an absolute-liability offense, the Model Penal Code created a presumption of recklessness when a homicide occurred in the course of the commission of certain felonies. If not rebutted, that presumption would support a conviction for murder.

Quicknotes

FELONY MURDER The unlawful killing of a human being while in the commission of, or attempted commission of, specified felonies.

People v. Washington

State (P) v. Convicted robber and murderer (D)

Cal. Sup. Ct., 62 Cal. 2d 777 (1965)

NATURE OF CASE: Appeal from conviction of murder of accomplice during a robbery where accomplice was killed by the robbery victim.

FACT SUMMARY: Washington (D), whose accomplice, Ball, was killed during a robbery by the robbery victim, was convicted of murder for Ball's death. Washington (D) contended that, under the circumstances, his murder conviction should be set aside because he lacked malice aforethought, and, since Ball did not kill anyone, the felony-murder doctrine was inapplicable.

RULE OF LAW

A robber cannot be convicted of murder for the killing of any person by another who is resisting the robbery.

FACTS: Washington (D) and his accomplice Ball held up a gas station. When Carpenter, the station owner, heard someone yell "robbery," he took out his revolver, and, when Ball entered Carpenter's office and pointed a pistol at Carpenter, Carpenter immediately shot Ball and killed him. Carpenter also shot, and hit, Washington (D), who was unarmed and who was running away with a money bag. Washington (D) was convicted of robbery, and was also convicted of first-degree murder under the felony-murder rule for Ball's death, for which he was sentenced to life imprisonment. Washington (D) challenged his conviction on the grounds that in cases where the felony-murder rule was applied, the murder victim was not a participant in the underlying felony. The state's highest court granted review.

ISSUE: Can a robber be convicted of murder for the killing of any person by another who is resisting the robbery?

HOLDING AND DECISION: (Traynor, C.J.) No. A robber cannot be convicted of murder for the killing of any person by another who is resisting the robbery. Washington (D) would hold that surviving felons are not guilty of murder when their accomplices are killed by persons resisting the felony. A distinction based on the person killed, however, would make the defendant's criminal liability turn upon the marksmanship of victims and police officers, and that is not an appropriate basis for a legal rule. Murder is the unlawful killing of a human being, with malice aforethought. Except when the common-law felony-murder doctrine is applicable, an essential element of murder is intent to kill or intent with conscious disregard for life to commit acts likely to kill. Where a killing during the robbery is not committed by the robber or their accomplice, malice aforethought is not attributable to the robber, because the killing is not committed by the robber in the perpetration or attempt to perpetrate robbery, as required by the felony-murder statute. It is not enough that the killing was a reasonably foreseeable risk of the robbery, since such a killing does not come within the statute's requirement that the murder be committed in the perpetration of the robbery. The purpose of the felony-murder rule is to deter felons from killing negligently or accidentally by holding them strictly responsible for killings they commit. This purpose is not served by punishing them for killings committed by their victims or others attempting to thwart the felony. Moreover, there is no support for the proposition that an additional purpose of the rule is to deter robbery. Instead, felons are guilty of murder when one of their accomplices kills in furtherance of the felony. A felon is also liable for murder when the felon intends to kill or intentionally commits acts that are likely to kill with a conscious disregard for life, even though the felon uses another person to accomplish their objective. Felons who initiate gun battles may also be found guilty of murder if their victims resist and kill, because initiating a gun battle involves a high degree of probability that it will result in death, and in such instances it is unnecessary to imply malice by invoking the felony-murder doctrine. Although the felony-murder rule is the law of the State, it should not be extended beyond any rational function that it is designed to serve; to apply the felony-murder doctrine when the killing is not committed by the defendant or by his accomplice could lead to absurd results, and the rule should not be invoked under such circumstances. The murder conviction is reversed.

ANALYSIS

The felony-murder rule has been criticized on the grounds that in almost all cases in which it is applied it is unnecessary and that it erodes the relation between criminal liability and moral culpability. It has been abolished in some common-law countries, such as England, and it has been converted to a rebuttable presumption of malice by the Model Penal Code. Nonetheless, as this case illustrates, despite its shortcomings, the rule is still in use to one degree or another.

Continued on next page.

Quicknotes

COMMON-LAW CRIME An activity that has been defined as a crime not by legislative enactment but by the courts through case law.

FELONY MURDER The unlawful killing of a human being while in the commission of, or attempted commission of, specified felonies.

MALICE AFORETHOUGHT The intention to commit an unlawful act without justification or excuse.

People v. Hernandez

State (P) v. Individual convicted of felony murder (D)

N.Y. Ct. App.*, 624 N.E. 2d 661 (1993)

NATURE OF CASE: Appeal from conviction for felony murder. [The procedural posture of the case is not presented in the casebook extract.]

FACT SUMMARY: Santana (D) and Hernandez (D), who were convicted of felony murder for the killing of a police officer in a gun battle following their attempt to rob an undercover police officer, contended that their felony murder convictions should have been dismissed because the dead officer had been shot and killed by a fellow officer, not by either one of them.

RULE OF LAW

A conviction of felony murder can be sustained where the homicide victim, a police officer, was shot not by the defendant or any codefendants but by a fellow officer during a gun battle initiated by the defendants following the defendants' attempted robbery of an undercover police officer.

FACTS: Santana (D) and Hernandez (D) conspired to ambush and rob a man who was coming to an apartment building in New York City to buy drugs. The plan was to have Santana (D) lure him into the building stairwell where Hernandez (D) waited with a gun. In fact, the man was an undercover state trooper, wearing a transmitter, and backed up by fellow officers. Once the undercover trooper was inside the building, Hernandez (D) accosted him and pointed a gun at his head. A fight ensued during which the officer announced that he was a policeman, pulled out his service revolver and began firing. In the confusion, Hernandez (D), still armed, ran from the building into a courtyard where he encountered members of the police back-up unit. They ordered him to halt. Instead, he aimed his gun at one of the officers and moved toward him. The officers began firing, and one was fatally shot. Hernandez (D) was apprehended and Santana (D) was arrested. They were charged with, inter alia, felony murder for the death of the officer, even though evidence clearly showed neither of them was the shooter that killed the officer. They were tried separately, and each was convicted of felony murder. On appeal, they each contended that the felony murder charges should have been dismissed because neither one of them fired the fatal shot.

ISSUE: Can a conviction of felony murder be sustained where the homicide victim, a police officer, was shot not by the defendant or any codefendants but by a fellow officer during a gun battle initiated by the defendants following the defendants' attempted robbery of an undercover police officer?

HOLDING AND DECISION: (Simon, J.) Yes. A conviction of felony murder can be sustained where the homicide victim, a police officer, was shot not by the defendant or any codefendants but by a fellow officer during a gun battle initiated by the defendants following the defendants' attempted robbery of an undercover police officer. In *People v. Wood*, 8 N.Y.2d 48, 201 N.Y.S.2d 328, 167 N.E.2d 736 (1960), this Court affirmed the dismissal of a felony murder charge on the grounds that neither the defendant nor a codefendant fired the weapon that caused death. At the time, the definition of murder in the first degree (the felony-murder antecedent) was "[t]he killing of a human being . . . without a design to effect death, by a person engaged in the commission of, or in an attempt to commit a felony." The court concluded that by the plain terms of the statute defendant could not be liable for murder, because the killing of the two men was not committed by a person "engaged in the commission of" a felony or a felony attempt. A few years later, the felony-murder statute was revised when the state's penal code was recast, by removing the language that had been dispositive in *Wood* and replacing it with a provision holding a person culpable for felony murder when, during the commission of an enumerated felony or attempt, either the defendant or an accomplice "causes the death of a person other than one of the participants." Thus, the key issue here is whether *Wood* remains good law despite the change in the definition of felony murder. The People (P) contend that the established construction of the term "causes the death" is dispositive. That term is used consistently throughout the homicide statutes and has been construed to mean that homicide is properly charged when the defendant's culpable act is "a sufficiently direct cause" of the death so that the fatal result was reasonably foreseeable. Accordingly, the People (P) maintain that it was highly foreseeable that someone would be killed in a shootout when Hernandez (D) refused to put down his gun and instead persisted in threatening the life of one of the back-up officers. Thus, under the People's (P) theory, Hernandez "caused

*The New York Court of Appeals is New York State's highest court.

Continued on next page.

the death" of the officer who was fatally shot. Because Hernandez's (D) attempt to avoid arrest was in furtherance of a common criminal objective shared with Santana (D), the People (P) contend that the murder was properly attributed to Santana (D) as well under principles of accomplice liability. In construing the felony-murder provision, courts have consistently held that an accused need not commit the final, fatal act to be culpable for causing death. To adopt Hernandez's (D) and Santana's (D) interpretation would require giving "causes the death" a different meaning than in other provisions of the same section. In light of the statutory language, the felony-murder provision should be accorded the same meaning it is given in those other provisions. That meaning accords with the view of causality, based on a proximate cause theory, that is consistent with fundamental principles of criminal law. The basic tenet of felony-murder liability is that the mens rea of the underlying felony is imputed to the participant responsible for the killing. By operation of that legal fiction, the transferred intent allows the law to characterize a homicide, though unintended and not in the common design of the felons, as an intentional killing. Thus, the presence or absence of the requisite mens rea is an issue turning on whether the felon is acting in furtherance of the underlying crime at the time of the homicide, not on the proximity or attenuation of the death resulting from the felon's acts. Contrary to Hernandez's (D) and Santana's (D) argument, using a proximate cause theory of causality will not extend criminal liability unreasonably. First, felony murder is limited to those deaths caused by one of the defendants in furtherance of their crime, and no felony-murder liability will be imposed only when the defendant's acts are a sufficiently direct cause of the death(s) involved. When the intervening acts of another party are supervening or unforeseeable, the necessary causal chain is broken, and there is no criminal liability for the defendants. Second, the felony-murder statute spells out the affirmative defense available to an accomplice who does not cause the death involved. These factors provide adequate boundaries to felony-murder liability. Applying these principles here, it is implausible that Hernandez (D) and Santana (D) could not have foreseen a bullet going astray when Hernandez (D) provoked a gun battle outside a residential building in an urban area. Affirmed.

ANALYSIS

The common-law view of causality in the felony murder context, and a view of some states, as well as the view upheld in *Wood,* is known as the agency theory of causality. Under the agency theory, no party to the underlying felony has the requisite mens rea when a nonparticipant is the shooter. Thus, under the agency theory, the presence or absence of the requisite mens rea for the homicide turns on the proximity or attenuation of the death resulting from the defendant's acts. As the court in *Wood* indicated, for a felon to be guilty of the homicide, the act (as in agency) must be either actually or constructively the felon's, and it cannot be the felon's act in either sense unless committed by the felon's own hand or by someone acting in concert with the felon or in furtherance of a common object or purpose. As the court in *Hernandez* notes, this view was replaced in New York State by a proximate cause view of causality, with the goal of extending liability broadly to those who commit serious crimes in ways that endanger the lives of others. In keeping with the latter view, the *Hernandez* court abrogated *Wood.*

Quicknotes

ABROGATE Annul; cancel; void.

ACCOMPLICE LIABILITY Liability of an individual who knowingly, purposefully or voluntarily combines with the main actor in the commission, or attempted commission, of a criminal offense.

FELONY MURDER The unlawful killing of a human being while in the commission of, or attempted commission of, specified felonies.

FELONY-MURDER RULE Common law rule that the unlawful killing of a human being while in the commission of, or attempted commission of, specified felonies constitutes murder.

INTERVENING CAUSE A cause, not anticipated by the initial actor, sufficient to break the chain of causation and relieve the initial actor of liability.

MENS REA Criminal intent.

PROXIMATE CAUSE The natural sequence of events without which an injury would not have been sustained.

SUPERVENING CAUSE An independent cause, which is the proximate cause of an act.

State v. Shock

State (P) v. Murderer (D)

Mo. Sup. Ct., 68 Mo. 552 (1878)

NATURE OF CASE: Appeal from murder conviction.

FACT SUMMARY: When Shock (D) was convicted of murder for beating a small boy to death, he argued the trial court had erred in instructing the jury on the felony-murder doctrine.

RULE OF LAW

The words "other felony" in a felony-murder statute refer to some collateral felony and not to those acts of personal violence to the deceased that constitute an element of the murder itself.

FACTS: Shock (D) severely beat a five-year-old boy to death. He was convicted of first-degree murder. Shock (D) appealed, arguing that the trial judge had erred in instructing the jury that if it believed that it was not the intention of Shock (D) to kill the child, but that he did intend to do him great bodily harm, and in so whipping him, death ensued, Shock (D) would be guilty of murder in the first degree.

ISSUE: Do the words "other felony" in a felony-murder statute refer to some collateral felony and not to those acts of personal violence to the deceased that constitute an element of the murder itself?

HOLDING AND DECISION: (Hough, J.) Yes. The words "other felony" in a felony-murder statute refer to some collateral felony and not to those acts of personal violence to the deceased that constitute an element of the murder itself, and are, therefore, merged into it, and which do not, when consummated, constitute an offense distinct from the homicide. Since this legislation includes only such murders as were murders at common law, it may well be doubted whether the words "other felony" can be held to include offenses that were not felonies at common law. The statute evidently contemplates such "other felony" as could be consummated, although the murder should also be committed. The arson, rape, robbery, and burglary may each be perpetrated and the murder also be committed. But when great bodily harm has been inflicted, and death immediately or speedily ensues therefrom, no felony has been committed, either at common law or under statutes, in addition to the murder. Here, the jury might properly have been instructed as to the law of first-degree murder on the theory of a willful, deliberate, and premeditated killing, and also as to the law of manslaughter. Reversed and remanded.

ANALYSIS

Without some kind of independent felony or merger limitation, every manslaughter would be murder.

Quicknotes

COMMON LAW A body of law developed through the judicial decisions of the courts as opposed to the legislative process.

FELONY MURDER The unlawful killing of a human being while in the commission of, or attempted commission of, specified felonies.

FIRST-DEGREE MURDER The willful killing of a person with deliberation and premeditation; first-degree murder also encompasses those situations in which a person is killed within the perpetration of, or attempt to perpetrate, specified felonies.

MANSLAUGHTER The killing of a person without premeditation or deliberation, or with the intent to kill or to commit a felony, which may be reasonably expected to result in death or serious bodily injury; manslaughter is characterized by reckless conduct or by some adequate provocation on the part of the actor, as determined by a subjective standard.

CHAPTER 7

Capital Murder and the Death Penalty

Quick Reference Rules of Law

Olsen v. State

Murderer (D) v. State (P)

Wyo. Sup. Ct., 67 P.3d 536 (2003)

NATURE OF CASE: Appeal from sentence of death.

FACT SUMMARY: When Olsen (D) was sentenced to death for murders he committed, he argued that the jury instructions as to mitigating circumstances did not correctly state the law.

RULE OF LAW

When jury instructions as to mitigating circumstances do not correctly state the law, a sentence of death will be set aside.

FACTS: Martin Olsen (D) entered a bar, instructed two patrons to lie down on the floor, and robbed the bar. After ordering the bartender to also lie face down on the floor, he shot all three in the back of the head, firing a fourth shot seconds later when it appeared that one victim was not dead. He was tried and found guilty of three counts of premeditated first-degree murder and three counts of first-degree felony murder. At the penalty phase of his trial, the jury sentenced Olsen (D) to death. Olsen (D) appealed, arguing that the jury instructions as to mitigating circumstances did not correctly state the law.

ISSUE: When jury instructions as to mitigating circumstances do not correctly state the law, will a sentence of death be set aside?

HOLDING AND DECISION: (Golden, J.) Yes. When jury instructions as to mitigating circumstances do not correctly state the law, a sentence of death will be set aside. Here, there were errors in the sentencing phase in the form of (1) insufficient evidence that the murders were especially atrocious or cruel; (2) insufficient evidence that Olsen (D) knowingly created a great risk of death to two or more persons; and (3) improper jury instructions on the law of mitigating circumstances and the decision-making process. There was no sufficient evidence of physical or mental torture. It was insufficient, under this aggravated circumstance, to argue simply that the victims suffered anguish because of uncertainty as to their ultimate fate. Nor was there sufficient evidence of great risk of death since the lives of bystanders, other than the intended victims, were not directly endangered during Olsen's (D) crimes. Furthermore, Olsen's (D) sentencing jury received inconsistent instructions as to how it should consider mitigating circumstances in that it was not clearly instructed that it was to consider mitigating circumstances even where all the mitigating evidence was not thoroughly proven. It is not sufficient "simply to allow" the defendant to present mitigating evidence to the sentencer. The sentencer "must also be able to consider and give effect" to that evidence in imposing sentence. The Wyoming death penalty statute intends the jury's consideration to be a mental balancing process, "a reasoned judgment," and a consideration of the "substantiality and persuasiveness" of all the circumstances, not the mere numbers of aggravating as opposed to mitigating circumstances. The weighing of aggravating and mitigating circumstances does not mean a mere mechanical counting of factors on each side of an imaginary scale, or the arbitrary assignment of weights to any of them. Additionally, the jury should have been instructed that, under the death penalty statute, a sentence of life imprisonment means that Olsen (D) would never be eligible for parole. Vacated and remanded.

ANALYSIS

The United States Supreme Court requires that a jury's discretion in sentencing defendants to death must be genuinely narrowed. However, once that is accomplished, the jury must be allowed the widest possible discretion to not choose death. Aggravating circumstances must meet certain requirements: (1) the circumstance may not apply to every defendant convicted of murder; (2) it must apply only to a subclass of defendants convicted of murder (genuine narrowing); and (3) the circumstance must not be unconstitutionally vague. The selection decision determines whether an eligible defendant should receive the death penalty and requires an "individualized determination" on the basis of the character of the individual and the circumstances of the crime.

Quicknotes

JURY INSTRUCTIONS A communication made by the court to a jury regarding the applicable law involved in a proceeding.

MITIGATING CIRCUMSTANCES OR EVIDENCE Circumstances that may be considered as extenuating or reducing the degree of moral culpability; although they do not constitute a justification or excuse for the offense in question, they are considered in light of fairness and mercy.

Tison v. Arizona

Jailbreak brothers (D) v. State (P)

481 U.S. 137 (1987)

NATURE OF CASE: Review of death sentence imposed subsequent to conviction under the felony-murder rule.

FACT SUMMARY: Ricky and Raymond Tison (D), charged with felony murder after they orchestrated a jailbreak to free their father that resulted in four homicides, contended that the imposition of the death penalty was unconstitutional since they had not actually taken a life themselves.

RULE OF LAW:
The death penalty may be imposed upon a felony-murder defendant whose acts constituted reckless disregard for life.

FACTS: Raymond Tison (D) and Ricky Tison (D) participated in the violent jailbreak of their father, Gary. After smuggling a cache of guns into the prison, Raymond (D), Ricky (D), and several others shot their way out and fled by automobile. Their getaway car broke down. Several members of the gang then flagged down a vehicle and killed the occupants. Neither Raymond (D) nor Ricky (D) participated in the murders. After a shootout with police, Raymond (D) and Ricky (D) were apprehended. They were charged and convicted of felony murder and sentenced to die. The Arizona Supreme Court affirmed. The United States Supreme Court granted review.

ISSUE: May the death penalty be imposed upon a felony-murder defendant whose acts constituted reckless disregard for life?

HOLDING AND DECISION: (O'Connor, J.) Yes. The death penalty may be imposed upon a felony-murder defendant whose acts constituted reckless disregard for life. The Eighth Amendment requires some proportionality between a crime and a sentence. The Tisons (D) argue that the death penalty is commensurate only with intent to kill and, therefore, cannot be imposed in a felony-murder rule. This is incorrect. Reckless indifference to human life can be just as threatening and blameworthy as intent to kill. The present case is an excellent example. The Tisons (D) purposefully entered into a situation where a death was not only possible but quite likely. The level of their blameworthiness is not materially less than that of a defendant who intends to kill, so the imposition of the death penalty was permissible. Affirmed.

ANALYSIS

The Eighth Amendment has put some limitations on the felony-murder rule. In *Enmund v. Florida*, 458 U.S. 782 (1982), a defendant whose role in a robbery resulting in death was tangential (he drove the getaway car) was sentenced to death for felony murder. The United States Supreme Court reversed, holding the penalty disproportionate to the crime.

Quicknotes

FELONY MURDER The unlawful killing of a human being while in the commission of, or attempted commission of, specified felonies.

MALICE The intention to commit an unlawful act with the intent to inflict injury without justification or excuse.

RECKLESSNESS Conduct that is conscious and that creates a substantial and unjustifiable risk of harm to others.

McCleskey v. Kemp

Convicted murderer (P) v. State (D)

481 U.S. 279 (1987)

NATURE OF CASE: Review of order dismissing habeas corpus petition.

FACT SUMMARY: McCleskey (P) contended that statistics demonstrating that capital punishment was more severely applied against Black people made capital punishment unconstitutional.

RULE OF LAW

Statistical evidence of racial bias in the imposition of capital punishment does not make capital punishment unconstitutional.

FACTS: McCleskey (P), a Black man, was convicted of murder in the course of robbery and sentenced to death. This was affirmed on appeal. In a federal habeas proceeding, McCleskey (P) introduced evidence of statistical studies showing that capital punishment was more likely to be applied when the perpetrator was Black and/or the victim was White. McCleskey (P) argued that this made the death penalty unconstitutional as cruel and unusual punishment and a violation of equal protection. The district court dismissed the habeas petition, and the Eleventh Circuit Court of Appeals affirmed. The United States Supreme Court granted review.

ISSUE: Does statistical evidence of racial bias in the imposition of capital punishment make capital punishment unconstitutional?

HOLDING AND DECISION: (Powell, J.) No. Statistical evidence of racial bias in the imposition of capital punishment does not make capital punishment unconstitutional. To show an equal protection violation, a party challenging such a sentence must show a discriminatory intent. Statistics show, at best, a result. This does make an equal protection violation. With respect to McCleskey's (P) Eighth Amendment claim, this court's decisions have held that, for a violation to occur, a state system of meting out death sentences must be arbitrary in such a fashion as to there being no rhyme or reason as to application of the punishment. A system that sets clear guidelines but at the same time permits discretion as to aggravation and leniency will not violate the Eighth Amendment. Some bias will almost naturally result from a system permitting discretion, but this does not raise a constitutional violation. Here, Georgia's system for implementing the death penalty falls well within accepted parameters, and no constitutional violation has been shown. Affirmed.

ANALYSIS

The Court's test for what constitutes an unacceptable death penalty system was largely announced in *Furman v. Georgia*, 408 U.S. 238 (1972). At that time, Georgia had no guidelines for when death could or could not be imposed on a convict. This sort of unbridled discretion the Court could not reconcile with the Eighth Amendment.

Quicknotes

CAPITAL PUNISHMENT Punishment by death.

EIGHTH AMENDMENT The Eighth Amendment to the federal constitution prohibits the imposition of excessive bail, fines, and cruel and unusual punishment.

EQUAL PROTECTION A constitutional guarantee that no person shall be denied the same protection of the laws enjoyed by other persons in life circumstances.

HABEAS CORPUS A proceeding in which a defendant brings a writ to compel a judicial determination of whether the defendant is lawfully being held in custody.

CHAPTER 8

Sexual Assault

Quick Reference Rules of Law

People v. Dorsey

State v. Rapist

N.Y. Sup. Ct., 429 N.Y.S.2d 828 (1980)

NATURE OF CASE: Motion to dismiss.

FACT SUMMARY: Dorsey (D) raped a woman in an elevator, having manipulated the controls to stall the elevator between floors.

RULE OF LAW

In proving a case of forcible compulsion, a woman has to exert only earnest resistance of a type reasonably to be expected from a person who genuinely refuses to participate in sexual intercourse, deviate sexual intercourse, or sexual contact, under all the attendant circumstances.

FACTS: A petite, middle-aged woman entered the lobby of her apartment building after work. She entered the elevator and pressed the button for the tenth floor on which her apartment was located. A large, heavy teenage male entered the elevator after her and pressed the button for another floor. The woman noticed that the elevator had stopped and looked up to see Dorsey (D) manipulating the buttons so that the elevator had stopped between floors; the alarm bell did not go off. Dorsey (D) ordered the woman to take off her clothes. She did not respond, but Dorsey (D) repeated his demand. The woman complied and was subjected to acts of sexual intercourse and sodomy during the next ten to fifteen minutes. Afterwards, Dorsey (D) told the woman to get dressed and started the elevator back up, eventually getting off on the twenty-second floor. As he was leaving the elevator, Dorsey (D) threatened that if anything happened to him in the next couple of days, his friends would get her. The woman got back to her floor, went to her apartment, and immediately called the apartment's security police force who then contacted the New York Police Department. Dorsey (D) was identified and arrested later that evening.

ISSUE: In proving a case of forcible compulsion, does a woman have to exert only earnest resistance of a type reasonably to be expected from a person who genuinely refuses to participate in sexual intercourse, deviate sexual intercourse, or sexual contact, under all the attendant circumstances?

HOLDING AND DECISION: (Schackman, J.) Yes. In proving a case of forcible compulsion, a woman has to exert only earnest resistance of a type reasonably to be expected from a person who genuinely refuses to participate in sexual intercourse, deviate sexual intercourse, or sexual contact, under all the attendant circumstances. The intent of the legislation was set forth in the preamble which stated: "It is the legislature's intention to modify the resistance requirement in the definition of forcible compulsion so that the victim need only offer so much resistance as is reasonable under the circumstances." The reasonable-under-the-circumstances approach, with language to make clear that the woman need not incur serious risk of death or serious bodily injury, is as low as the standard can be set and remain consistent with fair treatment of defendants. The issue before this court is to determine from the facts of this case whether Dorsey (D) either exerted physical force capable of overcoming this complainant's reasonable, earnest resistance, or whether the complainant was overcome by fear of immediate death or serious physical injury due to threat from the defendant. Both of these questions must be measured by all of the attendant circumstances in this case. Here, instead of being faced with four big men in a lonely place, the complainant was faced with a husky teenager, who was seven inches taller and outweighed her by 70 pounds. She was trapped in a stalled elevator, between floors, with no place to retreat to, or from which help could arrive. The law did not require that she ascertain what the defendant would do to her if she refused to take off her clothes. Nor does it take but a brief recognition of the everyday events in this city to reasonably conclude that a gun, knife or other deadly weapon might quickly and savagely be used if she did not yield to Dorsey (D). Therefore, the court finds, as a matter of law, that the People (P) presented sufficient trial evidence from which the jury could conclude, beyond a reasonable doubt, that Dorsey (D) engaged in sexual acts with the complainant by means of forcible compulsion, in that there was an implied threat which placed the complainant in fear of immediate death or serious physical injury. Motion to dismiss indictment denied.

ANALYSIS

Rape victims were no longer required to demonstrate a show of physical force in resisting the attack, although courts still looked for earnest and reasonable resistance. The requirement for fear of or actual force remains even when the sexual activity was nonconsensual. That means, the victim remains the one who has to prove they did not quietly acquiesce to escape serious injury even without the judicial requirement of "utmost resistance."

Quicknotes

RAPE Unlawful sexual intercourse by means of fear or force and without consent.

People v. Barnes

State (P) v. Convicted rapist (D)

Cal. Sup. Ct., 42 Cal. 3d 284, 228 Cal. Rptr. 228 (1986)

NATURE OF CASE: Review of reversal of rape conviction.

FACT SUMMARY: Barnes's (D) rape conviction was reversed on the basis that the alleged victim had not resisted.

RULE OF LAW

To sustain a rape conviction, evidence of resistance need not be presented.

FACTS: Barnes (D) invited one Marsha M. to his residence. Marsha, wishing to purchase marijuana, came over. According to Marsha, Barnes (D) began demonstrating aberrant behavior, acting belligerent one moment and then rational the next. Barnes (D) made several threats toward her. After several attempts at seduction, Barnes (D) demanded that they have intercourse. Marsha complied, which she later ascribed to fear for her safety. Barnes's (D) version was that she consented, which was his defense at trial. Barnes (D) was convicted. A court of appeals reversed due to the lack of resistance. The California Supreme Court granted review.

ISSUE: To sustain a rape conviction, must evidence of resistance be presented?

HOLDING AND DECISION: (Bird, C.J.) No. To sustain a rape conviction, evidence of resistance need not be presented. In 1980, the California Legislature amended Penal Code § 261, the section defining rape. Rape is now defined as intercourse accomplished against a person's will by means of force or fear of immediate and unlawful bodily injury on the person. Certain references to resistance that existed in the prior law were deleted, and the legislative history makes it clear that these deletions were intentional. This was consistent with the modern trend in the law, which recognizes that resisting a rape puts the victim in danger of further battery. In view of this, the court of appeals incorrectly read a resistance element into the offense, and this was erroneous. Reversed.

ANALYSIS

Rape is one of the more politicized offenses in the legal area. The evidentiary requirements for a rape conviction have been significantly altered. The present case illustrates such a change. Another change is that many states no longer permit evidence of a complainant's sexual history.

Quicknotes

BATTERY Unlawful contact with the body of another person.

RAPE Unlawful sexual intercourse by means of fear or force and without consent.

State v. Barela

State (P) v. Convicted first-degree rapist (D)

Utah Sup. Ct., 2015 UT 22, 349 P.3d 676 (2015)

NATURE OF CASE: Appeal from conviction of first-degree rape.

FACT SUMMARY: Barela (D), a massage therapist who was convicted of the first-degree rape of K.M., challenged the conviction on several grounds, including the sufficiency of the evidence. In doing so, Barela (D) raised a threshold question of statutory interpretation as to whether the state's nonconsent statute ("section 406"), which enumerated 12 circumstances where a sexual encounter was nonconsensual, was exhaustive or merely foreclosed the factfinder from deeming sex to be consensual in circumstances deemed substantively out of bounds as a matter of public policy.

RULE OF LAW

A state's nonconsent statute that enumerates specific circumstances where a sexual encounter is deemed nonconsensual is not exhaustive so as to preclude the factfinder from considering other circumstances of nonconsent.

FACTS: Barela (D) had a massage session with K.M. at a Massage Envy studio, where Barela (D) was employed as a massage therapist and K.M. was a client. K.M. had received one previous massage from Barela (D) at the studio. And when she arrived on the date in question, she had not requested Barela (D) as her therapist. K.M. removed all of her clothing for the massage. During the massage she was covered only by a sheet and blanket. In Barela's (D) version of the encounter, K.M. became aroused and initiated sexual contact by humping the table and grabbing Barela's (D) crotch. The two then began having sex, in which K.M. showed active engagement by giving him oral sex, rolling over on the table, and playing with her breasts. In contrast, in K.M.'s version, she was receiving a massage from Barela (D) when he unexpectedly started massaging her inner thigh, which made her feel very uncomfortable because she had never had a massage therapist do that in previous massages, and she "didn't know how to respond." Then, before she knew it, Barela (D) pulled her to the end of the table, dropped his pants and penetrated her vagina with his penis. K.M. reported that everything happened very fast and that Barela (D) may have touched or penetrated her vagina with his finger, but that she wasn't sure. According to K.M., Barela (D) went from rubbing her thigh to penetrating her vagina within a matter of seconds. K.M. said that she had not flirted with Barela (D) and did not say or do anything to suggest that she wanted to have sex with him. She did not physically resist or verbally tell Barela (D) "no"; she said nothing at all. Instead, she clung to the blanket and "just froze." She said she felt fearful because she was alone, and because the only other person in the massage parlor was a male receptionist. She repeatedly stressed that everything happened very fast, and she elaborated that she "checked out," "kind of withdrew," "was scared," and just "kind of froze." In K.M.'s version of the events, she heard Barela (D) make an alarmed and profane exclamation and then saw him looking at semen in his hand. Then he told her "this concludes your massage" and left the room. K.M. got up as quickly as she could, wiped herself with a towel, and got dressed. Her main concern was getting out of Massage Envy as quickly as she could. Barela (D) met her in the hallway, where he offered her water, which she accepted. She checked out as normal, told the receptionist the massage was fine, paid her bill (including a tip), and took a mint. Barela (D) was charged with first-degree rape. The defense's primary theory at trial was that K.M. had been the instigator and that the sex was consensual. In addition, the defense also asserted that K.M. had lied about the encounter in an effort to protect her relationship with Trista, with whom K.M. had one child together (conceived by K.M. through artificial insemination), and that at the time of the massage K.M. was taking fertility medication and had been artificially inseminated only a few days earlier. The evidence also indicated that the sperm donor was an African American friend of K.M. and Trista. Thus, the defense theory was that K.M. had consensual sex with Barela (D), worried that she had conceived and that the baby would resemble him (a light-skinned Hispanic), and that a "serious problem" would ensue when Trista realized that the baby did not resemble their African American donor. Barela (D) was convicted, and, on appeal to the state's highest court, challenged the conviction on several grounds, including ineffective assistance of counsel, and the insufficiency of the evidence. The high court agreed that Barela's (D) counsel had been ineffective when failing to object to a key jury instruction, and that such ineffectiveness was prejudicial. Therefore, the court overturned the verdict and ordered a new trial on that ground alone, and did not need to rule on the sufficiency of the evidence. However, the court addressed a threshold issue of statutory interpretation raised by Barela's (D) challenge to the sufficiency of the evidence on the element of K.M.'s nonconsent, an element that would have to be considered in a new trial. Barela (D) had asserted that the state's statute regarding nonconsent ("section 406"), which stated that "abuse is without consent of the victim"

Continued on next page.

under "any of" 12 "circumstances" listed in the statute, did not encompass the notion of K.M.'s becoming "frozen" during the alleged rape.

ISSUE: Is a state's nonconsent statute that enumerates specific circumstances where a sexual encounter is deemed nonconsensual exhaustive so as to preclude the factfinder from considering other circumstances of nonconsent?

HOLDING AND DECISION: [Judge not stated in casebook extract.] No. A state's nonconsent statute that enumerates specific circumstances where a sexual encounter is deemed nonconsensual is not exhaustive so as to preclude the factfinder from considering other circumstances of nonconsent. Section 406 statute does not define nonconsent, nor does it purport to set forth any sort of formula or criteria for the establishment of nonconsent. Generally, nonconsent is a fact-intensive, context-dependent question, decided on a case-by-case basis by the factfinder, and nothing in section 406 changes that. Instead, section 406 prescribes policy-based exceptions to this general approach by deeming certain circumstances beyond the case-by-case discretion of the factfinder. If, as Barela (D) urges the Court to hold, section 406 were construed to be exclusive and to identify the sum and substance of all circumstances in which nonconsent could be established, a jury would be foreclosed from finding nonconsent in a case where the settled understanding of nonconsent in the criminal law would easily support a guilty verdict. Because section 406 does not prevent a jury from finding nonconsent in circumstances properly understood to qualify as such, the jury in Barela's (D) new trial may conclude that K.M.'s "freezing" under the circumstances of the case was nonconsensual. Reversed and new trial ordered.

ANALYSIS

The question of consent is highly nuanced and context dependent. Thus, the outward indicators of consent in one context may suggest nonconsent in another. A person who had previously been a victim of sexual assault might well respond to unwanted sexual contact in a post-traumatic-stress response of "freezing." Under such circumstances, it would be reasonable for a jury to infer that a victim's freezing reaction was indicative of nonconsent, and a jury might also reasonably conclude that if the defendant was aware of the victim's past, the defendant knew or might have known such a reaction indicated nonconsent. However, that does not mean that a "freezing" response would always support such a determination, since, as Barela (D) suggests, freezing or nonparticipation may well be indistinguishable from normal sexual activity for some people, so that, in context, under certain circumstances, it might be possible for a defendant to establish that a putative victim's nonparticipation indicated consent.

Quicknotes

CONSENT A voluntary and willful agreement by an individual possessing sufficient mental capacity to undertake an action suggested by another.

RAPE Unlawful sexual intercourse by means of fear or force and without consent.

STATUTORY CONSTRUCTION The examination and interpretation of statutes.

In the Interest of M.T.S.

State (P) v. Rapist (D)

N.J. Sup. Ct., 609 A.2d 1266 (1992)

NATURE OF CASE: Prosecution for rape.

FACT SUMMARY: M.T.S. (D) was a houseguest in C.G.'s family's home. After engaging in consensual kissing and heavy petting, M.T.S. (D) engaged in sexual penetration of C.G. to which she had not consented.

RULE OF LAW

Any act of sexual penetration engaged in by the defendant, without the affirmative and freely given permission of the victim to the specific act of penetration, constitutes the offense of sexual assault.

FACTS: Fifteen-year-old C.G. was living with her family and seven other people, including 17-year-old M.T.S. (D) and his girlfriend. One evening, C.G. went upstairs to sleep after watching television with her mother, M.T.S. (D), and his girlfriend. At around 1:15 a.m., M.T.S. (D) entered C.G.'s bedroom as she was walking to the bathroom. C.G. returned from the bathroom, and the two engaged in kissing and heavy petting. According to M.T.S. (D), once they were in bed, they undressed each other and continued to kiss and touch for about five minutes, then proceeded to engage in sexual intercourse. According to M.T.S. (D), who was on top of C.G., he penetrated her three times and on the fourth time, she pushed him off of her. As she pushed him off, she said "stop, get off," and he got off immediately. After about one minute, he asked C.G. what was wrong and she replied with a back-hand to his face. M.T.S. (D) said that he proceeded to get dressed and told C.G. to calm down, but that she then told him to get away from her and began to cry. He left the room and went to sleep downstairs. The trial court determined that the juvenile was delinquent for committing a sexual assault. The Appellate Division reversed. The State (P) appealed.

ISSUE: Does any act of sexual penetration engaged in by the defendant, without the affirmative and freely given permission of the victim to the specific act of penetration, constitute the offense of sexual assault?

HOLDING AND DECISION: (Handler, J.) Yes. Any act of sexual penetration engaged in by the defendant, without the affirmative and freely given permission of the victim to the specific act of penetration, constitutes the offense of sexual assault. The New Jersey Code of Criminal Justice does not refer to force in relation to "overcoming the will," "physical overpowering," or the "submission" of the victim. It does not require the demonstrated non-consent of the victim. In reforming rape laws, the legislature placed primary emphasis on the assaultive nature of the crime, altering its constituent elements so that they focus exclusively on the forceful or assaultive conduct of the defendant. Thus, by eliminating all references to the victim's state of mind and conduct, and by broadening the definition of penetration to cover not only sexual intercourse between a man and a woman but a range of acts that invade another's body or compel intimate contact, the legislature emphasized the affinity between sexual assault and other forms of assault and battery. Under the new law, the victim is no longer required to resist and therefore need not have said or done anything in order for the sexual penetration to be unlawful. The alleged victim is not put on trial, and their responsive or defensive behavior is rendered immaterial. In a case such as this one, in which the State (P) does not allege violence or force extrinsic to the act of penetration, the factfinder must decide whether the defendant's act of penetration was undertaken in circumstances that led the defendant reasonably to believe that the alleged victim had freely given affirmative permission to the specific act of sexual penetration. Such permission can be indicated either through words or through actions that, when viewed in the light of all the surrounding circumstances, would demonstrate to a reasonable person affirmative and freely given authorization for the specific act of sexual penetration. In this case, the trial court concluded that the victim had not expressed consent to the act of intercourse, either through her words or actions. Reversed.

ANALYSIS

This case provides a definition of the actus reus of rape as sexual penetration absent some kind of affirmative expression of consent.

Quicknotes

ACTUS REUS The unlawful act that gives rise to criminal liability, as distinguished from the required mental state.

ASSAULT AND BATTERY Any unlawful touching of another person without justification or excuse.

RAPE Unlawful sexual intercourse by means of fear or force and without consent.

Commonwealth v. Lopez

State (P) v. Convicted rapist (D)

Mass. Sup. Jud. Ct., 745 N.E.2d 961 (2001)

NATURE OF CASE: Appeal from rape convictions.

FACT SUMMARY: Lopez (D), who was convicted of rape, contended that the trial court erred in refusing to give a mistake of fact instruction to the jury.

RULE OF LAW

A defendant's honest and reasonable belief as to a complainant's consent is not available as a defense to the crime of rape in all cases.

FACTS: A putative rape victim, a 17-year-old girl living in a foster home, claimed that Lopez (D) had raped her. She claimed that she encountered Lopez (D) on her way to a restaurant and that she agreed that he accompany her. She met her biological mother at the restaurant and introduced Lopez (D) as her friend. When she left the restaurant, Lopez (D) was waiting for her, and she agreed to his offer to walk her home. They walked to a park across the street from her home and talked for around half an hour. To avoid being heard by her foster family, they walked deep into nearby woods. At one point, she told Lopez (D) that she wanted to go home, but he assured her that he would do her no harm, and then he led her to a secluded area. Lopez (D) asked her why she was so distant and said that he wanted to start a relationship with her. She said that she did not want to "get into any relationship." Lopez (D) began making sexual innuendos to which she did not respond. He grabbed her by her wrist and began kissing her on the lips. She pulled away and said, "No, I don't want to do this." In response to his overtures, she repeated, "No, I don't want to. I don't want to do this." He raised her shirt and touched her breasts. She immediately pulled her shirt down and pushed him away. Lopez (D) then pushed her against a slate slab, unbuttoned her pants, and pulled them down. Using his legs to pin down her legs, he produced a condom and asked her to put it on him. She said, "No." Lopez (D) put the condom on and told her that he wanted her to put his penis inside her. She said, "No." He then raped her, and she began to cry. A few minutes later, she made a jerking move. Lopez (D) became angry, turned her around, pushed her face into the slate, and raped her again. Lopez (D) told her that she would get into a lot of trouble if she said anything. She then went home, showered, and told her foster mother what had happened. They called 911, and she cried hysterically as she spoke to the operator. The treating physician described the bruising to her knees as significant and opined that there had been excessive force and trauma to the vaginal area. Lopez's (D) version of the encounter was very different. According to him, the putative victim had been a willing and active partner in consensual sexual intercourse. He claimed that she had initiated the intimate activity and never once told him to stop. She had also invited him to a party that evening so he could meet her friends, and she appeared mildly upset when he told her he would be unable to attend. At trial, before the jury retired, defense counsel requested a mistake of fact instruction as to consent, but the trial judge declined, concluding that because Lopez's (D) theory was that the putative victim actually consented, the question for the jury was simply whether they believed the victim's or Lopez's (D) version of the encounter. The jury convicted Lopez (D) of rape. He appealed, on the basis that the trial court had erred in refusing to give the mistake of fact instruction. The state's highest court granted review.

ISSUE: Is a defendant's honest and reasonable belief as to a complainant's consent available as a defense to the crime of rape in all cases?

HOLDING AND DECISION: [Judge not stated in casebook excerpt.] No. A defendant's honest and reasonable belief as to a complainant's consent is not available as a defense to the crime of rape in all cases. The mistake of fact defense is available where the mistake negates the existence of a mental state essential to a material element of the offense. The state's rape statute follows the common-law definition of rape, and has been interpreted to require the State (P) to prove beyond a reasonable doubt that the defendant committed sexual intercourse (1) by means of physical force, nonphysical, constructive force, or threats of bodily harm, either explicit or implicit; and (2) at the time of penetration, there was no consent. Thus, although the State (P) must prove lack of consent, it does not need to prove that the defendant intended the intercourse to be without consent. Accordingly, because a defendant's knowledge of the victim's lack of consent or intent to engage in nonconsensual intercourse is not a material element of the offense, a mistake as to that consent cannot negate a mental state required for commission of the prohibited conduct. Other jurisdictions, however, have held that a mistake of fact instruction is necessary to prevent injustice where the force necessary for rape is not anything more than what is necessary to accomplish penetration. In those jurisdictions, an instruction as to a defendant's honest and reasonable belief as to consent is available to mitigate the undesirable and unforeseen consequences that may

Continued on next page.

flow from this construction. By contrast, in this jurisdiction, force, whether physical, constructive or threatened, must be proved, and this provides a defendant with some protection against mistakes as to consent. The mistake of fact defense in this state would also tend to eviscerate the long-standing rule that victims need not use any force to resist an attack. A shift in focus from the victim's to the defendant's state of mind might require victims to use physical force in order to communicate an unqualified lack of consent to defeat any honest and reasonable belief as to consent. Although a majority of other jurisdictions provide a mistake of fact as to consent defense, the minority of states that do not is significant. The case at bar does not provide a reason to depart from prior law in this regard: mistake of fact as to consent may not be recognized as defense to rape in all cases. Whether such a defense might, in some circumstances, be appropriate is a difficult question that may be considered in a future case where a defendant's claim of reasonable mistake of fact is at least arguably supported by the evidence. This is not such a case. Affirmed.

ANALYSIS

Because the mistake of fact defense is available where the mistake negates the existence of a mental state essential to a material element of the offense, a mistake of fact is not truly a defense, but rather a means of demonstrating that the prosecution has failed to prove beyond a reasonable doubt the essential elements of the crime. Nevertheless, the showing of mistake of fact is referred to as a "defense."

Quicknotes

CONSENT A voluntary and willful agreement by an individual possessing sufficient mental capacity to undertake an action suggested by another.

MISTAKE OF FACT An unintentional mistake in knowing or recalling a fact without the will to deceive.

RAPE Unlawful sexual intercourse by means of fear or force and without consent.

People v. Hernandez

State (P) v. Rapist (D)

Cal. Ct. App., 200 Cal. App. 4th 1000 (2011)

NATURE OF CASE: Appeal from conviction by jury for rape of an unconscious person.

FACT SUMMARY: Ramon Ruiz Hernandez (D) was convicted of rape of an unconscious person for having sex with victim A.B. while she was passed out after a party.

RULE OF LAW

A defendant may be convicted of rape for sexual intercourse with an unconscious or asleep person when the defendant is aware of the unconsciousness of the victim.

FACTS: Ramon Ruiz Hernandez (D) attended a birthday party at a cousin's apartment. He and another guest, A.B., stayed the night due to heavy drinking. A.B. slept in a bedroom, while Hernandez (D) slept on the couch. A.B. woke up at 4 a.m. and noticed evidence of sexual violation that she did not remember. A.B. went for a sexual assault examination and the nurse found evidence of sexual activity more severe than would be expected with consensual sex. Hernandez (D) told the police initially that A.B. was awake when he entered the bedroom; he later changed his story that A.B. was asleep when he entered but woke when he started kissing her and they had consensual sex. Ultimately, Hernandez (D) told police that A.B. was "knocked out" and "out cold" and did not consent to sexual intercourse. A.B. did not remember the assault. The State (P) charged Hernandez (D) with rape of an unconscious person. Hernandez (D) was convicted by a jury and appealed his conviction.

ISSUE: May a defendant be convicted of rape for sexual intercourse with an unconscious or asleep person when the defendant is aware of the unconsciousness of the victim?

HOLDING AND DECISION: [Judge not stated in casebook excerpt.] Yes. A defendant may be convicted of rape for sexual intercourse with an unconscious or asleep person when the defendant is aware of the unconsciousness of the victim. Hernandez (D) testified at trial that he and A.B. had consensual sex and that she was merely drunk rather than asleep or unconscious. However, Hernandez (D) had provided statements to police that A.B, was "knocked out" and "out cold" and that she did not wake up and "barely moved." Hernandez (D) had also given statements that A.B. never gave him permission to have sexual intercourse and that he knew she did not want to have sexual intercourse with him. A contention that a victim was merely drunk rather than unconscious is not enough for an appellate court to overturn the reasonable inference of the trier of fact that Hernandez (D) was aware A.B. was unconscious and had sexual intercourse with her anyway. Affirmed.

ANALYSIS

A victim that is unconscious or asleep cannot give consent or resist the offender. An offender that has sexual intercourse with a victim that is unconscious commits rape. Even in states that require a victim to resist for liability for rape to attach, such resistance is excused when the victim is unconscious and unable to resist. While Hernandez (D) originally claimed that he had consensual sex with A.B. and testified at trial that the encounter was consensual, his prior statements to police as well as other testimony provided a basis for a reasonable trier of fact to infer that A.B. was unconscious, and Hernandez (D) was aware.

Quicknotes

INCAPACITY Lack of capacity or ability to function legally, physically or mentally.

RAPE Unlawful sexual intercourse by means of fear or force and without consent.

State v. Jones

State (P) v. Rapist (D)

S.D. Sup. Ct., 804 N.W.2d 409 (2011)

NATURE OF CASE: Appeal for conviction by jury of two counts of third-degree rape.

FACT SUMMARY: Christopher Jones (D) was convicted of raping E.B. who testified she was too intoxicated to consent.

RULE OF LAW

Rape by intoxication is not a strict liability offense.

FACTS: Jones (D) met up with his friends and their friend E.B. after 1 A.M. Jones (D) and his friends had been celebrating a birthday and drinking. They socialized for a few hours and then E.B. went to sleep on the couch and Jones (D) went to sleep on the ottoman near the couch. E.B. testified that she woke up to Jones (D) penetrating her and she resisted verbally and physically. Due to her intoxication, E.B. testified she then went back to sleep on a chair but woke up again to Jones (D) penetrating her again. E.B. testified she again refused and resisted and stayed in the bathroom until Jones (D) left. E.B. subsequently went to the hospital for a sexual assault examination. A witness testified that E.B. was able to carry on normal conversation before the parties went to sleep and did not appear to be "wasted or drunk." E.B. consumed at least four drinks in Jones's (D) presence and had been drinking before she met him. Jones (D) testified he was unaware that E.B. was intoxicated and he believed they had consensual sex. The State (P) charged Jones (D) with rape in the third-degree due to the intoxication of E.B. Jones (D) requested a jury instruction that knowledge of the victim's intoxication was necessary for conviction, which was refused by the trial court. Jones (D) was convicted by the jury on two counts of third-degree rape of an intoxicated person and appealed.

ISSUE: Is rape by intoxication a strict liability offense?

HOLDING AND DECISION: (Konenkamp, J.) No. Rape by intoxication is not a strict liability offense. The prosecution must prove the offender knew or should have known the victim was intoxicated. The change to the language of the statute removing the requirement that the rapist administer the intoxicating agent to the victim did not render the crime one of strict liability. Because rape by intoxication is a serious felony, and the legislature did not make it clear it was eliminating the mens rea requirement, the statute should be interpreted to include the requirement of knowledge of intoxication for conviction. Reversed and remanded for a new trial. The circuit court will instruct the jury that the State (P) must prove the defendant knew or reasonably should have known that the complainant's intoxicated condition rendered her incapable of consenting.

ANALYSIS

Due to the severe nature of the crime of rape by intoxication, the silence of the legislature on the knowledge of the perpetrator of the victim's intoxication did not transform the crime into one of strict liability. The court read into the statute a requirement that the perpetrator had actual knowledge or should have reasonably known the victim was intoxicated. Mere removal of the requirement that the perpetrator administer the intoxicating agent to the victim was not sufficient to transfer the crime into one of strict liability, such as statutory rape. Here, the State (P) must prove that the assailant knew or reasonably should have known that the victim was intoxicated. The line between conscious intoxication, such that the victim drank too much to be able to properly consent, and incapacitating intoxication, where the victim could not consent at all, was too blurry for the court to impose strict liability in the case of rape of an intoxicated person.

Quicknotes

INTOXICATION The inability to act with full mental and physical capabilities because of alcohol or drug consumption.

MENS REA Criminal intent.

RAPE Unlawful sexual intercourse by means of fear or force and without consent.

STRICT LIABILITY Liability for all injuries proximately caused by a party's conducting of certain inherently dangerous activities without regard to negligence or fault.

Commonwealth v. Mlinarich

Commonwealth (P) v. Rapist (D)

Pa. Sup. Ct., 518 Pa. 247, 542 A.2d 1335 (1988)

NATURE OF CASE: Appeal from rape conviction.

FACT SUMMARY: Mlinarich (D), victim's adult guardian, threatened to recommit the victim, a 14-year-old girl, to a juvenile detention facility unless she agreed to sexual intercourse and other sexual acts with him.

RULE OF LAW

Rape is when a person engages in sexual intercourse with another person not his spouse by forcible compulsion or by threat of forcible compulsion that would prevent resistance by a person of reasonable resolution.

FACTS: Mlinarich (D) was an adult guardian to a 14-year-old girl. He threatened to recommit her to a juvenile detention facility unless she agreed to sexual intercourse and other sexual acts with him. Mlinarich (D) was arrested and charged with multiple counts of attempted rape, involuntary deviate sexual intercourse, corruption of a minor, indecent exposure, and endangering the welfare of a minor. A jury convicted him of all the charges. On appeal, the superior court reversed. The prosecution appealed the reversals.

ISSUE: Is rape when a person engages in sexual intercourse with another person not his spouse by forcible compulsion or by threat of forcible compulsion that would prevent resistance by a person of reasonable resolution constitute rape?

HOLDING AND DECISION: (Nix, C.J.) Yes. Rape is when a person engages in sexual intercourse with another person not his spouse by forcible compulsion or by threat of forcible compulsion that would prevent resistance by a person of reasonable resolution. The critical distinction is where the compulsion overwhelms the will of the victim in contrast to a situation where the victim can make a deliberate choice to avoid the encounter even though the alternative may be an undesirable one. Indeed, the victim in this instance apparently found the prospect of being returned to the detention home a repugnant one. Notwithstanding, she was left with a choice and therefore the submission was a result of a deliberate choice and was not an involuntary act. It does not meet the test of "forcible compulsion" as required by statute. The purpose of the term "forcible compulsion" was to distinguish between assault upon the will and the forcing of the victim to make a choice regardless how repugnant. Certainly difficult choices have a coercive effect but the result is the product of the reason, albeit unpleasant and reluctantly made. The fact cannot be escaped that the victim has made the choice and the act is not involuntary. Affirmed.

DISSENT: (Larsen, J.) Has civilization fallen so far, have our values become so distorted and misplaced, as to leave a 14-year-old child without protection when she is forced to make such an awful "choice"? Here, the victim's "choice" was in no way a "deliberate" exercise of her free will and the product of reason.

ANALYSIS

Justice Larsen was rightly incensed by this shocking decision when he wrote in his dissent, "Has civilization fallen so far, have our values become so distorted and misplaced, as to leave a 14-year-old child without protection when she is forced to make such an awful 'choice'?"

Quicknotes

RAPE Unlawful sexual intercourse by means of fear or force and without consent.

Boro v. People

Rapist (D) v. State (P)

Cal. Ct. App., 163 Cal. App. 3d 1224, 210 Cal. Rptr. 122 (1985)

NATURE OF CASE: Petition for writ of prohibition to restrain further prosecution of count II of the information on file against petitioner.

FACT SUMMARY: Boro (D) deceived Ms. R. into sexual intercourse with him by telling her he was a doctor and that her blood tests showed she had a fatal disease that could be cured by having sexual intercourse with an anonymous donor who had been injected with a disease-curing serum.

RULE OF LAW

Under California statutory law, rape is an act of sexual intercourse with a nonspouse accomplished where the victim is at the time unconscious of the nature of the act.

FACTS: Ms. R., the victim, received a telephone call from a "Dr. Stevens" (D) who said that he worked at Peninsula Hospital. He told Ms. R. that he had results of her blood test and that she had contracted a dangerous, highly infectious and perhaps fatal disease, that she could be sued as a result, and that the disease came from using public toilets. "Dr. Stevens" (D) further explained that there were only two ways to treat the disease. The first was a painful surgical procedure costing $9,000 and requiring her uninsured hospitalization for six weeks. The second alternative, "Dr. Stevens" (D) explained, was to have sexual intercourse with an anonymous donor who had been injected with a serum which would cure the disease. This procedure would cost only $4,500. When the victim replied she lacked sufficient funds, "Dr. Stevens" (D) suggested that $1,000 would suffice. Ms. R. agreed to the nonsurgical alternative and consented to intercourse with the mysterious donor, believing it was the only choice she had. After discussing her intentions with her work supervisor, the victim proceeded to the Hyatt Hotel in Burlingame as instructed and contacted "Dr. Stevens" (D) by telephone. He was furious that she had informed her employer of the plan, threatened to terminate treatment, and instructed her to inform her employer she had decided not to go through with the treatment. Ms. R. did so, then withdrew $1,000 from her bank, and checked into another hotel and called "Dr. Stevens" to give him her room number. About a half hour later, the "donor" (D) arrived at her room. When Ms. R. had undressed, the "donor" (D) had sexual intercourse with her. Boro (D) was apprehended when police arrived at the hotel room, having been called by Ms. R.'s supervisor. The People (P) contend that at the time of the intercourse, Ms. R. was unconscious of the nature of the act because of the misrepresentation that the act was a medical treatment and not a simple, ordinary act of sexual intercourse. Boro (D) contends that the victim was plainly aware of the nature of the act in which she was voluntarily engaged, so that her motivation is irrelevant.

ISSUE: Under California statutory law, is rape an act of sexual intercourse with a nonspouse accomplished where the victim is at the time unconscious of the nature of the act?

HOLDING AND DECISION: [Judge not stated in textbook excerpt.] Yes. Under California statutory law, rape is an act of sexual intercourse with a nonspouse accomplished where the victim is at the time unconscious of the nature of the act. If deception causes a misunderstanding as to the fact itself (fraud in the factum) there is no legally recognized consent because what happened is not that for which consent was given, whereas consent induced by fraud is as effective as any other consent, so far as direct and immediate legal consequences are concerned, if the deception relates not to the thing done but merely to some collateral matter (fraud in the inducement). In California, the language of the statute is plain. Rape does not include sexual intercourse with a nonspouse that has been brought about by deception. We cannot entertain the slightest doubt that the legislature well understood how to draft a statute to encompass fraud in the factum and how to specify certain fraud in the inducement as vitiating consent. Ms. R. precisely understood the nature of the act, but motivated by a fear of disease and death, succumbed to Boro's (D) fraudulent blandishments. To so conclude is not to vitiate the heartless cruelty of Boro's (D) scheme, but to say that it comprised crimes of a different order than rape under the statute in question. Let a peremptory writ of prohibition issue restraining the State (P) from further action on count II.

ANALYSIS

Boro (D), who engaged in the same conduct with several other women, became notoriously known as "Dr. Feelgood" in the California media. He proved unrepentant and repeated this scheme with another victim. In the interim, however, the California legislature had enacted law specifically criminalizing this kind of conduct. In 1987, Boro (D) was prosecuted under the new statute.

Continued on next page.

Quicknotes

RAPE Unlawful sexual intercourse with a woman by a man by means of fear or force and without her consent.

WRIT OF PROHIBITION A writ issued by a superior court prohibiting a lower court from exceeding its jurisdiction or from usurping jurisdiction beyond that authorized by law.

CHAPTER 9

Defensive Force, Necessity, and Duress

Quick Reference Rules of Law

People v. La Voie

State (P) v. Driver charged with murder (D)

Colo. Sup. Ct., 395 P.2d 1001 (1964)

NATURE OF CASE: Appeal of directed verdict dismissing a murder charge.

FACT SUMMARY: La Voie (D), in apparent imminent peril from a group of strangers, shot and killed one of them.

RULE OF LAW

One reasonably in fear for one's safety may use deadly force against the source of the fear.

FACTS: La Voie (D) was driving home from work early one morning. His car was forced off the road from the rear by another vehicle. Four men got out making threatening remarks to La Voie (D). As they approached, La Voie (D) pulled out his gun, which he had a license to carry, and shot one of the group, who later died. La Voie (D) was charged with murder. After trial, the court granted a directed verdict for the defense. The State (P) appealed.

ISSUE: May one reasonably in fear for one's safety use deadly force against the source of the fear?

HOLDING AND DECISION: (Moore, J.) Yes. One reasonably in fear for one's safety may use deadly force against the source of the fear. When a person has reasonable grounds for believing, and does actually believe, that danger of great bodily harm is imminent, the person may act on that fear and defend themself, even to the point of using deadly force, provided that such force is not disproportionate to the threat. Here, La Voie (D) was forced off the road and approached by four strange men, who threatened him. This certainly was sufficient to establish a fear of imminent bodily harm in his mind, and he was entitled to protect himself. Affirmed.

ANALYSIS

Self-defense has both objective and subjective components. Subjectively, a person must actually be in fear for their safety. Objectively, the fear must be reasonable. The objective analysis is a bit like the "reasonable person" standard in tort law.

Quicknotes

DEADLY FORCE That degree of force that is likely to result in death or great bodily injury.

DIRECTED VERDICT A verdict ordered by the court in a jury trial.

SELF-DEFENSE The right to protect an individual's person, family, or property against attempted injury by another.

People v. Gleghorn

State (P) v. Assault and battery defendant (D)

Cal. Ct. App., 193 Cal. App. 3d 196 (1987)

NATURE OF CASE: Appeal from assault and battery conviction.

FACT SUMMARY: When Gleghorn (D) was convicted of assault and battery, he argued that he was simply using justified deadly force to repel deadly force.

RULE OF LAW

If an attacked person defends themself so successfully that the attacker is rendered incapable of inflicting injury, there is no justification for further retaliation.

FACTS: In the early morning hours, Kelsey Gleghorn (D) entered a garage rented by Michael Fairall as his dwelling and began beating with a stick the rafters where Fairall slept. He then set fire to the rafters, and yelled he wanted to kill Fairall, whereupon Fairall shot Gleghorn (D) in the back with an arrow from his bow. At this point, Gleghorn (D), greatly angered, began beating Fairall, who had descended from the rafters, and did so with such severity that Fairall nearly died. Gleghorn (D) was convicted of assault and battery with the infliction of serious bodily injury. He appealed, contending that since the jury found his acts prior to being shot constituted only a simple assault, Fairall was not justified in replying with deadly force, which therefore entitled Gleghorn (D) to "defend himself" with equally deadly force. Thus, he argued, he could not be convicted of battery with the intention to inflict serious bodily injury.

ISSUE: If an attacked person defends themself so successfully that the attacker is rendered incapable of inflicting injury, is there justification for further retaliation?

HOLDING AND DECISION: (Stone, J.) No. If an attacked person defends themself so successfully that the attacker is rendered incapable of inflicting injury, there is no justification for further retaliation. Not every assault gives rise to the right to kill in self-defense. To repel a simple assault, the person assaulted is not authorized to resort to unduly violent measures. Gleghorn (D) contends that since he initially committed only a simple assault, he was legally justified as a matter of law in standing his ground, even though he was the attacker, and justified in utilizing lethal force against his adversary. Gleghorn's (D) argument, however, is misplaced since the right of self-defense is based upon the appearance of imminent peril to the person attacked. The right to defend one's person or home with deadly force depends upon the circumstances as they reasonably appeared to that person. That right cannot depend upon Gleghorn's (D) supposedly nonfelonious secret intent. Similarly, justification does not depend upon the existence of actual danger, but rather upon appearances, namely, if a reasonable person would be placed in fear for their safety, and defendant acted out of that fear. Here, the jury could reasonably infer from the evidence that Fairall acted reasonably upon the appearance this his life was in danger, or, even if he acted unreasonably in shooting Gleghorn (D) with an arrow, Gleghorn (D) was unjustified in further attacks upon Fairall. Affirmed.

ANALYSIS

As illustrated in the *Gleghorn* case, generally if one makes a felonious assault upon another, or has created the appearance of imminent peril justifying the other to launch a deadly counterattack in self-defense, the original assailant cannot slay the adversary in self-defense unless the original assailant has first, in good faith, declined further combat, and has fairly notified the other that the original assailant has abandoned the affray. On the other hand, however, when the victim of simple assault responds in a sudden and deadly counterassault, the original aggressor need not attempt to withdraw and may use reasonable necessary force in self-defense.

Quicknotes

ASSAULT AND BATTERY Any unlawful touching of another person without justification or excuse.

DEADLY FORCE That degree of force that is likely to result in death or great bodily injury.

State v. Leidholm

State (P) v. Wife convicted of murder of husband (D)

N.D. Sup. Ct., 334 N.W.2d 811 (1983)

NATURE OF CASE: Appeal from conviction for manslaughter.

FACT SUMMARY: Leidholm (D) contended she acted in self-defense in stabbing her husband to death.

RULE OF LAW

A person acts in self-defense if, under the circumstances perceived by that person, such acts appeared necessary to protect themself from imminent harm.

FACTS: Leidholm (D) was involved in a stormy marriage marked by frequent violent altercations. On August 6, 1981, after a violent fight, she and her husband went to bed, and she stabbed him while he slept. She was charged with murder. She contended that she acted in self-defense, responding to the years of abuse and her expectation of further abuse. The trial court instructed the jury that self-defense must be judged on the basis of what a reasonable person, regardless of subjective perceptions, would believe to be imminent danger. Leidholm (D) was convicted and appealed.

ISSUE: Does a person act in self-defense if, under the circumstances perceived by that person, such acts appeared necessary to protect themself from imminent harm?

HOLDING AND DECISION: (VandeWalle, J.) Yes. A person acts in self-defense if, under the circumstances perceived by that person, such acts appeared necessary to protect themself from imminent harm. The evidence clearly showed a subjective belief by Leidholm (D) that she was in imminent danger. Thus she acted in a subjective manner adequate to allow her defense of self-defense to go to the jury. This court must also address the expert testimony on "battered woman syndrome." The elements of the syndrome include low self-esteem and "learned helplessness" on the part of an abused woman. An abused woman cannot bring herself to leave her batterer. This syndrome was offered as part of a proposed jury instruction for the jury to consider whether Leidholm's husband had abused her prior to her stabbing him and her accompanying mindset. This separate jury instruction is not necessary. The jury must consider the existence and reasonableness of Liedholm's imminent fear, so the expert testimony on battered woman syndrome is included in that analysis. Reversed and remanded.

ANALYSIS

This case illustrates a rejection of the objective test of self-defense and the application of a subjective test. The trial court instructed the jury on an objective test. This requires the jury to disregard peculiar sensitivities of a particular defendant. The subjective test allows consideration of such sensitivities and requires an evaluation of the perception of the actor.

Quicknotes

MANSLAUGHTER The killing of a person without premeditation or deliberation, or with the intent to kill or to commit a felony that may be reasonably expected to result in death or serious bodily injury; manslaughter is characterized by reckless conduct or by some adequate provocation on the part of the actor, as determined by a subjective standard.

REASONABLE PERSON STANDARD The standard of care exercised by one who possesses the intelligence, education, knowledge, attention, and judgment required by society of its members when governing behavior; the standard applies to a person's judgment when determining breach of a duty under the theory of negligence.

SELF-DEFENSE The right to protect one's person, family, or property against attempted injury by another.

SUBJECTIVE STANDARD A standard that is based on the personal belief of an individual.

People v. Goetz

State (P) v. Subway passenger (D)

N.Y. Ct. App., 68 N.Y.2d 96, 497 N.E.2d 41 (1986)

NATURE OF CASE: Appeal from dismissal of counts from an indictment on charges of attempted murder, assault, and illegal weapons possession.

FACT SUMMARY: Goetz (D) shot four unarmed teenagers on a subway train because he believed they were attempting to rob him.

RULE OF LAW

A person's use of force in self-defense must be objectively reasonable.

FACTS: In 1984, Goetz (D) was riding a subway in New York City when he was approached by a group of four teenagers. Believing they were going to rob him, Goetz (D) pulled out a handgun and shot all four boys. According to statements made by Goetz (D), he fired another shot at one of the boys, Cabey, although he was already lying on the ground defenseless. Goetz (D) was indicted for attempted murder but appealed, claiming that the prosecutor (P) had erroneously introduced an objective element in consideration of Goetz's (D) claim of self-defense. An appeals court ruled for Goetz (D), and New York (P) appealed.

ISSUE: Must a person's use of force for self-defense be objectively reasonable?

HOLDING AND DECISION: (Wachtler, C.J.) Yes. A person's use of force in self-defense must be objectively reasonable. New York Penal Law § 35.15 states that a person may act in self-defense when and to the extent that they reasonably believe it is necessary to defend themself against what they reasonably believe to be the imminent use of force. The language of this statute clearly shows an intent that self-defense at least be objectively reasonable, although incorrect in actuality. New York intentionally did not follow the Model Penal Code's rule with regard to self-defense, which allows a defense for the subjective belief in the necessity of defense. Instead, New York chose to follow the rule that a person's actions must be objectively reasonable under the circumstances. The situation and circumstances may include all relevant evidence, of course, including prior experiences that lead to reasonable beliefs. Accordingly, the prosecution's (P) use of the "reasonable person" standard during the indictment proceedings was proper. Reversed.

ANALYSIS

When Goetz (D) subsequently went to trial, the jury acquitted him of all charges except illegal gun possession. The jury's decision was probably influenced by the prevailing community feelings at the time about street crime. More recently, a New York jury ruled for one of the four boys in a civil trial against Goetz (D).

Quicknotes

OBJECTIVE STANDARD A standard that is not personal to an individual but is dependent on some external source.

SELF-DEFENSE The right to protect one's person, family, or property against attempted injury by another.

People v. Ceballos

State (P) v. Property owner (D)

Cal. Sup. Ct., 12 Cal. 3d 470, 116 Cal. Rptr. 233 (1974)

NATURE OF CASE: Appeal from conviction for assault with a deadly weapon.

FACT SUMMARY: Ceballos (D) was convicted of assault with a deadly weapon when a trap gun he set up in his garage fired into the face of a teenage boy who broke open the garage door.

RULE OF LAW

A person may be held criminally or civilly liable under statutes proscribing homicides with intent to injure if that person sets upon their premises a deadly mechanical device and that device kills or injures another.

FACTS: Ceballos (D) lived in his apartment over his garage. One month some tools were stolen from his garage. Later, he noticed the lock had been bent and that there were pry marks on the door. Ceballos (D) then set up a trap gun that would fire when someone opened the garage. Two boys, Robert, 15, and Stephen, 16, both unarmed, pried off the lock. When Stephen opened the door, he was shot in the face by the trap gun. Ceballos (D) was convicted of assault with a deadly weapon and appealed.

ISSUE: May a person be held criminally or civilly liable under statutes proscribing homicides with intent to injure if that person sets upon their premises a deadly mechanical device and that device kills or injures another?

HOLDING AND DECISION: (Burke, J.) Yes. A person may be held criminally or civilly liable under statutes proscribing homicides with intent to injure if that person sets upon their premises a deadly mechanical device and that device kills or injures another. An exception has been recognized where the intrusion is, in fact, such that the person, if present, would be justified in taking life or inflicting the bodily harm with their own hands. But if the actor is present, there is the possibility that the actor will realize that deadly force is not necessary, while a device lacks that discretion. Deadly devices should be discouraged; even though the law of torts recognizes an exception as stated above, that exception is not appropriate to criminal law, for it does not prescribe a workable standard of conduct; liability depends on fortuitous results. While burglary is a dangerous crime at common law, by statute that crime has a much wider scope, so where the character and manner of a burglary would not create a fear of great bodily harm, there is no cause for the use of deadly force. Affirmed.

ANALYSIS

Defense of property relies on the theory that a person's home is their castle. Deadly force may be used where it appears reasonable and necessary to prevent an unlawful trespass apparently committed to harm the occupants or commit a felony therein. A mere trespass without felonious intent or not creating a serious threat of danger to the occupants will not justify the use of deadly force. Notice that the exception being argued on appeal is a rule of tort law and that the court noted that its decision was against the position of the Restatement (Second) of Torts. The tort rule simply did not state a clear enough standard to be applicable to criminal situations.

Quicknotes

ASSAULT The intentional placing of another in fear of immediate bodily injury.

BURGLARY Unlawful entry of a building at night with the intent to commit a felony therein.

DEFENSE OF PROPERTY An affirmative defense to criminal liability for the use of force in the protection of one's property.

TRESPASS Unlawful interference with, or damage to, the real or personal property of another.

Tennessee v. Garner

State (P) v. Father of felon (D)

471 U.S. 1 (1985)

NATURE OF CASE: Appeal from a dismissal of an action for unnecessary use of deadly force.

FACT SUMMARY: Tennessee (D) contended its statute allowing the use of deadly force on unarmed non-violent fleeing suspects was constitutional.

RULE OF LAW

Deadly force may not be used by a police officer to prevent escape of a suspect unless the officer harbors a good-faith belief that the suspect poses a significant threat of death or serious injury to the officer or others.

FACTS: Garner was shot and killed by a Tennessee police officer while fleeing the scene of a felony. The officer saw Garner was unarmed, yet shot him to prevent escape. Garner's father sued, contending the use of deadly force in this situation, pursuant to Tennessee statute, was unconstitutional. The trial court entered judgment for Tennessee (D), holding the statute constitutional, the district court affirmed, and the court of appeals reversed. The State of Tennessee (D) appealed.

ISSUE: May deadly force be used by a police officer to prevent escape of an unarmed, nonviolent suspect?

HOLDING AND DECISION: (White, J.) No. Deadly force may not be used by a police officer to prevent escape of a suspect unless the officer harbors a good-faith belief that the suspect poses a significant threat of death or serious injury to the officer or others. The seizure, in a case of a nonviolent felon, occurs when the suspect is ordered to stop and relinquish themself to police. The use of deadly force when that order is ignored goes beyond the constitutional bounds of reasonableness, unless deadly force has been threatened. Thus, the statute allowing for such force is unconstitutional. Affirmed.

ANALYSIS

At common law, deadly force would be allowed in this situation. This is so because most felonies were punishable by death. Thus, the consequences, although obtained without trial, equaled those facing the felon. Today, this is outdated and the court recognized this in its decision.

Quicknotes

DEADLY FORCE That degree of force that is likely to result in death or great bodily injury.

The Queen v. Dudley & Stephens

Government (P) v. Shipwreck survivors (D)

Q. B., 14 Q.B.D. 273 (1884)

NATURE OF CASE: Judicial review of murder indictment.

FACT SUMMARY: Dudley (D) and Stephens (D), while shipwrecked, killed Parker and ate him in order to avoid starving to death.

RULE OF LAW

It is not legal justification to kill another to save oneself in the absence of self-defense.

FACTS: Dudley (D), Stephens (D), Brooks, and Parker were cast away when their ship was caught in a storm. They were floating on a small boat for several days without food or water. To avoid starving to death, Dudley (D) and Stephens (D) agreed that Parker, the youngest and weakest, and who had no dependent family, should be sacrificed to save the others. Brooks dissented, and Parker was not consulted. Dudley (D) killed Parker and the remaining three lived off the body until help came. Dudley (D) and Stephens (D) were indicted for murder, and the jury found that all would have died if the act had not been committed. The jury sought judicial advice as to whether the acts constituted murder.

ISSUE: Is it legally justified to take another's life to save oneself in the absence of self-defense?

HOLDING AND DECISION: (Per curiam) No. It is not legally justified to kill another to save oneself in the absence of self-defense. In this case, the acts performed were in no way justified by law, even though any other human being probably would have acted the same way. There is no unqualified justification for self-preservation. Thus, the killing constituted murder. Dudley (D) and Stephens (D) are sentenced to death.

ANALYSIS

The Crown subsequently commuted the sentences to six months' imprisonment. This indicates the difficulty society had, and still has, with this factual situation. Commentators have suggested that, had Parker assented to the killing, the result would have been different as the defense of consent might have been available.

Quicknotes

MURDER The unlawful killing of a person, either with deliberation and premeditation or by conduct demonstrating a reckless disregard for human life.

NECESSITY DEFENSE A defense to liability for unlawful activity where the conduct is unavoidable and is justified by preventing the occurrence of a more serious harm.

SELF-DEFENSE The right to protect one's person, family, or property against attempted injury by another.

People v. Unger

State (P) v. Escapee (D)

Ill. Sup. Ct., 362 N.E.2d 319 (1977)

NATURE OF CASE: Appeal from criminal escape conviction.

FACT SUMMARY: Unger (D) escaped from a minimum security honor farm to allegedly avoid homosexual assaults and threats of death.

RULE OF LAW

The defenses of necessity and compulsion are available in escape cases and the jury should be so instructed where evidence adduced at trial is sufficient to raise the defense.

FACTS: Unger (D) was repeatedly sexually assaulted and threatened with death and physical injury at a minimum security honor farm. Unger (D) left the farm and was apprehended several days later. Unger (D) alleged that his escape was not voluntary and had been caused by compulsion (the acts of others) and necessity (outside forces, e.g., natural conditions). The court refused to instruct the jury that these facts were a defense to the charge. Rather, the court instructed the jury that Unger's (D) reasons for escaping were immaterial. The jury convicted Unger (D) of criminal escape and Unger (D) was sentenced to 3–9 years consecutive with the term he was currently serving for auto theft. On appeal, the conviction was reversed and remanded for a new trial. The first jury trial resulted in a hung jury. The second jury convicted Unger (D), and he appealed.

ISSUE: Are the defenses of necessity and compulsion available in escape cases and should the jury be so instructed where evidence adduced at trial is sufficient to raise the defense?

HOLDING AND DECISION: (Ryan, J.) Yes. The defenses of necessity and compulsion are available in escape cases and the jury should be so instructed where evidence adduced at trial is sufficient to raise the defense. While escape situations do not fit within the traditional ambit of either compulsion or necessity defenses, they have been recognized by several jurisdictions in similar situations. Since compulsion requires an imminent threat of great bodily harm, many commentators suggest that the situation fits within the necessity defense. The prisoner is forced to choose between the lesser of two evils. We, likewise, find that compulsion and necessity are defenses to a charge of escape. Where the defendant raises sufficient evidence at trial, the jury should be instructed as to the availability of the defense. It is a limited defense and the jury may consider factors such as whether the defendant's fears were justified, whether the threat was imminent and sufficiently severe, whether there was time to resort to either the courts or prison officials and if this would be effective, and whether the prisoner immediately reported his escape to the police. These factors go to the weight of the defense. A jury might find the defense valid even if one or more of these factors are missing. Reversed.

ANALYSIS

Duress was recognized as a defense to escape in a situation similar to *Unger*. *People v. Harmon*, 53 Mich. App. 482 (1974). The traditional response by most jurisdictions is that the defense should not be available on public policy grounds. Other jurisdictions would allow the defense only on a limited basis if certain conditions existed, which are similar to those stated by the majority in *Unger*. *People v. Lovercamp*, 43 Cal. App. 3d 823 (1974).

Quicknotes

COMPULSION Imminent threat of great bodily harm or death by one party so as to induce the other to commit a criminal offense.

NECESSITY DEFENSE A defense to liability for unlawful activity where the conduct is unavoidable and is justified by preventing the occurrence of a more serious harm.

State v. Warshow

State (P) v. Demonstrators (D)

Vt. Sup. Ct., 410 A.2d 1000 (1980)

NATURE OF CASE: Appeal from trespass convictions.

FACT SUMMARY: Warshow (D) and other demonstrators contended they were justified in committing criminal trespass because they were fighting the danger of a nuclear accident in entering the complainant's nuclear power plant.

RULE OF LAW

Necessity will justify criminal behavior only where the danger sought to be avoided is imminent.

FACTS: Warshow (D) and others, while protesting nuclear power, demonstrated on property owned by a private company upon which was operated a nuclear power plant. They were arrested and convicted of criminal trespass. They appealed, contending that they were justified in their actions by the necessity of preventing a nuclear disaster.

ISSUE: Will necessity justify criminal behavior only where the danger sought to be avoided is imminent?

HOLDING AND DECISION: (Barney, C.J.) Yes. Necessity will justify criminal behavior only where the danger sought to be avoided is imminent. There clearly was no emergency forcing Warshow (D) and others to protest in order to save life immediately in danger. Their evidence showed long-range potential danger, which is an insufficient necessity. Affirmed.

CONCURRENCE: (Hill, J.) The evaluation of competing evils justifies the result reached.

DISSENT: (Billings, J.) The defendants offered to prove their imminent danger theory. They had expert testimony ready to produce demonstrating the immediate danger of nuclear reaction within seven seconds of the plant starting up. They also offered to prove that reaction would have resulted in severe radiation damage to persons and property. The defendants asserted they had no other alternative to prevent the start up of the plant. The majority wrongly found the defendants did not show imminent danger or that the legislature precluded this theory. The defendants should be permitted to offer the defense of necessity.

ANALYSIS

This case illustrates that the defense of justification based upon necessity is not broadly applied. The danger necessitating the activity must be shown to be immediate, actual, and imminent before criminal activity will be excused. Other acts, such as arson to combat a forest fire in order to save lives, would be considered necessary as a clear choice of evils resulting in the least harmful conclusion.

Quicknotes

NECESSITY DEFENSE A defense to liability for unlawful activity where the conduct is unavoidable and is justified by preventing the occurrence of a more serious harm.

TRESPASS Unlawful interference with, or damage to, the real or personal property of another.

State v. Crawford

State (P) v. Robber (D)

Kan. Sup. Ct., 253 Kan. 629, 861 P.2d 791 (1993)

NATURE OF CASE: Appeal of conviction for robbery.

FACT SUMMARY: Crawford (D) embarked on a robbery spree that included multiple criminal acts. Crawford (D) alleged he had been coerced into committing his crimes by another person to whom he owed money.

RULE OF LAW

The defense of duress requires an imminent threat to the person being coerced, and that the fear created by that threat be reasonable.

FACTS: Crawford (D), a habitual drug user, frequently purchased his drugs from Bateman on credit. After accruing a debt of nearly $10,000, Crawford (D) was told by Bateman to commit robberies in order to repay the debt or Bateman would injure him. Bateman then drove Crawford (D) to a nearby city and instructed him to approach a woman getting into her car for the purpose of committing a robbery. Crawford (D) complied, accosting the woman and hitting her on the head with his pistol, demanding money and valuables. Crawford (D) then began a series of criminal acts lasting several hours by hijacking a nearby car and its occupant. These acts included robbing two separate homes, loading valuables into a stolen car, eating food from the refrigerator, and forcing one homeowner to access his ATM account and provide Crawford (D) with additional money. Crawford (D) subsequently contacted Bateman, who was dissatisfied with the total value of the items and cash stolen. Bateman then threatened Crawford (D) by suggesting his son would be harmed if he did not commit additional robberies to secure more cash. The homeowner whose car had been initially hijacked eventually freed himself and reported Crawford (D) to the authorities (P), who later arrested him. In his response, Crawford (D) asserted the defense of duress, alleging that Bateman was in fact the primary motivation for his criminal behavior, and that imposing culpability on him would have no deterrent effect. The district court convicted Crawford (D) of robbery and other charges, and he appealed.

ISSUE: Does the defense of duress require an imminent threat to the person being coerced, and that the fear created by that threat be reasonable?

HOLDING AND DECISION: (Allegrucci, J.) Yes. The defense of duress requires an imminent threat to the person being coerced, and that the fear created by that threat be reasonable. Duress is a defense because it shifts culpability away from the perpetrator in recognition of their subordinate role and lack of requisite intent, in light of another person who coerces the perpetrator into acting. However, to successfully assert the defense requires that the coercion be imminent, leaving the perpetrator with no means of escaping or withdrawing from the coerced activity. In his defense, Crawford (D) alleges that he was completely dependent on Bateman due to his narcotic addiction. Here, there was no imminence to the threats imposed on Crawford (D) and his son. Crawford (D) engaged in a series of criminal acts that lasted several hours, a period where he was out of touch with Bateman completely. The compulsion imposed by Bateman was therefore not continuous. In addition, Crawford (D) could have escaped and reported the coercive activity to the authorities. This case is distinguishable from similar duress cases because of the dependency present between the perpetrator and the coercing party. However, this dependency does not bear on the imminence of the threat, but the reasonableness of the fear imposed. The facts as presented do not support a finding that the fear experienced by Crawford (D) was reasonable. The threats made by Bateman toward Crawford (D) and his son were indefinite. Furthermore, the argument could be made that Crawford (D) willingly placed himself into the dependent position in the first place by obtaining drugs from Bateman. The defense of duress may therefore not apply. Affirmed.

ANALYSIS

In drafting its opinion, the court relied on *State v. Harrison*, 228 Kan. 558, 618 P.2d 827 (1980), in which the defendant had in fact escaped from her aggressor (Heath) in her own car and committed the robbery. She did not drive to the police station and report the threats made to her by Heath. Her vague reference to her children was not sufficient to show there was a present, imminent, and impending threat of direct or serious bodily injury to herself or her children. Had her testimony indicated the children were in the custody of Heath at his house when she committed the robbery, the defense of compulsion would have been a factual issue for the jury.

Quicknotes

DURESS Unlawful threats or other coercive behavior by one person that causes another to commit acts they would not otherwise do.

ROBBERY The unlawful taking of property from the person of another through the use of force or fear.

State v. Hunter

State (P) v. Convicted felon (D)

Kan. Sup. Ct., 740 P.2d 559 (1987)

NATURE OF CASE: Appeal of conviction of felony murder.

FACT SUMMARY: Hunter (D), accused of felony murder, was not permitted to raise the defense of duress.

RULE OF LAW
Duress is a defense to felony murder.

FACTS: Hunter (D), while hitchhiking, was picked up by two men. A series of events ensued in which several people were kidnapped and robbed and two were killed. Hunter (D) was charged with robbery, battery, kidnapping, and murder under the felony-murder rule. Hunter (D) claimed he had been compelled to join the criminal activity by threats from one of the two men. The court rejected a proffered instruction, holding that duress is not available as a defense to a felony-murder charge. Hunter (D) was convicted, and he appealed.

ISSUE: Is duress a defense to felony murder?

HOLDING AND DECISION: [Judge not stated in casebook excerpt.] Yes. Duress is a defense to felony murder. Duress is available as a defense to all crimes other than voluntary homicide. Since the felony-murder rule imposes homicide liability for actions which were not expected or intended to result in death, it is improper to deny the defense to one who, through fortuity, becomes involved in an enterprise resulting in a death not so expected. Here, Hunter's (D) homicide liability, if any, would be by way of felony murder. Therefore, he should have been able to raise duress as a defense. Reversed.

ANALYSIS

Duress is a universally recognized defense to a criminal charge, although the amount of duress necessary to make the defense available varies. Murder and voluntary manslaughter generally do not afford the defense. The rationale behind this exception is that one is not free to kill another to save their own life.

Quicknotes

DURESS Unlawful threats or other coercive behavior by one person that causes another to commit acts they would not otherwise do.

FELONY MURDER The unlawful killing of a human being while in the commission of, or attempted commission of, specified felonies.

CHAPTER 10

Mental Illness as a Defense

Quick Reference Rules of Law

People v. Serravo

State (P) v. Delusional husband (D)

Colo. Sup. Ct. 823 P.2d 128 (1992)

NATURE OF CASE: State supreme court certiorari of state law defining defense based on insanity.

FACT SUMMARY: Serravo (D) stabbed his wife following a paranoid delusion that he was instructed by God to do so. At trial the court issued a jury instruction on a defense of insanity based on the *M'Naghten* rule that the prosecution later disputed on the grounds that the instruction drew an erroneous distinction between legal and moral wrong.

RULE OF LAW

A defense of insanity based on the *M'Naghten* rule is defined by a defendant's inability to distinguish right from moral wrong as opposed to legal wrong.

FACTS: Serravo (D) was a union employee of King Soopers who harbored plans to construct and build a sports complex based on instructions from God. After visiting with several other employees and believing he had received encouragement toward his endeavor, Serravo (D) went home and stabbed his wife, who was hospitalized. Serravo (D) explained to his wife and authorities that an intruder had committed the act, but his wife subsequently discovered letters written by Serravo (D) describing his intentions to stab his wife in an attempt to sever their marriage based on instructions from God. In addition, Serravo (D) later revealed under psychiatric examination that he believed his wife did not support his plan to build the sports complex and that there were inner "evil spirits" troubling him regarding how to deal with his wife's lack of encouragement. After reading his letters, Serravo's (D) wife called the authorities, who arrested him and charged him with attempted first-degree murder and first-degree assault. During trial, psychiatric testimony was offered from both sides. The prosecution's diagnosis was that Serravo (D) experienced a delusional disorder due to brain damage he had sustained in an auto accident some years earlier but was sane at the time he committed the crime. The defense presented testimony that Serravo (D) was in fact mentally ill at the time of the crime, and that a paranoid delusion about God affected his ability to tell right from wrong. At trial, the court issued a disputed jury instruction that is the basis of this review, which suggested that Serravo (D) would be protected by the defense of insanity if he believed the act he was committing was morally right. The jury returned a not guilty verdict, and the prosecution appealed, asserting that the defense of insanity should be evaluated on legal, not moral, grounds. On appeal, the court affirmed the trial court's decision, adding that the moral standard be based on the prevailing societal standard of morality. The prosecution then petitioned for review by the state supreme court.

ISSUE: Is the defense of insanity based on the *M'Naghten* rule defined by a defendant's inability to distinguish right from moral wrong as opposed to legal wrong?

HOLDING AND DECISION (Quinn, J.) Yes. A defense of insanity based on the *M'Naghten* rule is defined by a defendant's inability to distinguish right from moral wrong as opposed to legal wrong. The state law in question is based on the *M'Naghten* rule, [8 Eng. Rpt. 718 (1843)], which defines insanity as an inability to distinguish between right and wrong. We agree with the ruling in *M'Naghten* suggesting that a person be considered legally sane where a person commits an act they know to be morally wrong, regardless of the legal underpinning. Other courts have rejected the view that the term "wrong" as used in *M'Naghten* refers to an act that is contrary to the laws of the state, or a legal wrong. To base the definition of "wrong" on "legal wrong" removes a critical psychological component from the legal definition of insanity. However, this should not permit a person whose moral views are merely different from the laws of the state to avoid culpability based on insanity. Instead, the distinction this court draws between legal and moral wrong will void culpability in a mentally ill defendant who commits an act which the defendant is aware is contrary to law but commits anyway. In addition, the definition of morality may be based either objectively on prevailing social standards, or subjectively on the defendant's own moral beliefs. A person's awareness of right and wrong derives from their personal experiences but is not necessarily limited to the standards endorsed by society. Defining morality on a purely subjective standard thus ignores a part of social morality upon which acceptable behavior is built. We therefore conclude that the term "wrong" as used by *M'Naghten* and the applicable state statute's definition of insanity refer to moral and not legal wrong. In addition, we affirm the court of appeals' definition of moral wrong based on an objective social standard rather than a subjective one. The finding of not guilty on reason of insanity is therefore affirmed.

Continued on next page.

ANALYSIS

The opinion bases a part of its analysis on the distinction between subjective and objective moral standards. However, the *M'Naghten* rule was originally intended to limit a defendant's cognition to the legality of the act, and not to the prevailing moral standard. This ruling now shifts culpability away from persons who may not agree with the established law. Despite the fact that such a person may be insane, the court here did address the decisional balance that must exist to account for both legally and morally culpable perpetrators.

Quicknotes

CRIMINAL ASSAULT The intentional placing of another in fear of immediate bodily injury; criminal assault does not require that the victim suffer apprehension so long as the defendant has an intent to injure and commits an act in furtherance of that intent.

INSANITY DEFENSE An affirmative defense to a criminal prosecution that the defendant suffered from a mental illness, thereby relieving the defendant of liability for their conduct.

***M'NAGHTEN* RULE** A defense to a criminal prosecution that the defendant was not guilty due to a mental disease or defect that rendered them incapable of knowing the nature and quality of their conduct or that such conduct was wrong.

Smith v. State

Army private (D) v. State (P)

Alaska Sup. Ct., 614 P.2d 300 (1980)

NATURE OF CASE: Appeal of conviction of shooting with intent to kill or to cause great bodily harm.

FACT SUMMARY: A court rejected Smith's insanity plea, although a preponderance of expert medical testimony was to the contrary.

RULE OF LAW

A factfinder may hold a defendant to have been legally sane even when a preponderance of expert medical testimony is to the contrary.

FACTS: Smith (D), who was about to be dishonorably discharged from the army due to poor behavior, commandeered an army vehicle at gunpoint and fled the base. Police chased him into a wooded area where he fled on foot. He was eventually captured but not before shooting and seriously wounding a pursuer. He was civilly tried for shooting with intent to kill or cause great bodily harm. Evidence showed a history of aberrant behavior. Two experts testified that Smith (D) suffered from chronic schizophrenia and was legally insane at the time of the incident. One expert testified that while Smith (D) did have schizophrenia, he had not been legally insane. The court, sitting without a jury, held Smith (D) to have been legally sane and convicted him. Smith (D) appealed.

ISSUE: May a factfinder hold a defendant to have been legally sane even when a preponderance of expert medical testimony is to the contrary?

HOLDING AND DECISION [Judge not stated in casebook excerpt.] Yes. A factfinder may hold a defendant to have been legally sane even when a preponderance of expert medical testimony is to the contrary. Under Alaska law, when a defendant claiming the insanity defense produces substantial evidence thereof, the burden shifts to the prosecution to disprove insanity beyond a reasonable doubt. It does not follow, however, that conflicting testimony regarding sanity must be resolved in favor of the accused. A factfinder is free to give credence to one party's expert and not the other's, even if the number of experts on the side not believed is greater than the side believed. Here, the court was convinced by the State's (P) medical expert, and this was not clear error. Affirmed.

DISSENT: (Boochever, J.) The State (P), as a matter of law, did not disprove insanity beyond a reasonable doubt. Smith (D) lacked the capacity to conform his conduct to societal standards.

ANALYSIS

Alaska adopted a two-part test of insanity. A defendant could invoke the defense if (1) the defendant was unable to appreciate the wrongfulness of their conduct, or (2) was incapable of conforming their conduct to societal norms. That the first part was inapplicable was conceded; at issue was the second part of the test. An expert's credibility can be judged by the degree of the expert's experience and whether or not the expert is in the "business" of being a paid expert witness, among other factors.

Quicknotes

INSANITY DEFENSE An affirmative defense to a criminal prosecution that the defendant suffered from a mental illness, thereby relieving the defendant of liability for their conduct.

CHAPTER 11

Attempt

Quick Reference Rules of Law

State v. Lyerla

State (P) v. Murderer (D)

S.D. Sup. Ct., 424 N.W.2d 908 (1988)

NATURE OF CASE: Appeal of convictions for murder and attempted murder.

FACT SUMMARY: Lyerla (D) was convicted of attempted second-degree murder.

RULE OF LAW
There is no crime of attempted second-degree murder.

FACTS: Lyerla (D), driving on an interstate, fired three shots into a pickup truck carrying three girls. One girl was killed and two were injured. Lyerla (D) was charged with murder and attempted murder. The jury found him guilty of second-degree murder with respect to the homicide and attempted second-degree murder with respect to the injured girls. Lyerla (D) appealed.

ISSUE: Is there a crime of attempted second-degree murder?

HOLDING AND DECISION: (Konenkamp, J.) No. There is no crime of attempted second-degree murder. Second-degree murder is based on non-intentional killing; it is the result of acting in an extremely reckless manner, but without intent to kill. A crime of attempt, on the other hand, by its definition involves intent to bring about the thing attempted. "Attempted second-degree murder" may be translated as "attempted extreme recklessness," a logical impossibility. Therefore, there is no crime of attempted second-degree murder. Reversed as to the attempt convictions.

DISSENT: (Sabers, J.) Attempted second-degree murder may exist in any situation where, had fortuity not resulted in the victim surviving, a second-degree murder conviction would have been sustainable.

ANALYSIS

The rule announced here would appear to be that of the majority of jurisdictions that have ruled on the issue. The general consensus is that "attempted second-degree murder" in most situations amounts to assault and/or battery. This would be the situation in the instant case.

Quicknotes

ATTEMPT An intent combined with an act falling short of the thing intended.

SECOND-DEGREE MURDER The unlawful killing of a person, without premeditation, and characterized by either an intent to kill or by a reckless disregard for human life.

People v. Bland

State (P) v. Convicted murderer (D)

Cal. Sup. Ct., 28 Cal. 4th 313 (2002)

NATURE OF CASE: Appeal from reversal of attempted murder conviction.

FACT SUMMARY: Bland (D) shot at a car, killing Wilson and injuring two passengers. It was clear that Bland (D) intended to kill Wilson, but it was unclear whether he intended to kill the passengers. Nonetheless, Bland (D) was convicted of attempted murder of the two passengers. After the conviction was reversed, the prosecutor (P) contended that the doctrine of transferred intent was correctly applied in reaching the attempted murder conviction.

RULE OF LAW

(1) Transferred intent extends to everyone actually killed even when a defendant kills the intended target.

(2) The transferred intent doctrine does not apply to an inchoate crime like attempted murder.

FACTS: Wilson, a gang member of the Rolling 20's Crips, was driving a car with two non-gang passengers, Morgan and Simon. They encountered Bland (D), a member of the rival gang, the Insane Crips, and another man. Wilson made it clear to them that Morgan and Simon were not gang members. After a brief exchange of words, Bland (D) and the other man started to shoot their guns at Wilson's car. Wilson managed to drive away, but crashed into a pole and died of gunshot wounds. Passengers Simon and Morgan had gunshot injuries but survived. A jury convicted Bland (D) of the first-degree murder of Wilson and the premeditated attempted murders of Simon and Morgan. It also found that Bland (D) intentionally and personally discharged a firearm and proximately caused great bodily injury or death to any person other than an accomplice. The state's intermediate appellate court reversed the two attempted murder convictions, finding the trial court erroneously instructed the jury on the doctrine of transferred intent. On appeal, the prosecutor contended that the doctrine of transferred intent had been properly applied. The state's highest court granted review.

ISSUES:

(1) Does transferred intent extend to everyone actually killed even when a defendant kills the intended target?

(2) Does the transferred intent doctrine apply to an inchoate crime like attempted murder?

HOLDING AND DECISION: [Judge not stated in casebook extract.]

(1) Yes. Transferred intent extends to everyone actually killed even when a defendant kills the intended target. Under the classic formulation of the doctrine of transferred intent, a defendant who shoots with the intent to kill a certain person and hits a bystander instead is subject to the same criminal liability that would have been imposed had the intended target been killed. That classic formulation did not address what happens—as here—when the intended target is killed and the defendant injures, but does not kill, unintended victims. One issue is whether the defendant's intent is transferred to others the defendant has shot and killed when the defendant successfully kills their intended victim. The answer is that the intent is not "used up" and may be transferred. Regardless of how one conceptualizes the transfer, either that the intent to kill the intended target transfers to others also killed, or that intent to kill need not be directed at a specific person, the result is the same: assuming legal causation, a person maliciously intending to kill is guilty of the murder of all persons actually killed. If the intent is premeditated, the murder or murders are first degree. Here, however, Simon and Morgan were not killed, so there is no transfer of intent to them.

(2) No. The transferred intent doctrine does not apply to an inchoate crime like attempted murder. There is nothing to suggest that the legislature intended to extend liability for unintended victims to an inchoate crime. The crime of attempt seeks to punish a person for what the person intended to do but did not accomplish, not unintended and unaccomplished potential consequences of the person's actions. Also, the mental states for murder and attempted murder are different. Murder does not necessarily require intent to kill—such intent may be implied in some circumstances—whereas attempted murder does require the intent to kill. Thus, where a defendant does not intend to kill a person, the defendant cannot be guilty of that person's attempted murder even if the crime would have been murder—due to transferred intent—if the person were killed. To be guilty of attempted murder, the defendant must intend to kill the alleged victim, not someone else. It should be

Continued on next page.

kept in mind that notwithstanding that transferred intent does not apply to inchoate crimes, a defendant can still be punished for shooting at a group of people, even if the defendant primarily targeted only one of them. In fact, the defendant may still be guilty of attempted murder of everyone in the group, just not on a transferred intent theory. One theory under which the defendant could be prosecuted for attempted murder is a "kill zone" theory, where the nature and scope of the attack, while directed at a primary victim, are such that it can be concluded that the defendant intended to ensure harm to the primary victim by harming everyone in that victim's vicinity, or "kill zone." In such cases, the defendant has intentionally created a kill zone to ensure the death of their primary victim, and the trier of fact may reasonably infer from the method employed an intent to kill others concurrent with the intent to kill the primary victim. In such cases, the intent to kill not only the primary victim but also those in the kill zone is direct, and need not be transferred from the primary victim to others affected by the shooting. The case at bar compels the inference that Bland (D) intended to kill everyone in the car that Wilson was driving so as to be sure to kill Wilson, since he and his cohort sprayed a flurry of bullets at the fleeing car and thereby created a kill zone. Accordingly, such a finding would support convictions of attempted murder of Simon and Morgan. Contrary to the prosecutor's (P) assertion, this conclusion does not create an anomaly in the law of transferred intent. When a defendant attempts to kill one person but instead kills another, there are always two victims: the intended target and the one actually killed. However, when the defendant kills the intended target, the result may vary depending on the circumstances. It is clear that one victim exists, but whether a second victim also exists may be less clear. The defendant may be convicted of the attempted murders of any within the kill zone, although on a concurrent, not transferred, intent theory. Persons not within the kill zone are not necessarily victims in the same sense as the intended target of a shooting that kills the wrong person. Therefore, convicting the defendant of a crime other than attempted murder, or no crime at all, as to unintended targets, who are neither killed nor within the kill zone, creates no anomaly. Applying these principles here, whether Bland (D) is guilty of attempted premeditated murder of Morgan or Simon depends on his mental state as to them, not on his mental state as to Wilson. The jury instruction given referred to a mistaken killing, but not to injuries. Although it was referred to as a transferred intent instruction, it told the jury that it did not need to determine intent when someone other than, or in addition to, the intended victim was killed, but it did not allow the jury to transfer intent to someone who was only injured. The evidence shows that the jury understood and followed these instructions, and that it determined each charge separately. Given that the instruction correctly stated the law, and that the evidence virtually compelled a finding that, even if Bland (D) primarily wanted to kill Wilson, he also, concurrently, intended to kill the others in the car by intending to create a kill zone, the trial court did not commit prejudicial error. The lower appellate court's judgment is reversed and the conviction for attempted murder is upheld.

ANALYSIS

Judge Kennard, dissenting, argued that the majority erred in cursorily concluding that any instructional error was harmless because "the evidence here virtually compelled a finding that, even if defendant primarily wanted to kill Wilson, he also, concurrently, intended to kill the others in the car" because he "intended to create a kill zone." Judge Kennard agreed that Bland (D) had a motive to kill Wilson because he knew the latter to be a member of a rival gang, but there was no evidence that Bland (D) had any motive to kill Simon and Morgan, who Bland (D) knew were not gang members. Judge Kennard thus reasoned that although the jury certainly could have concluded that Bland (D) intended to kill all of the occupants in the car, it could not be said beyond a reasonable doubt that the jury would necessarily have reached such a conclusion.

Quicknotes

INCHOATE Impartial or incomplete.

TRANSFERRED INTENT When a perpetrator acts with the intent to commit a crime against one person, and instead commits that crime against another person, the perpetrator's intent is transferred to the actual victim for the purposes of liability.

People v. Murray

State (P) v. Man who tried to marry his niece (D)

Cal. Sup. Ct., 15 Cal. 159 (1859)

NATURE OF CASE: Appeal of conviction for attempt to contract an incestuous marriage.

FACT SUMMARY: Murray (D) insisted that his conviction for attempt to contract an incestuous marriage was improper in that his actions had not crossed the line from mere preparation to attempt.

RULE OF LAW

An actual attempt to commit an offense is manifested by acts that would end in the consummation of the particular offense but for the intervention of circumstances independent of the will of the defendant.

FACTS: In appealing his conviction for attempt to contract an incestuous marriage, Murray (D) claimed that he had made certain preparations to attempt to marry his niece, but that he had not crossed the line between that and making an actual attempt to commit the offense. They had eloped for the purpose of marrying, and he had requested one of the witnesses to go for the magistrate to perform the ceremony. That, however, was as far as it went.

ISSUE: Is an actual attempt to commit an offense manifested by acts that would end in the consummation of the particular offense but for the intervention of circumstances independent of the will of the defendant?

HOLDING AND DECISION: (Field, C.J.) Yes. An actual attempt to commit an offense is manifested by acts that would end in the consummation of the particular offense but for the intervention of circumstances independent of the will of the defendant. There exists a wide difference between preparation for an attempt to commit an offense and the attempt itself. Preparation consists in devising or arranging the means or measures necessary for the commission of the offense. Attempt is the direct movement toward the commission after the preparations are made. Thus, in this case, the attempt contemplated by the statute must be manifested by acts which would end in the consummation of the particular offense but for the intervention of circumstances independent of Murray's (D) will. Preparations to attempt the marriage had been made, but until the officer was engaged and the parties stood before him ready to take the marriage vows, it cannot be said, in strictness, that the attempt was made. Clearly, Murray (D) cannot be held to have attempted to contract an incestuous marriage. Reversed and remanded.

ANALYSIS

Model Penal Code §5.01 contains the rules for determining whether an attempt to commit a crime has been made. An attempt can be established if the defendant, acting with the kind of culpability otherwise required for commission of the crime, purposefully does or omits to do anything that is an act or omission constituting a "substantial step" in the course of conduct planned to culminate in the commission of the crime. Such acts or omissions include lying in wait, searching for, or following the intended victim, and reconnoitering the scene where the crime is to be committed.

Quicknotes

ATTEMPT An intent combined with an act falling short of the thing intended.

OMISSION The failure to perform an act or obligation that one is required to perform by law.

McQuirter v. State

Alleged intending rapist (D) v. State (P)

Ala Ct. App., 63 So. 2d 388 (1953)

NATURE OF CASE: Appeal from conviction for attempt to commit an assault with intent to commit rape.

FACT SUMMARY: McQuirter (D), a Black man, followed a White woman down the street and then up the street.

RULE OF LAW

An attempt to commit assault with intent to commit rape is merely an attempt to commit rape that has not proceeded far enough to constitute an assault.

FACTS: Mrs. Allen, a White woman, and her two children walked down the street at eight p.m. on a summer evening. McQuirter (D) was sitting in a truck as they walked by. He said something unintelligible as they walked past and then got out of the truck and followed her down the street. Allen turned into a friend's house when McQuirter (D) was two or three feet behind her. She waited ten minutes for McQuirter (D) to pass and then she proceeded on her way. She then observed McQuirter (D) walking toward her from behind a telephone pole. Allen sent the children to get another friend. When the friend appeared, McQuirter (D) went across the street and waited there for thirty minutes. He then left and Allen went home. McQuirter (D) testified that he had just been walking up the street to go to another part of town and that Mrs. Allen just happened to be in front of him. When he got to the telephone pole, he waited, trying to decide whether to go on or not. After thinking a few minutes, he went on to the other part of town. He came back after thirty minutes. He denied saying anything or making any gestures toward Allen. A police chief testified that McQuirter (D) told him that he was sitting in the truck, that he wanted a woman, and that he was going to have the first woman that came by whether he had to rape her or not. McQuirter (D) was found guilty of an attempt to commit an assault with intent to commit rape.

ISSUE: Is an attempt to commit assault with intent to commit rape merely an attempt to commit rape that has not proceeded far enough to constitute an assault?

HOLDING AND DECISION: (Price, J.) Yes. An attempt to commit assault with intent to commit rape is merely an attempt to commit rape that has not proceeded far enough to constitute an assault. The jury need only be satisfied that the accused actually intended to rape Mrs. Allen. In determining intent, the jury may look at all the circumstances, including social conditions and customs founded upon racial differences. Here, Mrs. Allen was a White woman and McQuirter (D) was a Black man, and the jury may take this into account when deciding whether McQuirter's (D) actions indicated intent to rape. Conviction affirmed.

ANALYSIS

Attempt to commit rape is a recognized offense that requires only that the defendant have the apparent ability to do so, and intent is proven. As such, proof of conduct that a jury believes to manifest the intent to commit a crime is sufficient to convict. By Hornbook law, assault is the attempted battery (e.g., rape) of another with the apparent ability to succeed. Where no act in furtherance of a battery occurs, however, no assault will arise. However, acts in furtherance of the object of the contemplated assault (e.g., rape) may be sufficient to establish an attempt to accomplish that object (e.g., following Mrs. Allen). Hence, an attempted attempt arises. Note, however, that since such a rule permits criminal liability merely for manifesting intent in one's actions, this case borders on a violation of the universal criminal law requirement of actus reus.

Quicknotes

ACTUS REUS The unlawful act that gives rise to criminal liability, as distinguished from the required mental state.

ASSAULT The intentional placing of another in fear of immediate bodily injury.

ATTEMPT An intent combined with an act falling short of the thing intended.

BATTERY Unlawful contact with the body of another person.

RAPE Unlawful sexual intercourse by means of fear or force and without consent.

People v. Rizzo

State (P) v. Attempted robber (D)

N.Y. Ct. App., 246 N.Y. 334, 158 N.E. 888 (1927)

NATURE OF CASE: Appeal from conviction for attempt to commit robbery in the first degree.

FACT SUMMARY: Rizzo (D) and three others set out with the intention to commit a robbery but they were arrested before they found the person they intended to rob.

RULE OF LAW

An attempt to commit a crime requires an act "tending," but failing, to effect its commission, which encompasses only those acts that are so near to the accomplishment of the crime that in all reasonable probability the crime itself would have been committed but for timely interference.

FACTS: Rizzo (D) and three others set out in a car to rob one Charles Rao of a payroll he was to carry from the bank for the United Lathing Company. Rizzo's (D) job was to point out Rao to the others. In fact, the police were following the four as they rode around looking for Rao. They were arrested at the site of one of the buildings being constructed by United Lathing as they were canvassing the buildings looking for Rao. Neither Rao nor another man, who was supposed to carry a payroll, was at the building at the time of the arrest. Rizzo (D) appealed his conviction for attempt to commit robbery in the first degree, asserting that his conduct had not been sufficient to constitute an "attempt."

ISSUE: Does an attempt to commit a crime require an act "tending," but failing, to effect its commission, which encompasses only those acts that are so near to the accomplishment of the crime that in all reasonable probability the crime itself would have been committed but for timely interference?

HOLDING AND DECISION: (Crane, J.) Yes. An attempt to commit a crime requires an act "tending," but failing, to effect its commission, which encompasses only those acts that are so near to the accomplishment of the crime that in all reasonable probability the crime itself would have been committed but for timely interference. However, the line is drawn between acts which are remote and those which are proximate and near to the consummation. That is, the law considers those acts "tending" to the commission of the crime to be the ones that are so near to its accomplishment that, in all reasonable probability, the crime itself would have been committed but for timely interference. Here, the defendants had not even found or seen the man they intended to rob. Their acts were not so near to the result that the danger of success was very great. Thus, no "attempt" was made to commit the crime. Reversed and new trial ordered.

ANALYSIS

It is interesting that the Model Penal Code provision dealing with criminal attempt lists certain acts that shall not be insufficient as a matter of law to constitute an "attempt." The list includes lying in wait, searching for, or following the contemplated victim of the crime, and reconnoitering the place contemplated for the commission of the crime.

Quicknotes

ATTEMPT An intent combined with an act falling short of the thing intended.

ROBBERY The unlawful taking of property from the person of another through the use of force or fear.

People v. Staples

State (P) v. Attempted burglar (D)

Cal. Ct. App., 6 Cal. App. 3d 61, 85 Cal. Rptr. 589 (1970)

NATURE OF CASE: Appeal from conviction for attempted burglary.

FACT SUMMARY: Staples (D) offered evidence to show he had abandoned any attempt to commit a burglary before he was arrested, contending such abandonment would preclude his being found guilty of attempted burglary.

RULE OF LAW

Abandonment is no defense to a criminal charge of attempting to commit a particular offense.

FACTS: While his wife was away, Staples (D), a mathematician, rented an office he knew was directly over the vault of a bank. He brought in drilling tools and drilled two groups of holes in the floor, but stopped drilling before they went through the floor. He brought in acetylene gas tanks, a blow torch, a blanket, and linoleum. According to his later confession, he came back to the office a number of times, covered the holes with a linoleum rug, and installed a hasp lock on a closet where he intended to, or did, place his tools. The landlord, who had been coming and going to do repair work, had notified the police of the strange goings on. Staples (D), who was convicted of attempted burglary, made a voluntary oral statement in which he admitted that he kept going back to the office while his wife was away, that he still had not given up his plan to rob the bank, but that his wife came back after two weeks or so and his life as a bank robber seemed more and more absurd. Thus, he claimed, he abandoned the idea of committing the robbery.

ISSUE: Is abandonment a defense to a criminal charge of attempting to commit a particular crime?

HOLDING AND DECISION: (Reppy, J.) No. Abandonment is no defense to a criminal charge of attempting to commit a particular offense. Once it is found that a person attempted to commit a particular offense, there can be no exculpatory abandonment. One of the purposes of criminal law is to protect society from those who intend to injure it. Once it is established that a defendant intended to commit a specific crime and that in carrying out this intention the defendant committed an act that caused harm or sufficient danger of harm, it is immaterial that for some collateral reason the defendant could not complete the intended crime. In the case at bar, the acts committed by Staples (D) reached such a stage of advancement that they could be classified as an attempt. Thus, any later abandonment of his plan is of no significance. Affirmed.

ANALYSIS

The Model Penal Code is different in that it provides in §5.01(4) for a limited defense of abandonment. It specifically requires "a complete and voluntary renunciation" of criminal purpose by the defendant. It has not been an easy defense for defendants to prove.

Quicknotes

ABANDONMENT The voluntary relinquishment of a right without the intent of reclaiming it.

BURGLARY Unlawful entry of a building at night with the intent to commit a felony therein.

People v. Lubow

State (P) v. Solicitor (D)

N.Y. Ct. App., 29 N.Y.2d 58, 272 N.E.2d 331 (1971)

NATURE OF CASE: Appeal from convictions for solicitation to commit a felony.

FACT SUMMARY: Lubow (D) was convicted of solicitation to commit a felony under a state statute.

RULE OF LAW

One is guilty of statutory criminal solicitation if one "solicits, requests, commands, importunes or otherwise attempts to cause" another person to engage in conduct constituting a crime with the intent that said other person engage in such conduct.

FACTS: Silverman confronted Lubow (D), who owed him a considerable sum on notes covering the purchase of diamonds. Both were in the jewelry business. Lubow (D) suggested that they engage in a scheme whereby they would purchase diamonds partially on credit, sell them for less than cost, and use the proceeds to keep buying and selling until they established a great credit rating for Silverman. At that point, they would claim that Silverman lost the proceeds of the sales gambling and would file for bankruptcy, dividing the proceeds between the three involved in the scheme. Silverman reported it to the district attorney and cooperated in having a recording device planted on him to record incriminating conversations with Lubow (D). Lubow (D) was convicted of solicitation to commit a felony under an applicable state statute making it a crime to solicit, request, command, importune or otherwise attempt to cause another person to engage in conduct constituting a crime, with the intent that they engage in such conduct.

ISSUE: Is one guilty of criminal solicitation if one solicits another to engage in conduct constituting a crime, with the intent that the other person engage in such conduct?

HOLDING AND DECISION: (Bergan, J.) Yes. One is guilty of criminal solicitation if one solicits another to engage in conduct constituting a crime, with the intent that the other person engage in such conduct. The statute speaks in terms of soliciting, requesting, commanding, importuning or otherwise attempting to cause another to engage in conduct constituting a crime. It thus makes communication itself, with the intent the other person engage in the unlawful conduct, sufficient to uphold a conviction. There need be no corroboration. There is sufficient evidence here to find that Lubow (D) intended that Silverman engage in conduct constituting a felony by means of grand larceny, and that he importuned Silverman to engage in such conduct. The proof meets the actual terms of the statute. Affirmed.

ANALYSIS

There are instances in which the intent is to communicate with another to solicit the commission of a crime, but there is no actual communication effected. The Model Penal Code treats this situation in § 5.02, which provides that it is immaterial to the criminal solicitation provisions that the actor fails to communicate with the person the actor solicits to commit a crime if the actor's conduct was designed to effect such communication.

Quicknotes

FELONY A criminal offense of greater seriousness than a misdemeanor; felonies are generally defined pursuant to statute as any crime that is punishable by death or by a term of imprisonment exceeding one year.

Booth v. State

Buyer (D) v. State (P)

Okla. Ct. Crim. App., 398 P.2d 863 (1964)

NATURE OF CASE: Appeal from conviction for attempting to receive stolen property.

FACT SUMMARY: Booth (D) purchased a coat he believed had been stolen, but which in fact had been recovered by the owner.

RULE OF LAW

A person cannot be convicted of attempt when the act attempted would not have been criminal if completed.

FACTS: Booth (D) agreed to buy a coat stolen by Stanford. However, Stanford was apprehended before delivery. Stanford agreed with the police to go through with the purported sale. Booth (D) received the coat and was promptly arrested. Booth (D) was charged with, and convicted of, attempting to receive stolen property. Booth (D) appealed.

ISSUE: Can a person be convicted of attempt when the act attempted would not have been criminal if completed?

HOLDING AND DECISION: (Nix, J.) No. A person cannot be convicted of an attempt when the act attempted would not have been criminal if completed. This situation is what is known as "legal impossibility." It is settled law that if one having a criminal intent commits an act that is not illegal, no crime exists. It follows that if one is attempting to commit an act one believes is illegal, but which in fact is not illegal, no attempt exists. Here, the coat was no longer stolen property when Booth (D) received it, the coat having been recovered. Since no substantive crime could have been committed, an attempted crime could not have been either. Reversed.

ANALYSIS

Legal impossibility is one of the most confusing areas of criminal law. Legal impossibility occurs when an act, if completed as intended, would not be criminal. This sounds simple in theory, but in practice it can lead to some serious hair-splitting.

Quicknotes

ATTEMPT An intent combined with an act falling short of the thing intended.

LEGAL IMPOSSIBILITY An activity that the defendant believes to be unlawful, but that does not constitute a crime; legal impossibility is a defense to criminal liability.

People v. Thousand

State (P) v. Obscene materials distributor (D)

Mich. Sup. Ct., 631 N.W.2d 694 (2001)

NATURE OF CASE: Appeal of the dismissal of a charge of attempted distribution of obscene materials to a minor.

FACT SUMMARY: When Thousand (D) was charged with attempted distribution of obscene materials to a minor, he argued that because the person to whom he attempted the distribution was an adult police officer, not a child, he could not be guilty of the offense.

RULE OF LAW

Impossibility is not a defense to a crime of attempt.

FACTS: A deputy sheriff, conducting an undercover investigation for the sheriff department's Internet crimes bureau, made computer contact with Thousand (D) in a chat room. The deputy online posed as a fourteen-year-old girl. After a series of sexually explicit chat room conversations initiated by Thousand (D), the sheriff, still pretending to be the young girl, agreed to meet with Thousand (D) at a McDonald's. When Thousand (D) arrived, he was arrested and charged with the attempted distribution of obscene materials to a minor. Thousand (D) moved to quash the indictment, arguing that since the existence of a child victim was an element of the charge, the evidence was legally insufficient to support the charges. The trial court agreed and dismissed the charges. The intermediate appellate court affirmed, and the State (P) appealed.

ISSUE: Is impossibility a defense to a crime of attempt?

HOLDING AND DECISION: (Young, J.) No. Impossibility is not a defense to a crime of attempt. Under Michigan statute, an "attempt" consists of (1) an attempt to commit an offense prohibited by law, and (2) any act toward the commission of the intended offense. This court is unable to discern from the words of the attempt statute any legislative intent that the concept of "impossibility" provides any impediment to charging a defendant with, or convicting a defendant of, an attempted crime, notwithstanding any factual mistake—regarding either the attendant circumstances or the legal status of some factor relevant thereto—that the defendant may harbor. The attempt statute carves out no exception for those who possessing the requisite criminal intent to commit an offense prohibited by law and taking action toward the commission of that offense have acted under an extrinsic misconception. Here, Thousand (D) is not charged with the substantive crime of distributing obscene material to a minor. It is unquestioned that he could not be convicted of that crime, because he allegedly distributed obscene material not to a "minor," but to an adult man. Instead, Thousand (D) is charged with the distinct offense of attempt, which requires only that the prosecution prove intention to commit an offense prohibited by law, coupled with conduct toward the commission of that offense. Because the nonexistence of a minor victim does not give rise to a viable defense to the attempt charge in this case, the circuit court erred in dismissing this charge on the basis of legal impossibility. Reversed.

ANALYSIS

Courts and legal scholars have drawn a distinction between two categories of impossibility: "factual impossibility" and "legal impossibility." At common law, legal impossibility was a defense to a charge of attempt, but factual impossibility was not. However, after struggling unsuccessfully over the years to articulate an accurate rule for distinguishing between categories of "impossibility," the vast majority of American jurisdictions have now simply abolished impossibility as a defense.

Quicknotes

ATTEMPT An intent combined with an act falling short of the thing intended.

CRIMINAL INTENT An intention to carry out a criminal offense.

FACTUAL IMPOSSIBILITY A circumstance in which a person commits an act that would otherwise constitute a criminal offense, however, the attendant facts and circumstances unknown to the actor make it impossible to commit the crime; factual impossibility does not constitute a defense to criminal liability.

LEGAL IMPOSSIBILITY An activity that the defendant believes to be unlawful, but that does not constitute a crime; legal impossibility is a defense to criminal liability.

People v. Dlugash

State (P) v. Convicted murderer (D)

N.Y. Ct. App., 41 N.Y.2d 725, 363 N.E.2d 1155 (1977)

NATURE OF CASE: Appeal of reversal of murder conviction.

FACT SUMMARY: Dlugash (D) fired several shots into the head of Geller, already mortally wounded and possibly dead.

RULE OF LAW

Impossibility is not a defense to a crime of attempt.

FACTS: A disagreement arose between Bush, Geller, and Dlugash (D). Bush took a .38 pistol and shot Geller three times in the chest. Two to five minutes later Dlugash (D) took a pistol and fired multiple shots into the head of the prostrate Geller. Dlugash (D) was convicted of murder. Medical evidence was unable to prove or disprove that Geller had been alive when Dlugash (D) shot him. Dlugash (D) contended that he believed Geller had been dead when he shot him. The appellate court reversed the conviction, stating that the evidence did not prove that Geller was alive when Dlugash (D) shot him. The State (P) appealed.

ISSUE: Is impossibility a defense to a crime of attempt?

HOLDING AND DECISION: (Jasen, J.) No. Impossibility is not a defense to a crime of attempt. Legal scholars have argued for years over the merits of the impossibility defense. The modern trend, as reflected in the Model Penal Code and adopted by this state, is that the criminal mental state of a defendant is, in itself, a danger to society and should be punished if steps toward the attainment thereof are taken, even if the crime was legally impossible. Here, the State (P) was unable to prove that Dlugash (D) killed Geller, so the murder conviction was properly reversed. However, the lesser included offense of attempted murder was not barred by impossibility. Reversed.

ANALYSIS

The variations on the impossibility doctrine are many. The distinctions between legal and factual impossibility are subtle, and often it seems a situation could be described as involving either. When one considers the confusion engendered by the doctrine and the danger to society of criminal intent, abolishing the doctrine does seem to be the trend.

Quicknotes

ATTEMPT An intent combined with an act falling short of the thing intended.

LEGAL IMPOSSIBILITY An activity that the defendant believes to be unlawful, but that does not constitute a crime; legal impossibility is a defense to criminal liability.

CHAPTER 12

Complicity

Quick Reference Rules of Law

PAGE

1. *State v. Ochoa.* When one in a group altercation becomes aware that deadly force is being used, that person becomes an accessory to the use of that force. 134
2. *State v. Tally.* One who interferes with the relaying of potentially life-saving information is an abettor if a homicide results. 135
3. *State v. Formella.* An individual can be held criminally liable as an accomplice where the individual terminates complicity prior to the commission of the offense but does not wholly deprive the complicity of its effectiveness. 136
4. *People v. Beeman.* An aider or abettor must act with knowledge of the criminal purpose and with intent to facilitate the commission of the offense. 138
5. *Wilson v. People.* One cannot be an accessory to a crime unless one has the intent for the crime to actually proceed successfully. 139
6. *State v. Anthony.* A defendant is subject to conviction as an accomplice to negligence-based crimes. 140
7. *Rosemond v. United States.* To obtain a conviction of aiding or abetting a crime under 18 U.S.C. §924(c), which criminalizes the use or carrying of a gun in the commission of a drug trafficking or violent crime, the government must prove that the defendant actively participated in the underlying crime with advance knowledge that a confederate would use or carry a gun during the crime's commission. 141
8. *People v. Kessler.* Where an accomplice aids another in the planning or commission of a criminal offense, the accomplice can be legally accountable for the conduct of the person the accomplice aids for any criminal act done in furtherance of the planned and intended act, even absent specific intent to commit that act. 143
9. *State v. Christy Pontiac-GMC, Inc.* A corporation may be held criminally liable for a specific-intent crime. 145
10. *United States v. Hilton Hotels Corp.* As a general rule, a corporation is liable under the Sherman Act for the acts of its agents in the scope of their employment, even though such acts are contrary to general corporate policy and/or express instructions to the agent. 146

State v. Ochoa

State (P) v. Protesters (D)

N.M. Sup. Ct., 41 N.M. 589, 72 P.2d 609 (1937)

NATURE OF CASE: Appeal of second-degree murder convictions based on principles of aiding and abetting.

FACT SUMMARY: A riot erupted in which a sheriff was shot to death, although the individual who pulled the trigger was never identified.

RULE OF LAW

When one in a group altercation becomes aware that deadly force is being used, that person becomes an accessory to the use of that force.

FACTS: A group of about 125 people gathered outside a courthouse to support a criminal defendant. The sheriff and his deputies tried to covertly transport the prisoner through the rear entrance. The crowd became aware of this and went around to the back of the building. A melee ensued and shots were fired. The sheriff was killed and several deputies wounded. The shots came from a group including Ochoa (D) and Avitia (D). Evidence showed that Ochoa (D) and Avitia (D) remained in the group while the shots were being fired, beating a downed deputy. Avitia (D), Ochoa (D), and Velarde (D), who had not been in the group, were convicted of second-degree murder, and they appealed.

ISSUE: When one in a group altercation becomes aware that deadly force is being used, does that person become an accessory to the use of that force?

HOLDING AND DECISION: (Sadler, J.). Yes. When one in a group altercation becomes aware that deadly force is being used, that person becomes an accessory to the use of that force. One is rendered an aider or abettor if a common purpose is shown. In a group altercation situation, it would be unfair to hold one to be an abettor if a common purpose is not shown. Moreover, in a group altercation situation, it would be unfair to hold one to be an abettor in the use of deadly force if they are unaware that their companions plan to use it. However, once the individual becomes aware of the force, they may be held to be an aider. Here, Ochoa (D) and Avitia (D) continued to beat the deputy after they knew that deadly force was being used by the group, so they had the common purpose. There was no evidence of this as to Velarde (D). Reversed as to Velarde (D); affirmed as to the others.

ANALYSIS

Although convicted as aiders and abettors, the defendants were sentenced as would a principal have been. At common law, distinctions in culpability between principals and abettors existed. Many jurisdictions have modified or abolished these distinctions, as had New Mexico.

Quicknotes

ACCESSORY An individual who combines with the main actor in the commission or attempted commission of a criminal offense, either before or after its performance.

AIDING AND ABETTING Assistance given in order to facilitate the commission of a criminal act.

PRINCIPAL A person or entity that authorizes another (the agent) to act on its behalf and subject to its authority to the extent that the principal may be held liable for the actions of the agent.

SECOND-DEGREE MURDER The unlawful killing of a person, without premeditation, and characterized by either intent to kill or by a reckless disregard for human life.

State v. Tally

State (P) v. Convicted murderer (D)

Ala. Sup. Ct., 15 So. 722 (1894)

NATURE OF CASE: Appeal of murder conviction grounded on aiding and abetting.

FACT SUMMARY: Tally (D) prevented the transmission of a warning message to Ross, who was subsequently killed by the men about whom the message warned.

RULE OF LAW

One who interferes with the relaying of potentially life-saving information is an abettor if a homicide results.

FACTS: A feud had erupted between Ross and the Skeltons. Ross slipped out of town in a coach, unaware that four Skeltons pursued him on horseback. A relative of Ross sent a telegram to Ross at the next town warning him. Tally (D), who knew the telegraph operator in the next town, immediately sent a telegram to the operator requesting he not deliver the message to Ross. When Ross arrived in town, the operator did not give him the message. Ross was ambushed by the Skeltons and was shot to death. Tally (D), who was convicted of aiding and abetting the murder, appealed.

ISSUE: Is one who interferes with the relaying of potentially life-saving information an abettor if a homicide results?

HOLDING AND DECISION: (McClellan, J.) Yes. One who interferes with the relaying of potentially life-saving information is an abettor if a homicide results. To be guilty of aiding a crime, the defendant must do an act in furtherance of the criminal design, the act must contribute to the effectuation of the crime, and the act must actually help bring about the victim's death. The answer on all three counts must be yes, since the relaying of information to Ross that he was being pursued was done with both the intent and effect of helping the Skeltons in their criminal plan. It is hard to conclude that Ross was more vulnerable in his ignorant state than he would have been otherwise. Affirmed.

DISSENT: (Head, J.) Proof beyond a reasonable doubt that Tally's (D) acts contributed to Ross's death does not exist.

ANALYSIS

The court appeared to be of the opinion that any decrease in the victim's chances of survival was sufficient to satisfy the requirement that the act contribute to the crime. The court used the term "depriving him of some disadvantage." Exactly how much would be sufficient was not stated, but the implication seemed to be that very little is needed since the court noted in passing that there was a strong probability that Ross would have been killed anyway.

Quicknotes

AIDING AND ABETTING Assistance given in order to facilitate the commission of a criminal act.

REASONABLE DOUBT Enough doubt on the part of a factfinder to acquit a defendant based on the absence of evidence.

State v. Formella

State (P) v. Convicted accomplice to theft (D)

N.H. Sup. Ct., 960 A.2d 722 (2008)

NATURE OF CASE: Appeal from conviction of theft as an accomplice.

FACT SUMMARY: Formella (D), who initially served as a lookout for others who stole exams but then decided that participating in the crime was wrong and stopped serving as a lookout before the crime was committed, contended that he could not be convicted of theft as an accomplice since he had withdrawn in time from the crime.

RULE OF LAW

An individual can be held criminally liable as an accomplice where the individual terminates complicity prior to the commission of the offense but does not wholly deprive the complicity of its effectiveness.

FACTS: Formella (D), a high school student, and his friends were asked by a group of other students to serve as lookouts while the group stole mathematics exams from within the high school. Formella (D) and his friends agreed, and, on their way to their lockers, looked around to "confirm or dispel" whether anyone was there. After getting their books from their lockers, Formella (D) and his friends decided that serving as lookouts was wrong, and they left the school building. The other group succeeded in stealing the exams. Formella (D), who admitted his involvement in the theft, was convicted of theft based on criminal liability for the conduct of another, as an accomplice. Formella (D) appealed, contending that the trial court had erred in failing to make findings of fact relative to the timing of his withdrawal from the theft and the completion of the theft since the accomplice liability statute provides that a person is not an accomplice if he "terminates his complicity prior to the commission of the offense and wholly deprives it of effectiveness in the commission of the offense or gives timely warning to the law enforcement authorities or otherwise makes proper effort to prevent the commission of the offense." The state's highest court granted review.

ISSUE: Can an individual be held criminally liable as an accomplice where the individual terminates complicity prior to the commission of the offense but does not wholly deprive the complicity of its effectiveness?

HOLDING AND DECISION: (Galway, J.) Yes. An individual can be held criminally liable as an accomplice where the individual terminates complicity prior to the commission of the offense but does not wholly deprive the complicity of its effectiveness. It is undisputed that Formella (D) became an accomplice when he agreed to serve as a lookout. The issue, therefore, is whether his later acts terminated his accomplice liability. Formella (D) neither timely warned the police, nor otherwise made a "proper effort" to prevent the offense. The question, therefore, is whether his termination "wholly deprived his complicity of effectiveness." The accomplice statute does not define what is required for a person to wholly deprive their complicity of effectiveness. The State (P) argues that there must be an overt act aimed at undermining the prior complicity, and Formella (D) argues no such act is required. The statute is ambiguous as to this requirement, and the legislative intent must be determined. The Model Penal Code, on which the statute is based, indicates that to deprive complicity such as is involved here of effectiveness, the withdrawing participant must not only withdraw from the commission of the offense, but also must communicate their disapproval to the principals sufficiently in advance of the commission of the crime to allow the principals time to reconsider as well. Here, even though Formella (D) timely withdrew before the commission of the theft, he nonetheless did not wholly deprive his complicity of its effectiveness because he made no affirmative act, such as communicating his withdrawal to the principals, which would give them a chance to reconsider committing the offense. Instead, the principals remained unaware of his withdrawal. While it is true that Formella (D) no longer served as an effective lookout after he withdrew, he did nothing to counter the effect of his prior complicity. His agreeing to serve as a lookout encouraged the principals to engage in the offense, and it was this encouragement that needed to be undone or undermined. Because there was no evidence that Formella (D) had wholly deprived his complicity of its effectiveness, it was not error for the trial court to refuse to make findings on the timing of the offense because such findings would not have altered the result. Affirmed.

ANALYSIS

As this case demonstrates, a mere change of heart, flight from the crime scene, apprehension by the police, or an uncommunicated decision not to carry out his part of the scheme will not suffice to relieve a withdrawing accomplice of criminal liability. However, as the case also notes, while the terminating accomplice does not actually have to prevent the crime from occurring, he must take some affirmative action that communicates

Continued on next page.

disapproval to the principals in time for them to consider changing course.

Quicknotes

ACCOMPLICE An individual who knowingly, purposefully or voluntarily combines with the main actor in the commission, or attempted commission, of a criminal offense.

ACCOMPLICE LIABILITY Liability of an individual who knowingly, purposefully, or voluntarily combines with the main actor in the commission, or attempted commission, of a criminal offense.

COMPLICITY The act of conspiring to, or participating in, the commission of an unlawful act.

THEFT The illegal taking of another's property with the intent to deprive the owner thereof.

People v. Beeman

State (P) v. Informant (D)

Cal. Sup. Ct., 35 Cal. 3d 547 (1984)

NATURE OF CASE: Appeal from conviction of aiding and abetting a robbery.

FACT SUMMARY: Beeman (D) gave others certain information that was used by them to facilitate the robbery of a relative of Beeman (D), although Beeman (D) claimed he did not want the robbery to occur.

RULE OF LAW

An aider or abettor must act with knowledge of the criminal purpose and with intent to facilitate the commission of the offense.

FACTS: Beeman (D) knew Burk and Gray. Burk learned from Beeman (D) of certain valuables owned by Beeman's aunt. Beeman (D) gave Burk other information about the aunt and her possessions. At some point, Burk and Gray decided to rob the aunt, which they did. Charged with aiding the robbery, Beeman (D) contended that the information was given casually, that he never expected that a robbery would occur, and that he later declined an invitation to join in the crime. The jury returned a guilty verdict after being instructed that an aider is one who knowingly aids the commission of a crime. Beeman (D) appealed.

ISSUE: Must an aider or abettor act with knowledge of the criminal purpose and with intent to facilitate the commission of an offense?

HOLDING AND DECISION: (Reynoso, J.) Yes. An aider or abettor must act with knowledge of the criminal purpose and with intent to facilitate the commission of an offense. The weight of authority and sound legal principles dictate that to be an aider one must have a concert of mind with the principal. One who gives aid to the commission of a criminal act without wishing to promote the act should not be liable. The jury instruction here did not take that into account. It allows for an interpretation that by giving the information alone, Beeman (D) could have been liable. Reversed.

ANALYSIS

Not all jurisdictions have this requirement, at least not so clearly spelled out. For instance, Model Penal Code § 2.06(3)(a) only requires knowledge that a criminal purpose existed, not a desire that it proceed. This was subsequently changed.

Quicknotes

AIDING AND ABETTING Assistance given in order to facilitate the commission of a criminal act.

ROBBERY The unlawful taking of property from the person of another through the use of force or fear.

Wilson v. People

Accessory (D) v. State (P)

Colo. Sup. Ct., 100 Colo. 441, 87 P.2d 5 (1939)

NATURE OF CASE: Appeal of conviction of burglary based on aiding and abetting.

FACT SUMMARY: Wilson (D) "set up" Pierce to commit burglary to exact revenge on Pierce.

RULE OF LAW

One cannot be an accessory to a crime unless one has the intent for the crime to actually proceed successfully.

FACTS: Wilson (D) met Pierce in a café and they spent time drinking together. Pierce talked about some of his criminal acts. At one point, Wilson (D) noticed his watch missing and accused Pierce of stealing it, which Pierce denied. At some point, they developed a plan to rob a drugstore. Wilson (D) boosted Pierce through a window. Wilson (D) then called his father, a prosecutor, who summoned the police. Both Pierce and Wilson (D) were arrested. Wilson (D) was charged with aiding and abetting. Wilson (D) contended that he wanted to "set up" Pierce so that he could be arrested and have Wilson's (D) watch returned. The trial judge did not allow this defense, and Wilson (D) was convicted. He subsequently appealed.

ISSUE: Can one be an accessory to a crime if one does not have the intent for the crime to actually proceed successfully?

HOLDING AND DECISION: (Bock, J.) No. One cannot be an accessory to a crime unless one has the intent for the crime to actually proceed successfully. An accessory must share the criminal intent with the principal. If a person does not share that intent, then that individual is not an accessory. Here, Wilson (D) contended that he did not want the burglary to succeed but merely wanted his watch back—an intent hardly concurrent with that of Pierce. This defense should have gone to the jury. Reversed and remanded.

ANALYSIS

The flip side of the issue here is whether someone can be guilty of aiding and abetting when the principal actor is not guilty. An example would be when one aids in the commission of a crime with another who is not mentally competent for criminal liability. Logic would dictate that one could not be liable, but the law gets around this by considering the "abettor" to be the true principal.

Quicknotes

ACCESSORY An individual who combines with the main actor in the commission or attempted commission of a criminal offense, either before or after its performance.

AIDING AND ABETTING Assistance given in order to facilitate the commission of a criminal act.

BURGLARY Unlawful entry of a building at night with the intent to commit a felony therein.

PRINCIPAL A person or entity that authorizes another (the agent) to act on its behalf and subject to its authority to the extent that the principal may be held liable for the actions of the agent.

State v. Anthony

State (P) v. Accomplice (D)

N.H. Sup. Ct., 861 A.2d 773 (2004)

NATURE OF CASE: Appeal from conviction by jury of accomplice to negligent cruelty to animals.

FACT SUMMARY: Virginia Anthony (D) was convicted of accomplice to negligent cruelty to animals for assisting her husband in binding a colt's legs.

RULE OF LAW

A defendant is subject to conviction as an accomplice to negligence-based crimes.

FACTS: Anthony (D) assisted her husband in binding a colt's legs together to restrain the animal. The colt was left bound on the ground, in pain, and injured itself. The State (P) brought a felony charge of accomplice to cruelty to animals against Anthony (D). The lesser-included offense in felony accomplice to cruelty to animals is accomplice to negligent cruelty to animals. Anthony (D) was convicted by the jury on the lesser-included offense and appealed her conviction.

ISSUE: Is a defendant subject to conviction as an accomplice to negligence-based crimes?

HOLDING AND DECISION: [Judge not stated in casebook excerpt.] Yes. A defendant is subject to conviction as an accomplice to negligence-based crimes. Anthony (D) argued that accomplice to negligent cruelty to animals was not a recognized crime based on *State v. Etzweiler*, 480 A.2d 870 (N.H. 1984), which held that a person could not be an accomplice to negligent homicide. The *Etzweiler* court interpreted the statute on accomplice to commission of an offense to require both the intention to aid the primary offender commit the act and the purpose to make the crime succeed. Because negligence requires unawareness on the part of the principal offender, the *Etzweiler* court concluded an accomplice could not provide intentional aid for a crime the principal offender was unaware they were committing. The legislature amended the accomplice statute in 2001, in part to clarify its intent in response to *Etzweiler*. An offender is subject to accomplice liability if (1) the accomplice intended to enable the principal's unlawful conduct and (2) the accomplice acted with the mental state of the relevant statute with respect to the result. Therefore, the law does allow for conviction as an accomplice for negligence-based crimes. Affirmed.

ANALYSIS

The *Etzweiler* case was seen as error that promoted an illogical result. Namely, that because liability as an accessory is not a distinct crime, it would not be logical to hold the principal offender liable while precluding liability for the accessory when both possessed the relevant mental state for commission of the crime. The 2001 amendment to the accomplice statute clarified the original intent of the statute in response to *Etzweiler* but did not alter it. Accomplice liability is available for negligence-based crimes when the accomplice intends to facilitate the principal's unlawful conduct and acts with the mental state required with respect the result.

Quicknotes

ACCOMPLICE An individual who knowingly, purposefully, or voluntarily combines with the main actor in the commission, or attempted commission, of a criminal offense.

NEGLIGENCE Conduct falling below the standard of care that a reasonable person would demonstrate under similar conditions.

Rosemond v. United States

Criminal convicted of aiding or abetting the use or carrying of a gun in the commission of a drug trafficking crime (D) v. Federal government (P)

562 U.S. 65 (2014)

NATURE OF CASE: Appeal from affirmance of conviction under 18 U.S.C. § 924(c) of aiding or abetting the use or carrying of a gun in the commission of a drug trafficking crime.

FACT SUMMARY: Rosemond (D), an accomplice to a drug deal, was convicted, inter alia, of aiding and abetting the violation of 18 U.S.C. § 924(c), which criminalizes the use or carrying a gun in connection with a drug trafficking or violent crime. Rosemond (D) contended that the district court's instructions as to what the Government (P) had to prove to sustain the conviction was erroneous because it failed to require proof that he had advance knowledge a gun would be present or used at the drug deal.

RULE OF LAW

To obtain a conviction of aiding or abetting a crime under 18 U.S.C. § 924(c), which criminalizes the use or carrying of a gun in the commission of a drug trafficking or violent crime, the government must prove that the defendant actively participated in the underlying crime with advance knowledge that a confederate would use or carry a gun during the crime's commission.

FACTS: Perez sought to sell a pound of marijuana to Gonzalez and Painter. Joseph and Rosemond (D) accompanied her to the meeting place in her car. It was unclear whether Joseph or Rosemond (D) was in the front passenger seat, and which of them was in the back seat. When they got to the designated meeting place, Gonzales climbed into the car's back seat while Painter waited outside. The backseat passenger allowed Gonzales to inspect the marijuana. Rather than handing over money, Gonzales punched that man in the face and fled with the drugs. As Gonzales and Painter ran away, either Rosemond (D) or Joseph (it was not clear who) exited the car and fired several shots from a semiautomatic handgun. The shooter then re-entered the vehicle, and all three would-be drug dealers gave chase after the buyers-turned-robbers. However, before they could catch Gonzalez and Painter, a police officer, responding to a dispatcher's alert, pulled their car over. Rosemond (D) was prosecuted for inter alia, violating 18 U.S.C. § 924(c), which criminalizes the use or carrying of a gun in the commission of a drug trafficking or violent crime, or, alternatively, aiding and abetting that offense. The Government (P) proceeded on these two alternative theories because it was unclear whether it was Rosemond (D) or Joseph who had and used the firearm during the events of the failed drug deal. The district court judge instructed the jury on the principles of aiding and abetting and informed the jury that it could convict Rosemond (D) if it found that "(1) the defendant knew his cohort used a firearm in the drug trafficking crime, and (2) the defendant knowingly and actively participated in the drug trafficking crime." The jury convicted Rosemond of violating § 924(c). The court of appeals rejected Rosemond's (D) argument that the district court's aiding and abetting instructions were erroneous. The United States Supreme Court granted certiorari.

ISSUE: To obtain a conviction of aiding or abetting a crime under 18 U.S.C. § 924(c), which criminalizes the use or carrying of a gun in the commission of a drug trafficking or violent crime, must the government prove that the defendant actively participated in the underlying crime with advance knowledge that a confederate would use or carry a gun during the crime's commission?

HOLDING AND DECISION: (Kagan, J.) Yes. To obtain a conviction of aiding or abetting a crime under 18 U.S.C. § 924(c), which criminalizes the use or carrying of a gun in the commission of a drug trafficking or violent crime, the government must prove that the defendant actively participated in the underlying crime with advance knowledge that a confederate would use or carry a gun during the crime's commission. The federal aiding and abetting statute, 18 U.S.C. § 2, which derives from common-law standards for accomplice liability, has two components: a person is liable under § 2 only if that person (1) takes an affirmative act in furtherance of the underlying offense (2) with the intent to facilitate that offense's commission. Section 924(c) has two elements: a drug deal or violent crime element, and the element of using or carrying a firearm in connection with that crime. The instructions correctly permitted the jury to convict Rosemond (D) of aiding and abetting even if he facilitated only the drug element, and not the gun element, since the common law imposed aiding and abetting liability on a person who facilitated any element of a criminal offense, even if he did not facilitate all elements, and that principle continues to govern § 2. In addition to conduct extending to some part of the crime, aiding and abetting requires intent extending to the whole crime. The defendant must not just associate themself with the venture but must also participate in it as something that the defendant wishes

Continued on next page.

to bring about and seek by their actions to make succeed. That requirement is satisfied when a person actively participates in a criminal venture with full knowledge of the circumstances constituting the charged offense. An active participant in a drug transaction has the intent needed to aid and abet a § 924(c) violation when that individual knows that one of the confederates will carry a gun. This must be advance knowledge—meaning, knowledge at a time when the accomplice has a reasonable opportunity to walk away. Thus, when an accomplice knows nothing of a gun until it appears at the scene, that person may already have completed acts of assistance, or may at that late point have no realistic opportunity to quit the crime. When that is the case, the defendant lacks the requisite intent to assist a crime involving a gun. The trial court's jury instructions were, therefore, erroneous because they failed to require that Rosemond (D) knew in advance that one of his cohorts would be armed. In telling the jury to consider merely whether Rosemond (D) "knew his cohort used a firearm," the court did not direct the jury to determine when Rosemond obtained the requisite knowledge—i.e., to decide whether he knew about the gun in sufficient time to withdraw from the crime. Remanded to the circuit court to consider the possible consequences of the district court's error.

ANALYSIS

The United States Supreme Court rejected Rosemond's (D) suggestion that an accomplice should be guilty of aiding and abetting a 18 U.S.C §924(c) violation only when the accomplice affirmatively desires one of their confederates to use a gun. In rejecting this higher standard, the Court explained that what matters for purposes of gauging intent is that the defendant has chosen, with full knowledge, to participate in the illegal scheme – not that, if all had been left to the defendant, they would have planned the identical crime. In this regard, the Court said: "The law does not, nor should it, care whether the defendant participates with a happy heart or a sense of foreboding. Either way, the individual has the same culpability, because either way he or she has knowingly elected to aid in the commission of a peculiarly risky form of offense."

Quicknotes

ACCOMPLICE LIABILITY Liability of an individual who knowingly, purposefully, or voluntarily combines with the main actor in the commission, or attempted commission, of a criminal offense.

AIDING AND ABETTING Assistance given in order to facilitate the commission of a criminal act.

People v. Kessler

State (P) v. Convicted burglar and attempted murderer (D)

Ill. Sup. Ct., 315 N.E.2d 29 (1974)

NATURE OF CASE: Appeal from reversal of convictions of attempted murder.

FACT SUMMARY: Kessler (D)—the getaway driver for accomplices who initially were unarmed and burglarized a tavern, but who then shot and wounded the owner with a gun obtained during the burglary and then shot at a police officer while fleeing—was convicted, inter alia, of two counts of attempted murder. The People (P) contended that under the relevant statute, an accomplice to a criminal plan was liable for subsequent, unplanned criminal violations of that person's cohorts regardless of the accomplice's intent as to those violations.

RULE OF LAW

Where an accomplice aids another in the planning or commission of a criminal offense, the accomplice can be legally accountable for the conduct of the person the accomplice aids for any criminal act done in furtherance of the planned and intended act, even absent specific intent to commit that act.

FACTS: Kessler (D) told two cohorts where he had seen a large sum of money at a tavern. He remained in an automobile while the two cohorts burglarized the tavern, during the course of which one cohort shot and wounded the owner with a gun found on premises. As the cohorts were fleeing on foot, one of them also shot a police officer who was in pursuit. Kessler (D) was convicted of one count of burglary and two counts of attempted murder. State statutes made an accomplice liable for the conduct of another where "[e]ither before or during the commission of an offense and with the intent to promote or facilitate such commission, he solicits, aids, abets, agrees or attempts to aid, such other person in the planning or commission of the offense." The state's intermediate appellate court reversed the attempted-murder convictions, holding that Kessler (D) could not be liable for attempted murder absent his specific intent to commit the attempted murders committed by his cohorts. The court also stated that except in felony-murder cases, state statutes did not impose liability on accountability principles for all consequences and further crimes that could flow from participation in an initial criminal venture, absent a specific intent by the accomplice being held accountable to commit, or aid and abet the commission of, such further crimes. The People (P) appealed, arguing that a person is responsible for all criminal violations actually committed by another if that person assists another in the commission of a single criminal violation, and that if the legislature had intended to limit accomplice liability only to further criminal acts that had been specifically intended, the word "conduct" would not have been included in the relevant statutes. The state's highest court granted review.

ISSUE: Where an accomplice aids another in the planning or commission of a criminal offense, can the accomplice be legally accountable for the conduct of the person the accomplice aids for any criminal act done in furtherance of the planned and intended act, even absent specific intent to commit that act?

HOLDING AND DECISION: (Davis, J.) Yes. Where an accomplice aids another in the planning or commission of a criminal offense, the accomplice can be legally accountable for the conduct of the person the accomplice aids for any criminal act done in furtherance of the planned and intended act, even absent specific intent to commit that act. The word "conduct" encompasses any criminal act done in furtherance of the planned and intended act, regardless of whether the accomplice intended the act committed by their cohort. Here, Kessler (D) and his cohorts participated in a common design to commit a burglary, and each of them was legally accountable for the conduct of the other in connection with that common scheme. The result was the offense of attempted murder of the tavern owner and police officer who tried to apprehend the fleeing parties, and each of the participants, including Kessler (D), were accountable for these attempted murders. The intermediate appellate court's reversal of Kessler's (D) attempted-murder convictions is reversed, and the trial court's judgment is affirmed.

ANALYSIS

Illinois is in the minority of states that extend accomplice liability to secondary crimes that are foreseeable as a result of, or in furtherance of, a primary crime. The majority of states hold that accomplices to a primary crime are accomplices to a secondary crime only if they knowingly or purposely aid or encourage it. Even so, as this case illustrates, Illinois and some other jurisdictions extend accomplice liability to secondary crimes only where the secondary crimes are in furtherance of an agreement or "common design" to commit a primary crime, and, thus, in those jurisdictions accomplice liability does not

Continued on next page.

necessarily extend to all secondary crimes that relate to a primary crime.

Quicknotes

ACCOMPLICE LIABILITY Liability of an individual who knowingly, purposefully, or voluntarily combines with the main actor in the commission, or attempted commission, of a criminal offense.

SPECIFIC INTENT The intent to commit a specific unlawful act for which one is later charged. Specific intent is a required element for criminal liability for certain crimes.

State v. Christy Pontiac-GMC, Inc.

State (P) v. Corporation convicted of theft (D)

Minn. Sup. Ct., 354 N.W.2d 17 (1984)

NATURE OF CASE: Appeal from a conviction of a corporation for theft by swindle and aggravated forgery.

FACT SUMMARY: After an employee of Christy Pontiac-GMC, Inc. (Christy Pontiac) (D) forged the signatures of two customers on rebate applications, Christy Pontiac (D) was charged and convicted of theft by swindle and aggravated forgery.

RULE OF LAW

A corporation may be held criminally liable for a specific-intent crime.

FACTS: Christy Pontiac-GMC, Inc. (Christy Pontiac) (D), a Minnesota corporation, was solely owned by James Christy (D), its president and director. Christy Pontiac (D) made two car sales after a rebate offer from GM had expired. Both customers were told that the salesman would still try to get the rebate for them. Hesli (D), a salesman and fleet manager, forged the signatures of both customers on the rebate applications, and the purchase order forms were backdated to put them within the time frame of the rebate offers. When the purchasers learned of the forged rebate applications, they complained to Christy (D). Charges were filed against Hesli (D), Christy (D), and Christy Pontiac (D). In a separate trial, Hesli (D) was found guilty of theft for the second forgery and was given a misdemeanor disposition. An indictment against Christy (D) was dismissed. The corporation Christy Pontiac (D) was convicted as charged. This appeal followed.

ISSUE: May a corporation be held criminally liable for a specific-intent crime?

HOLDING AND DECISION: (Simonett, J.) Yes. A corporation may be held criminally liable for a specific-intent crime. Therefore, a corporation may be prosecuted and convicted for the crimes of theft and forgery. Criminal guilt, however, requires that the agent act in furtherance of the corporation's business interests. Moreover, it must be shown that corporate management authorized, tolerated, or ratified the criminal activity. Here, since Christy Pontiac (D) got the GM rebate money, Hesli (D) was acting in furtherance of the corporation's business interests. Hesli (D) himself had middle-management responsibilities for cash rebate applications. Swandy, a corporate officer, signed the backdated retail buyer's order form for the first sale. Christy (D), the president, attempted to negotiate a settlement with the second purchaser. The evidence thus establishes that the theft by swindle and the forgeries constituted the acts of the corporation. Affirmed.

ANALYSIS

The Model Penal Code provides that a corporation may be convicted of an offense if the conduct is performed by an agent of the corporation acting on behalf of the corporation within the scope of the agent's employment. See Model Penal Code 2.07(1). The conduct need not actually benefit the corporation to impart liability. However, if the agent acts only to further self-interests—for example, is embezzling funds from the corporation—such an act is not considered to be "on behalf of the corporation."

Quicknotes

AGENT An individual who has the authority to act on behalf of another.

FORGERY The false preparation or modification of a written document with intent to defraud another.

SPECIFIC INTENT The intent to commit a specific unlawful act for which one is later charged. Specific intent is a required element for criminal liability for certain crimes.

United States v. Hilton Hotels Corp.

Federal government (P) v. Corporation convicted under the Sherman Act (D)

467 F.2d 1000 (9th Cir. 1972)

NATURE OF CASE: Appeal from a conviction for violation of the Sherman Act.

FACT SUMMARY: Hilton Hotels (D) was convicted of violating the Sherman Act after the judge charged the jury that a corporation is responsible for the acts and statements of its agents, done or made within the scope of their employment, even if contrary to their actual instructions or to the corporation's stated policies.

RULE OF LAW

As a general rule, a corporation is liable under the Sherman Act for the acts of its agents in the scope of their employment, even though such acts are contrary to general corporate policy and/or express instructions to the agent.

FACTS: Although it was against the corporate policies of Hilton Hotels (D) and constituted a violation of instructions that he take no part in the boycott, the purchasing agent for its hotel in Portland, Oregon, had threatened a supplier with the loss of the hotel's business unless the supplier paid an assessment to an association which the local businesses had organized to attract convention business to Portland. The agreement among the members of the association was that those suppliers who would not pay their assessment would be "boycotted" (i.e., no purchases would be made from them). Hilton Hotels (D) was convicted of violating the Sherman Act, the judge charging the jury that a corporation is responsible for the acts and statements of its agents done or made within the scope of their employment, even if contrary to their actual instructions or to the corporation's stated policies. On appeal, Hilton Hotels (D) cited this as error.

ISSUE: As a general rule, is a corporation liable under the Sherman Act for the acts of its agents in the scope of their employment, even though such acts are contrary to general corporate policy and/or express instructions to the agents?

HOLDING AND DECISION: (Browning, J.) Yes. As a general rule, a corporation is liable under the Sherman Act for the acts of its agents in the scope of their employment, even though such acts are contrary to general corporate policy and/or express instructions to the agent. Congress may constitutionally impose criminal liability upon a business entity for acts or omissions of its agents within the scope of their employment, even without proof that the conduct was within the agent's actual authority and even though it may have been contrary to that agent's express instructions or the policies of the corporation. While the Sherman Act does not expressly impose such liability, the construction of the act that best achieves its purpose is that a corporation is liable for the acts of its agents within the scope of their authority, even when done against company orders. Affirmed.

ANALYSIS

Consider the argument that only individuals, not fictional entities, commit crimes. The entity is being held responsible as a group when it was a person's act that resulted in criminal charges. A person may be more likely to engage in criminal behavior if the person believes the company will have to accept the responsibility and defend against the actions. On the other hand, a corporation could always hide behind the veil if not held accountable for the actions of its agents. The entity could have individuals behaving criminally with no one person charged because of the group protection. The debate was silenced with legislation imposing liability on corporations for individual action.

Quicknotes

AGENT An individual who has the authority to act on behalf of another.

SHERMAN ACT Prohibits unreasonable restraint of trade.

CHAPTER 13

Conspiracy

Quick Reference Rules of Law

Chapline v. State

State legislator convicted of conspiracy (D) v. State (P)

Sup. Ct. Ark., 95 S.W. 477 (1906)

NATURE OF CASE: Appeal from conviction of conspiracy to bribe state legislators.

FACT SUMMARY: George Chapline (D), a state legislator, after being convicted of conspiracy with M. D. L. Cook, a lobbyist, to commit bribery of other state legislators, contended that the evidence was insufficient to support the conviction because it was almost entirely circumstantial.

RULE OF LAW

Evidence that is almost entirely circumstantial may be legally sufficient to support a conviction for conspiracy to commit a crime.

FACTS: After the Cache River Levee Bill came up for reconsideration in the state legislature after failing to pass by large margins for the third time, some citizens interested in the bill's passage assembled in a hotel in the state's capital to determine what could be done to get the bill passed. Chapline (D), a state legislator, came to the hotel, and a meeting was held with him and the citizens in the room of one of the citizens, Mayberry. Chapline (D) told the group he thought it would take around $1,000 to secure the bill's passage, and when asked by one of the citizens if the money was to be used for a "corruption fund," Chapline (D) indicated it would be used for expenses, not bribery. He said that someone would have to see certain members of the House, and that they ought to get a lobbyist for that purpose. Mayberry was selected to take charge of the money when raised, and to employ someone to assist in securing the passage of the bill. Chapline (D) then proposed to put Mayberry in touch with a man who could help their cause, and he did so by introducing Mayberry to M. D. L. Cook, a lobbyist. When Mayberry was introduced to Cook, he said to Cook: "You are the man I think I want to see." Mayberry complained to Cook of the necessity of having to raise money to secure the passage of the bill, and Cook replied by saying that "nearly all of these important bills are passed with the use of money"; and that it would take at least $1,500 to secure the passage of the bill. The money was not to be paid to legislators until the bill became a law. The group raised $1,475.00; Cook was employed; and the money was delivered to Oscar Davis to be paid to Cook, on the order of Mayberry, when the bill became a law. However, the bill did not become law, the money was not paid, and there was no crime of bribery. Chapline (D) was charged with, and convicted of, conspiring with Cook to commit the crime of bribery. On appeal to the state's highest court, Chapline (D) challenged the sufficiency of the evidence on the grounds that it was almost entirely circumstantial.

ISSUE: May evidence that is almost entirely circumstantial be legally sufficient to support a conviction for conspiracy to commit a crime?

HOLDING AND DECISION: [Judge not stated in the casebook extract.] Yes. Evidence that is almost entirely circumstantial may be legally sufficient to support a conviction for conspiracy to commit a crime. To establish a conspiracy, it is not necessary to prove the unlawful agreement by direct evidence, as such agreement may be proved by circumstantial evidence. Given the secrecy usually surrounding conspiracies, a conspiracy usually must be inferred by the jury from proof of facts and circumstances that, taken together, apparently indicate that they are merely parts of some complete whole. Thus, there is not a need to show by direct evidence that the alleged co-conspirators actually came together and agreed in express terms to enter into and pursue a common criminal design. Where the evidence shows a concert of action, between the persons alleged to have conspired to commit a crime or the person charged and another, that is sufficient to establish the necessary common object and intent, and the jury will be justified in concluding that they were engaged in a conspiracy to effect that object. Applying these principles here, the jury could have inferred that the money raised, which was not to be paid unless the bill passed, was to be used to bribe legislators. When Chapline (D) identified Cook as the one to assist the group, the jury could have inferred that Cook was to be hired to put into effect the group's object, which, along with the selection of Cook, should be considered together to determine the object of his employment. It can be inferred from the evidence that Chapline (D) knew that Cook could be hired for such a job, and had, before the meeting at the hotel, been in contact with Cook and told Cook of the criminal plan, which is why Chapline (D) was able to recommend Cook to the group. From this, the jury could reasonably have inferred that Chapline (D) promised Cook to do what Chapline (D) did, and Cook agreed to accept the employment if it was tendered. That is the prima facie evidence of the conspiracy, and what followed, after Chapline (D) introduced Cook to Mayberry, confirms the conspiracy. Affirmed.

Continued on next page.

ANALYSIS

With conspiracy, the primary focus is on the agreement between the alleged co-conspirators, which can be deemed to be the actus reus in the absence of a requirement that there be an overt act taken in furtherance of the conspiracy by one of the alleged co-conspirators. As Chapline (D) reinforces, the focus is on the agreement—the collusion, the secrecy, and the resulting threat to society that such criminal liaisons create. The act is required as a method of showing that some step has been taken toward executing the illicit agreement. Any action sufficient to corroborate the existence of the agreement and to show that it is being put into effect is sufficient to support the conspiracy.

Quicknotes

ACTUS REUS The unlawful act that gives rise to criminal liability, as distinguished from the required mental state.

BRIBERY The offering, giving, receiving, or soliciting of something of value for the purpose of influencing the action of an official in the discharge of the official's public or legal duties.

CIRCUMSTANTIAL EVIDENCE Evidence that, though not directly observed, supports the inference of principal facts.

CONSPIRACY Concerted action by two or more persons to accomplish some unlawful purpose.

INFERENCE A deduction from established facts.

United States v. Recio

Federal government (P) v. Drug conspirator (D)

537 U.S. 270 (2003)

NATURE OF CASE: Appeal from conviction for conspiracy to distribute drugs.

FACT SUMMARY: When Recio (D) was convicted of having conspired to possess and distribute unlawful drugs, he argued that the government could not prosecute drug conspiracy defendants unless they had joined the conspiracy before the government seized the drugs.

RULE OF LAW

A conspiracy does not end automatically when its object becomes impossible to achieve.

FACTS: Police stopped a truck and found and seized a large stash of illegal drugs. With the help of the truck's drivers, the police set up a sting in which the truck was taken to another location and the drivers paged Jimenez Recio (D) and another defendant to come and pick up the truck and the drugs. When Recio (D) and the other defendant arrived, they were arrested. They were convicted of having conspired to possess and distribute unlawful drugs. However, the trial judge determined the jury instructions had been erroneous in failing to inform the jury that it could not convict Recio (D) of the conspiracy unless the jury believed he had joined the conspiracy before the truck was stopped by the police. At the new trial, Recio (D) was again convicted and appealed.

ISSUE: Does a conspiracy end automatically when its object becomes impossible to achieve?

HOLDING AND DECISION: (Breyer, J.) No. A conspiracy does not end automatically when its object becomes impossible to achieve. In *United States v. Cruz*, 127 F.3d 791 (1997), the Ninth Circuit held that the government could not prosecute drug conspiracy defendants unless they had joined the conspiracy before the government seized the drugs. The Ninth Circuit thereby held that a conspiracy ends automatically when its object becomes impossible to achieve. In other words, the conspiracy ends through "defeat" when the government intervenes, making the conspiracy's goals impossible to achieve, even if the conspirators did not know that the government had intervened and are totally unaware that the conspiracy is bound to fail. In our view, this statement of the law is incorrect. To the contrary, a conspiracy does not automatically terminate simply because the government, unbeknownst to some of the conspirators, has defeated the conspiracy's object. The essence of a conspiracy is an agreement to commit an unlawful act. That agreement is a "distinct evil" that "may exist and be punished whether or not the substantive crime ensues." To hold otherwise would reach well beyond arguable police misbehavior, potentially threatening the use of properly run law enforcement sting operations. The conspiracy itself poses a threat to the public over and above the threat of the commission of the relevant substantive crime. Reversed.

ANALYSIS

The American Law Institute's Model Penal Code §5.03 (1985) provides that a conspiracy terminates when the crime or crimes that are its object are committed or when the relevant agreement is abandoned. The Model Penal Code would not find "impossibility" a basis for termination.

Quicknotes

CONSPIRACY Concerted action by two or more persons to accomplish some unlawful purpose.

People v. Lauria

State (P) v. Answering service proprietor (D)

Cal. Ct. App., 251 Cal. App. 2d 471, 59 Cal. Rptr. 628 (1967)

NATURE OF CASE: Appeal from indictment for conspiracy to further prostitution being set aside.

FACT SUMMARY: Lauria (D) knew that some of his answering service customers were prostitutes who used his service for business purposes.

RULE OF LAW

A supplier does not necessarily become a part of a conspiracy to further an illegal venture by furnishing goods or services that the supplier knows are to be used for criminal purposes, where the crime involved is a misdemeanor.

FACTS: Lauria (D) and three people who used his answering service were arrested for prostitution. Lauria (D) knew that one of the people was a prostitute. He said he did not arbitrarily tell the police about prostitutes who used his service for business purposes. Lauria (D) and three prostitutes were indicted for conspiracy to further prostitution. The trial court set aside the indictment as lacking reasonable or probable cause. The State (P) appealed.

ISSUE: Does a supplier necessarily become a part of a conspiracy to further an illegal venture by furnishing goods or services that the supplier knows are to be used for criminal purposes, where the crime involved is a misdemeanor?

HOLDING AND DECISION: (Fleming, J.) No. A supplier does not necessarily become a part of a conspiracy to further an illegal venture by furnishing goods or services that the supplier knows are to be used for criminal purposes, where the crime involved is a misdemeanor. Both the knowledge of the illegal use of the goods or services and the intent to further that use are necessary to support a conviction for conspiracy. Intent may be inferred from circumstances of the sale that show the supplier had acquired a special interest in the activity. Or a supplier may be liable on the basis of knowledge alone where the supplier furnishes goods that the supplier knows will be used to commit a serious crime. However, this does not apply to misdemeanors. Here, Lauria (D) was not shown to have a stake in the venture, and he is charged with a misdemeanor. Hence, he could not be charged with conspiracy to further prostitution. Affirmed.

ANALYSIS

In *U.S. v. Falcone*, 311 U.S. 205, the sellers of large quantities of sugar, yeast, and cans were absolved from participation in a moonlighting conspiracy. In *DirectSales Co. v. U.S.*, 319 U.S. 703, a wholesale drug company was convicted of conspiracy to violate the narcotic laws by selling large quantities of drugs to a physician who was supplying them to addicts. The court distinguished these two leading cases on the basis of the character of the goods. The restricted character of the goods in *Direct Sales* showed that the defendant knew of their illegal use and had taken the step from knowledge to intent and agreement.

Quicknotes

CONSPIRACY Concerted action by two or more persons to accomplish some unlawful purpose.

MISDEMEANOR A crime that does not constitute a felony. A misdemeanor is generally less severe and results in a lesser punishment.

United States v. Diaz

Federal government (P) v. Conspirator (D)

864 F.2d 544 (7th Cir. 1988)

NATURE OF CASE: Appeal of conviction of conspiracy, among others, to use a firearm in relation to commission of a drug trafficking crime.

FACT SUMMARY: Diaz (D) was convicted of conspiracy to use a firearm in relation to commission of a drug trafficking crime, even though he did not know his accomplice was bringing a gun.

RULE OF LAW

One may be convicted of conspiracy to use a firearm in relation to the commission of a drug trafficking crime even if one did not know that their accomplice was bringing a gun.

FACTS: Diaz (D) became involved in a drug deal set up by DEA officers. Diaz (D) was to meet with several accomplices to effect a sale of cocaine to an undercover DEA officer. At the scene of the sale, Peirallo (D), an accomplice, brought a gun. Diaz (D) had no knowledge that Peirallo (D) intended to bring a gun. Diaz (D) and the others were arrested at the scene. Diaz (D) was convicted of conspiracy to distribute cocaine, possession and distribution of cocaine, and conspiracy to use a firearm in relation to commission of a drug trafficking crime. Diaz (D) appealed the firearm conspiracy conviction.

ISSUE: May one be convicted of conspiracy to use a firearm in relation to the commission of a drug trafficking crime even if one did not know that their accomplice was bringing a gun?

HOLDING AND DECISION: (Ripple, J.) Yes. One may be convicted of conspiracy to use a firearm in relation to the commission of a drug trafficking crime even if one did not know that their accomplice was bringing a gun. It is a rule that when one enters a conspiracy, one becomes responsible for the acts of every other conspirator done in furtherance of the conspiracy. The only exception to this is when the act is not a foreseeable, reasonable consequence of the conspiracy. In the context of the drug industry, it hardly needs mention that possession of a gun is a foreseeable consequence of a "deal." This being so, the conviction was proper. Affirmed.

ANALYSIS

The leading case in this area is *Pinkerton v. United States*, 328 U.S. 640 (1946). Pinkerton broadly established the rule noted by the opinion. The circuits have varied as to how expansive the rule should be. Some circuits require more agreement as to the offense in question than other circuits. The Seventh Circuit, by its own admission, takes a broad view of the rule.

Quicknotes

ACCOMPLICE An individual who knowingly, purposefully, or voluntarily combines with the main actor in the commission or attempted commission of a criminal offense.

CONSPIRACY Concerted action by two or more persons to accomplish some unlawful purpose.

United States v. Caldwell

Federal government (P) v. Drug dealer Co-conspirator (D)

589 F.3d 1323 (10th Cir. 2009)

NATURE OF CASE: Appeal from conviction for a single conspiracy to distribute drugs.

FACT SUMMARY: Caldwell (D) was charged and convicted of engaging in a single conspiracy with Herrera and Anderson to sell drugs. An introduction by Caldwell (D) of Anderson to Herrera led to Herrera becoming the common source of drugs for both Caldwell (D) and Anderson.

RULE OF LAW

Having a common drug supplier does not constitute sufficient evidence of a single conspiracy.

FACTS: Caldwell (D) sold drugs and initially received them only from Herrera. Later, after Caldwell (D) set up an introduction of his friend Anderson (from whom Caldwell had also bought drugs) to Herrera, Caldwell (D) continued to receive drugs from Herrera, but not from Anderson. Ultimately, Caldwell was indicted for conspiring to distribute a large volume of drugs with both Herrera and Anderson as part of one conspiracy. After trial, Caldwell (D) was convicted and imprisoned.

ISSUE: Does having a common drug supplier constitute sufficient evidence of a single conspiracy?

HOLDING AND DECISION: (Lucero, J.) No. Having a common drug supplier does not constitute sufficient evidence of a single conspiracy. A jury convicted Caldwell (D) of being involved in a single conspiracy with two other individuals (Herrera and Anderson) to distribute drugs. In the present case, Caldwell (D) and Anderson were equal-level purchasers rather than links in a vertical chain. A vertical conspiracy, or "chain-and-link" conspiracy, involves a series of consecutive buyer-seller relationships. The classic vertical conspiracy involves Supplier A selling contraband to Supplier B, who then sells the contraband to Supplier C. But drug distribution organizations often do not fit neatly into the concept of vertical conspiracy. After Herrera was introduced by Caldwell (D) to Anderson, Herrera became their joint supplier. Neither Caldwell (D) nor Anderson bought or sold marijuana to the other. Instead, each independently sold marijuana to third parties. Thus, their relationship does not evince the characteristics of a vertical conspiracy. This relationship would fit more neatly into the concept of a "hub-and-spoke" conspiracy, in which several separate players all interact with a common central actor, here Herrera. Herrera's role as a common supplier, Caldwell's (D's) earlier purchase of marijuana from Anderson, and Caldwell's (D's) introduction of Anderson to Herrera do not constitute sufficient evidence of a single conspiracy among the three drug dealers. Instead, the evidence presented at trial demonstrates the existence of separate conspiracies between Caldwell (D) and Anderson, and between Caldwell (D) and Herrera. The sharing of a common supplier, without more, does not demonstrate that two drug dealers are acting together for their shared mutual benefit. Evidence showing that an alleged co-conspirator has an economic stake in the outcome of a drug transaction can demonstrate that a transaction is not merely casual. Of course, direct economic benefit for all individuals involved is not necessarily a prerequisite for a jury to find a single conspiracy. On the other hand, an act that merely facilitates the distribution of drugs may be insufficient to show that two individuals intend to act together for their mutual benefit. The facts surrounding this case demonstrate that it was friendly rather than conspiratorial. There was no evidence that Caldwell (D) received any economic benefit from the introduction, and Anderson testified that Caldwell (D) received no such benefit. Reversed.

ANALYSIS

The charge, and what the jury ultimately convicted Caldwell (D) of, indicated a single, or tripartite, conspiracy that all three (Caldwell, Herrera, and Anderson) acted in conspiratorial coordination. An examination by the court revealed different level of interactions, focusing on what each person did to establish the scope of the alleged conspiracy. However, and the court was quick to note this, Caldwell (D) admitted that he conspired only with Herrera and not Anderson. This distinction was fatal to the charges, which alleged a single conspiracy among all three men, a tripartite conspiracy, which did not occur.

Quicknotes

CONSPIRACY Concerted action by two or more persons to accomplish some unlawful purpose.

CHAPTER 14

Theft and Other Property Offenses

Quick Reference Rules of Law

Commonwealth v. Mitchneck

State (P) v. Coal mine owner (D)

Pa. Super. Ct., 198 A. 463 (1938)

NATURE OF CASE: Appeal from conviction for fraudulent conversion.

FACT SUMMARY: Mitchneck (D) contended that his actions in withholding payment of money may have been actionable civilly but were not criminal in nature.

RULE OF LAW

Fraudulent conversion is committed through the intentionally wrongful withholding of property from one who has a possessory interest therein.

FACTS: Mitchneck (D) owned a coal mine and agreed with a store owner to deduct from his employee's wages amounts used to purchase goods and then turn the amounts over to the storekeeper. Mitchneck (D) withheld the amounts but failed to turn the money over, and he was charged with and convicted of fraudulent conversion. He appealed, contending that his actions only constituted a civil rather than criminal breach.

ISSUE: Is fraudulent conversion committed through the intentionally wrongful withholding of property from one who has a possessory interest therein?

HOLDING AND DECISION: (Keller, P.J.) Yes. Fraudulent conversion is committed through the intentionally wrongful withholding of property from one who has a possessory interest therein. The employees in this case were owed a debt, yet they had no possessory interest in the money. Thus, the money did not belong to the employees and their assignment to the store transferred only the right to collect the debt. Thus no criminal conduct occurred. Reversed.

ANALYSIS

This case illustrates the difference between civil liability and criminal guilt. The creditor cannot invoke the power of the state to collect a private debt. To allow such would invite the return of the debtor's prison.

Quicknotes

POSSESSORY INTEREST The right to possess particular real property to the exclusion of others.

The Case of the Carrier Who Broke Bulk Anon v. The Sheriff of London

Bailee (D) v. Government (P)

Star Chamber (1473). YB. Pasch.13 Edw. IV, f.9, pl. 5 (1473), 64 Selden Soc. 30 (1945)

NATURE OF CASE: Trial for felony theft.

FACT SUMMARY: A bailee (D) broke open the package with which he was entrusted and converted the goods inside.

RULE OF LAW

Bailees who break open their entrusted packages and convert the contents are not guilty of felony theft.

FACTS: A man (D) agreed to carry bales of woad (a type of dye) and other goods to Southampton for another man. The bailee (D) then opened the bales, took the goods, and converted them to his own use. The issue at trial was whether this constituted felony theft. The defense argued that bailees with legal possession cannot feloniously steal those goods. The prosecution argued that by breaking open the bales the man committed a felony.

ISSUE: Are bailees who break open their entrusted packages and convert the contents guilty of felony theft?

HOLDING AND DECISION: (Bryan, C.J.C.P.) No. Bailees who break open their entrusted packages and convert the contents are not guilty of felony theft. The bailee (D) was given possession of the package and therefore cannot be guilty of anything except in an action of detinue.

(Chokke, J.C.P.) Possession of the goods within the bulk package is not given to a bailee. The bailee cannot be guilty of felony theft for converting the bulk package in their own possession; the package contents were not entrusted into the bailee's care. Accordingly, when a bailee breaks open a bulk package, the bailee commits felony theft of the contents. The bailee (D) in the present case is guilty.

(The Chancellor) All judges hold that bailees who break open their entrusted packages and convert the contents are not guilty of felony theft.

ANALYSIS

This case, decided in 1473, was a major decision in the development of theft and larceny. It was the first decision to consider a bailee's liability for larceny. A dissenting judge, Nedeham, opined that possession does not excuse the bailee's felonious conversion of the entrusted goods, giving the example that a man cannot convert the mug in which a tavern owner serves him a drink notwithstanding that the drink itself is the man's possession. The distinction between possession and custody of goods remains the foundation of modern statutory theft offenses.

Quicknotes

BAILEE Person holding property in trust for another party.

FELONY A criminal offense of greater seriousness than a misdemeanor; felonies are generally defined pursuant to statute as any crime that is punishable by death or by a term of imprisonment exceeding one year.

LARCENY The illegal taking of another's property with the intent to deprive the owner thereof.

Rex v. Chisser

Government (P) v. Customer (D)

K.B., T. Raym 275, 83 Eng. Rep. 142 (1678)

NATURE OF CASE: Appeal from jury verdict of guilty in felony larceny trial.

FACT SUMMARY: Chisser (D), after asking a sales clerk to see two items, ran out of the shop without paying for the merchandise.

RULE OF LAW

Leaving a store with merchandise a sales clerk has offered for inspection shows intent to steal and is a felony.

FACTS: Abraham Chisser (D) went into the shop of Anne Charteris and asked to see two crevats. She handed him the crevats to look at and told him the price. He offered her a lower price and immediately ran out of the shop with the crevats.

ISSUE: Does leaving a store with merchandise a sales clerk has offered for inspection show intent to steal and is it a felony?

HOLDING AND DECISION: [Judge not stated in casebook excerpt.] Yes. Leaving a store with merchandise a sales clerk has offered for inspection shows intent to steal and is a felony. There was no completed contract between the parties in this case, and the goods were still in Charteris's possession even though she had handed them to Chisser (D) to inspect. Chisser's (D) running away with the goods in the presence of Charteris reveals the same intent to steal as if he had taken the goods while no one was in the shop. Chisser (D) committed a felony.

ANALYSIS

The common-law elements of larceny were (1) a trespassory taking and carrying away of property (2) from the possession of another (3) with the intent to permanently deprive the owner of the property. Because of the "trespassory taking" requirement, determining when possession passed from the owner of the property to the thief was a critical issue. This case was among the first to expand the interpretation of the "trespassory taking" requirement from its literal meaning.

Quicknotes

FELONY A criminal offense of greater seriousness than a misdemeanor; felonies are generally defined pursuant to statute as any crime that is punishable by death or by a term of imprisonment exceeding one year.

LARCENY The illegal taking of another's property with the intent to deprive the owner thereof.

The King v. Pear

Government (P) v. Horse thief (D)

Ct. for Crown Cases Reserved, 1 Leach 211, 168 Eng. Rep. 208 (1779)

NATURE OF CASE: Appeal of larceny conviction.

FACT SUMMARY: Pear (D) hired a horse for a trip, but immediately sold it without going on the trip.

RULE OF LAW

Trespass for larceny may be accomplished by fraud where the taking involved is done by a trick to gain possession of property, and with the intent to steal.

FACTS: Pear (D) rented a horse from Samuel Finch, stating his intention to make a journey to another town and return that night. He never returned, but, rather, sold the horse that same day. Pear (D) was indicted for larceny (horse stealing). At trial, the jury found that Pear (D) had intended to sell the horse from the beginning. Upon conviction, he appealed, contending that his acts did not constitute the crime of larceny.

ISSUE: May trespass for larceny be accomplished by fraud where the taking involved is done by a trick to gain possession of property, and with the intent to steal?

HOLDING AND DECISION: (Ashhurst, J.) Yes. Trespass for larceny may be accomplished by fraud where the taking involved is done by a trick to gain possession of property, and with the intent to steal. The taking by fraud does not alter the nature of the victim's possession of the property at the time of the crime. Even though the victim's act of parting with the property is deliberate, the fact that they were induced to do so by fraud negates their intent to transfer possession. As such, the taking from the victim of their property is trespassory in that it is done against their actual will. Here, Pear (D) intended, at the time of renting the horse, to sell it. Finch did not give it to him for that purpose. As such, the taking of the horse with the intent to sell it was a trespass against the property of Finch. The conviction must stand.

ANALYSIS

This case points out the generally accepted relationship between the larceny requirement of a "trespass in the taking" and use of fraud to effect such a trespass. The trespass, of course, is to an interest in the property of another (possession or ownership). The crime was larceny in the case above because there was a trespass to the owner's "ownership" interest in the taking (legally) of his "possessory" interest in the property. If the taking had been of the full ownership interest (title), the crime would not have been larceny since there would have been no trespass to any property interest of the owner. Note, finally, that the word "stealing" when used in the name of a crime generally denotes the crime of larceny. Thus, horse stealing is larceny of a horse. "Intent to steal," however, for larceny, generally denotes the "intent to permanently deprive."

Quicknotes

FRAUD A false representation of facts with the intent that another will rely on the misrepresentation to their detriment.

LARCENY The illegal taking of another's property with the intent to deprive the owner thereof.

TRESPASS Unlawful interference with, or damage to, the real or personal property of another.

People v. Sattlekau

State (P) v. Solicitor (D)

N.Y. App. Div., 120 App. Div. 42, 104 N.Y.S. 805 (1907)

NATURE OF CASE: Appeal from conviction of grand larceny by false pretenses.

FACT SUMMARY: Sattlekau (D) induced a woman to give him $1,000 for a phony hotel investment after placing a personal ad in the newspaper for the possibility of marriage.

RULE OF LAW

The elements of larceny by false pretenses are a deliberate intention to defraud, the representation of false pretenses, and the reliance of the victim upon such pretenses.

FACTS: Sattlekau (D) placed a personal ad in the newspaper soliciting women for a housekeeping position in his hotel as well as the possibility of marriage. He signed the ad "Bachelor." Rosa Kaiser responded and they corresponded by mail before arranging to meet for an interview. Over the course of their correspondence, Sattlekau (D) told Kaiser that his name was Ernest Paul, that he was unmarried, that he owned a hotel, and that he was in need of $1,000 for the purposes of purchasing another hotel, which would become their home. Kaiser gave Sattlekau (D) the money and shortly thereafter received a letter stating that there had been a fire at the hotel and that she would need to wait for him for a while. Sattlekau (D) was arrested after setting up an "interview" with another woman, and a jury convicted him of larceny by false pretenses. Sattlekau (D) appealed, alleging that the indictment was defective and the elements of the charge had not been proven.

ISSUE: Are the elements of larceny by false pretenses a deliberate intention to defraud, the representation of false pretenses, and the reliance of the victim upon such pretenses?

HOLDING AND DECISION: (Clarke, J.) Yes. The elements of larceny by false pretenses are a deliberate intention to defraud, the representation of false pretenses, and the reliance of the victim upon such pretenses. Kaiser's testimony at trial, along with Sattlekau's (D) own admissions on several issues, fully supports the conviction. Sattlekau (D) made several key misrepresentations, i.e., that he was not married, that he was the proprietor of a hotel, and that the hotel he named and used in his ads and letterhead was located in Pennsylvania. Kaiser, in parting with her money, relied upon Sattlekau's (D) false representations. The deliberate intent to defraud, the falsity of the pretenses made, and the reliance by Kaiser were fully established at trial and alleged in the indictment. Affirmed.

ANALYSIS

This case was prosecuted under 18 U.S.C. § 1341, the mail fraud statute. The statute's broad scope has been used to prosecute numerous cases involving schemes to defraud sent or delivered through the U.S. Postal Service. In addition, there is a parallel wire fraud statute, 18 U.S.C. § 1343, which covers schemes to defraud transmitted via wire, radio, or television.

Quicknotes

FALSE PRETENSES The unlawful obtaining of money or property from another with intent to defraud and with the utilization of false representations.

Durland v. United States

Bond fund operator (D) v. Federal government (P)

161 U.S. 306 (1896)

NATURE OF CASE: Appeal from conviction of federal mail fraud.

FACT SUMMARY: Durland (D) was charged with running a dishonest bond fund for which he solicited participation through mailed brochures promising return rates of 50% in only six months.

RULE OF LAW

The fact that a scheme to defraud was not effective in that it did not induce reliance by any victim does not preclude prosecution for federal mail fraud.

FACTS: Durland (D) mailed brochures from the Provident Bond and Investment Company with which he would trick individuals into "investing" a small amount of money each month, promising very large returns. He claimed the rates went up the longer the money was left in the fund and that they would reach as high as 50 percent in six months. At trial, it was found that Durland (D) was running a scheme to defraud and that he had no intention of the "bonds" ever maturing. Durland (D) was convicted under the U.S. mail fraud statute, 18 U.S.C. § 1341. On appeal, Durland (D) argued that the statute does not apply to him because at common law the definition of false pretenses applied only to the representation of existing facts, not to a mere promise regarding the future.

ISSUE: Does the fact that a scheme to defraud was not effective in that it did not induce reliance by any victim preclude prosecution for federal mail fraud?

HOLDING AND DECISION: (Brewer, J.) No. The fact that a scheme to defraud was not effective in that it did not induce reliance by any victim does not preclude prosecution for federal mail fraud. The scope of the mail fraud statute is very broad, and a scheme can be promoted through representations or promises of future rewards. Just because no one was issued the phony bonds does not mean that Durland (D) can escape charges. The record clearly reflected that Durland (D) had no intention of making an honest effort at investing the money he received. Therefore, his intent to defraud was sufficient to justify punishment. Affirmed.

ANALYSIS

Following *Durland*, other courts have held that although actual injury need not be proven, the government does have to show that the defendant intended harm or injury. In *United States v. Regent Office Supply, Inc.*, 421 F.2d 1174 (2d Cir. 1970), a salesman who falsely stated that he had been referred by a customer's friends was found not guilty because the representations had no bearing on the quality of the merchandise he was selling. Even though the salesman's misrepresentations may have played a part in inducing his customers to make purchases, the court found no actual injury because the goods were what he said they were.

Quicknotes

FALSE PRETENSES The unlawful obtaining of money or property from another with intent to defraud and with the utilization of false representations.

United States v. Phillips

Federal government (P) v. Mortgage borrower convicted of making false statements to a bank (D)

731 F.3d 649 (7th Cir. 2013)

NATURE OF CASE: Rehearing en banc of affirmance of convictions under 18 U.S.C. § 1014 for knowingly making and conspiring to make false statements for the purpose of influencing a federally insured bank.

FACT SUMMARY: Phillips (D) and Hall (D), who were encouraged by a mortgage broker, Bowling, to make false statements on a mortgage application with a federally insured bank, Fremont Investment & Loan (Fremont), were convicted under 18 U.S.C. § 1014 for knowingly making and conspiring to make false statements for the purpose of influencing the bank. They contended that the court erroneously excluded as irrelevant evidence that either they had not made statements they knew to be false or, though knowing the statements to be false, they hadn't made them for the purpose of influencing the bank's action on their mortgage application.

RULE OF LAW

Under 18 U.S.C. § 1014, which criminalizes the knowing making of false statements for the purpose of influencing a federally insured bank, evidence is relevant, and therefore admissible, if it might show that either the defendant had not made statements the defendant knew to be false, or that, though knowing the statements to be false, the defendant had not made them for the purpose of influencing a bank.

FACTS: Phillips (D) and Hall (D), a financially unsophisticated couple, wanted to purchase a house that was beyond their means. After they were rejected for a mortgage by one bank (Associated), because Hall (D) had recently had a bankruptcy, and because their joint income was insufficient to qualify them for the amount they were seeking, they turned to Bowling, a mortgage broker, who, unbeknownst to them was in fact a crook who brokered fraudulent loans. Bowling steered them to a federally insured bank, Fremont Investment & Loan (Fremont), which made "stated income" loans—known to the knowing as "liars' loans" because in a stated-income loan the lender accepts the borrower's statement of their income without trying to verify it. Such loans were profitable despite the high risk of default because lenders sold them—usually to be securitized—as soon as they had made them. According to Phillips (D) and Hall (D), Bowling had told them, first, that Phillips (D) should be the only applicant for the stated-income loan because her credit history was good while Hall's (D) was bad; second, that Hall's (D) income should be added to hers on the line in the application that asked for the borrower's gross monthly income; and third, that this was proper in the case of a stated-income loan because what the bank was asking for was the total income from which the loan would be repaid rather than just the borrower's income. They also alleged that Bowling told them that Phillips (D) would need to change her job title to make her income look a little better; so on the loan application she was listed as a "sales manager," which was false. Finally, they claimed that Bowling filled out the application, and that they did not read it, so they did not know of the inaccuracies in it. Phillips (D) was the only one who signed the application. They eventually were convicted under 18 U.S.C. § 1014 for knowingly making and conspiring to make false statements for the purpose of influencing Fremont. They sought to introduce evidence of what they alleged Bowling had told them and had done, but the judge ruled that this evidence was irrelevant. Instead, the judge ruled that if the defendants "sign something and they send it in, they're attempting to influence the bank." Phillips (D) and Hall (D) contended that the court erroneously excluded as irrelevant evidence that either they had not made statements they knew to be false or, though knowing the statements to be false, hadn't made them for the purpose of influencing the bank's action on their mortgage application. The jury rendered a general verdict, simply finding the defendants guilty of both counts of the indictment (the second being the conspiracy count). The verdict did not reveal what false statements the jury attributed to the defendants. A divided court of appeals panel affirmed, and the full court granted a rehearing en banc.

ISSUE: Under 18 U.S.C. § 1014, which criminalizes the knowing making of false statements for the purpose of influencing a federally insured bank, is evidence relevant, and therefore admissible, if it might show that either the defendant had not made statements the defendant knew to be false, or that, though knowing the statements to be false, the defendant had not made them for the purpose of influencing a bank?

HOLDING AND DECISION: (Posner, J.) Yes. Under 18 U.S.C. § 1014, which criminalizes the knowing making of false statements for the purpose of influencing a federally insured bank, evidence is relevant, and therefore admissible, if it might show that either the defendant had not made statements the defendant knew to be false, or that, though knowing the statements to be false, the defendant had not made them for the purpose of

Continued on next page.

influencing a bank. The trial court's ruling was erroneous insofar as it suggested that making a statement that is false and influences a bank is a crime. That is not the law. The statement must be knowingly false. Thus, the trial judge excluded evidence that if believed might have convinced a jury that any false statements the defendants made were not made knowingly—that is, not known by them to be false. The evidence if believed might also have rebutted an inference of intent to influence the bank. As to the influencing requirement, if the defendants believed that all Fremont cared about was that the applicant for a loan had a decent credit rating, as did Phillips (D), who alone signed the application as borrower, they would not have thought the statement of income would influence the bank's decision. If one were to believe their version of what Bowling had told them—a version they were forbidden to present to the jury—they did not believe that including in the space for "borrower's income" a non-borrower's income would affect Fremont's decision, because all the bank cared about was the total income available to service the loan. Thus, if their version was presented and believed, it would have been meaningless to say that the defendants intended to influence the bank by telling it something they were confident would not influence its decision. The evidence they were prevented from giving was pertinent both to whether they had knowingly made a false statement and to whether, if so, their intention had been to influence the bank to grant them a mortgage. Although the defendants must have known that in a literal sense Hall's (D) income was not part of Phillips's (D) income, literal meanings are not the only true meanings of phrases or sentences or other linguistic units, and even the simplest sentences require interpretation. Accordingly, it should have been left to the jury to determine what the defendants understood to be the meaning that Bowling attached to "borrower's income," especially since in finance, words and phrases in everyday use often bear a specialized meaning of which ordinary people are ignorant. Another consideration was that Fremont, given its business model, was asking for either an individual's income or a combined income, rather than just for the former, so that by putting down the combined income, Phillips (D) was making a true statement. It could also have been that, given its model, Fremont did not care whether the defendants would be able to repay the loan, and a jury could have found that the defendants believed the bank had approved the loan to the couple, and was telling them through Bowling what to put on the loan application, or what he should put on it in their name, and that in complying with his directives the defendants were not trying to influence the bank because they knew the bank had already made up its mind to make the loan and were just following Bowling's directions, which they may not have understood. In other words, a jury could have found from such evidence that the defendants had not tried to influence Fremont. Or, it could have found that they were indeed attempting to influence the bank. Had Phillips (D) and Hall (D) been allowed to testify to what Bowling had told them the phrase "borrower's income" meant, the jury might well have concluded that the couple had believed that combining their income on the "borrower's income" line of the loan application was precisely what the application called for. In sum, the judge's evidentiary ruling left the jury with little choice but to convict the defendants on the basis of the (literal) meaning of "borrower's income" alone. Because this erroneous exclusion of evidence favorable to the defendants could thus have been decisive in the jury's decision to convict, the judgment is reversed and the case remanded for a new trial.

ANALYSIS

It should be noted that materiality is not an element of the offense punished by U.S.C. § 1014. As a practical matter, however, materiality is relevant, because if the loan applicant does not think the falsehood would influence the bank, it is unlikely that in making it the applicant intended to influence the bank. Hence the literal reading of the statute will not normally take the scope of § 1014 beyond the limit that a materiality requirement would impose, but such a reading will allow immateriality to be used as evidence that the false statement was not intended to influence the bank.

Quicknotes

EVIDENTIARY FACTS: Those facts that are necessary for the determination of the ultimate facts.

KNOWINGLY Intentionally; willfully; an act that is committed with knowledge as to its probable consequences.

MATERIALITY Importance; the degree of relevance or necessity to the particular matter.

People v. Dioguardi

State (P) v. Extortionist (D)

N.Y. Ct. App., 8 N.Y. 2d 260, 203 N.Y.S.2d 870 (1960)

NATURE OF CASE: Appeal from reversal of several extortion convictions.

FACT SUMMARY: Dioguardi (D) was convicted of extortion for taking money to ensure against labor disputes.

RULE OF LAW

Extortion is committed by obtaining property by a wrongful use of fear, induced by a threat to do an unlawful injury.

FACTS: Dioguardi (D), through a front man, guaranteed a peaceful resolution to Kerin's labor problems if he was retained as a labor consultant. Kerin paid the retainer for some time before going to the district attorney. Dioguardi (D) was convicted of extortion, yet his conviction was overturned on appeal. The State of New York (P) appealed the reversal.

ISSUE: Is extortion committed by obtaining property by a wrongful use of fear, induced by a threat to do an unlawful injury?

HOLDING AND DECISION: (Froessel, J.) Yes. Extortion is committed by obtaining property by a wrongful use of fear, induced by a threat to do an unlawful injury. Kerin was fearful that the labor problems would drive him out of business. Dioguardi (D) used this fear by wrongfully threatening continued problems unless payment was made. Thus the elements of the crime were established. Reversed and new trial ordered.

ANALYSIS

The court indicated that the defendant need not have created the events instilling the fear. Further, fear of economic injury is sufficient to meet the second element. It was sufficient that the defendant controlled the situation to an extent that they could end the problem causing the fear.

Quicknotes

EXTORTION The unlawful taking of property of another by threats of force.

Lear v. State

Robber (D) v. State (P)

Ariz. Sup. Ct., 39 Ariz. 313, 6 P.2d 426 (1931)

NATURE OF CASE: Appeal from a robbery conviction.

FACT SUMMARY: When Lear (D) was convicted of robbery for grabbing a bag of silver from the victim, Lear (D) argued that the elements of the crime of robbery were not present since he used no force or fear.

RULE OF LAW
A taking must be accomplished by force or fear to constitute robbery.

FACTS: Lear (D) entered the shop of George Gross. Gross had placed a bag of silver on the sales counter. While Gross was untying the bag, Lear grabbed the bag from Gross's hands and ran out the back door. Lear (D) said no word at the time, exhibited no arms, and used no force other than to grab the bag. Lear (D) was tried and convicted of robbery and appealed, arguing that the facts did not sustain a robbery conviction since there was no evidence that the taking of the bag was by force or fear.

ISSUE: Must a taking be accomplished by force or fear to constitute robbery?

HOLDING AND DECISION: (Ross, J.) Yes. A taking must be accomplished by force or fear to constitute robbery. The crimes of robbery and larceny are not the same. The former is classified as a crime against the person and the latter as a crime against property. In robbery there is, in addition to the felonious taking, a violent invasion of the person. If the victim is not made to surrender the possession of the personal property by means of force or fear, the key element of robbery is not present. In the instant case, the element of force or fear is absent. Lear (D) made no threat or demonstration. He simply grabbed the bag of silver from the hands of George Gross and ran away with it. There was no pulling or scrambling for possession of the bag. This was not the type of force necessary to constitute robbery because it was not of such a nature as to show it was intended to overpower the party robbed and prevent their resisting. "Snatching, as here, which is sufficient asportation in simple larceny, may or may not carry with it the added violence of robbery. . . ." (*Bishop on Criminal Law*, Ninth Edition, Vol. 2, page 864, section 1167.) In this case, no violence or fear was manifested; hence the evidence was insufficient to sustain the conviction for robbery. Reversed and remanded.

ANALYSIS

The force or intimidation of a robbery usually must occur during the course of the commission of the theft. Common-law courts often interpreted this rule narrowly to require that the harmful or threatening behavior occur during the actual "taking" and, further, that the taking be successfully completed. In contrast, Model Penal Code § 222.1 has interpreted this requirement broadly to include force or intimidation occurring during an attempted theft or during flight from a completed or attempted crime. The Model Penal Code takes the position that the primary concern is with the physical danger or threat of danger to the citizen and not the property aspects of the crime.

Quicknotes

FORCE The exercise of power over a person or thing.

ROBBERY The unlawful taking of property from the person of another through the use of force or fear.

State v. Colvin

State (P) v. Burglar (D)

Minn. Sup. Ct., 645 N.W.2d 449 (2002)

NATURE OF CASE: Appeal from a burglary conviction.

FACT SUMMARY: When Peter Colvin (D) was convicted of burglary for violating the no-entry provision of a protective order, he argued that his mere entry was insufficient to establish the independent crime of burglary.

RULE OF LAW

Violation of the no-entry provision of a protective order is not sufficient to establish the independent crime element of burglary.

FACTS: Michelle obtained an emergency statutory order for protection (OFP) against her ex-husband, Peter Colvin (D), containing a provision that Colvin (D) was not permitted to enter Michelle's residence. When Colvin (D) violated the order by entering her residence, he was charged with, and convicted of, violation of the OFP and first-degree burglary. The intermediate appellate court affirmed, and Colvin (D) appealed, arguing that his wrongful entry with the intent to violate the OFP was insufficient to establish the crime of burglary absent the commission of, or intent to commit, any crime other than the OFP violation.

ISSUE: Is violation of the no-entry provision of a protective order sufficient to establish the independent crime element of burglary?

HOLDING AND DECISION: (Lancaster, J.) No. Violation of the no-entry provision of a protective order is not sufficient to establish the independent crime element of burglary. Trespass cannot serve as the crime committed or intended to be committed to establish burglary. To allow intent to commit a trespass to satisfy the requirement of intent to commit a crime would mean that a mere trespassor who had no intent other than to enter or remain in a building without the consent of the owner could be convicted of burglary. Like trespass, the violation of a no-entry provision of an order for protection is excluded from the crimes that can be the bases for the independent crime of burglary. Both offenses are designed to protect the interests that are invaded by the unauthorized entry that the burglar makes. Thus both trespass and violation of the no-entry provision of an OFP satisfy the legal entry element of burglary. Further, both offenses are complete upon entry. However, the same entry is insufficient to satisfy both the illegal entry element of the burglary statute and the independent-crime requirement. Under the statute, for a burglary conviction to stand, the state must prove that a defendant intended to commit some independent crime other than mere trespass. Reversed.

DISSENT: (Anderson, J.) If the state has misused its charging authority given the facts in this case, that action should be addressed directly rather than through a strained interpretation of the district court's straightforward ruling.

ANALYSIS

In *Colvin*, the court noted that if the legislature wanted to sanction violation of an OFP based solely on entering a home similarly to first-degree burglary—with a presumptive sentence of 48 months for a first-time offender—it could do so by amending the appropriate statute.

Quicknotes

BURGLARY Unlawful entry of a building at night with the intent to commit a felony therein.

PROTECTIVE ORDER Court order protecting a party against potential abusive treatment through use of the legal process.

TRESPASS Unlawful interference with, or damage to, the real or personal property of another.

In re Jason Allen D.

State (P) v. Delinquent trespasser (D)

Md. Ct. App., 127 Md. App. 456 (1999)

NATURE OF CASE: Appeal from finding of delinquency as to trespass.

FACT SUMMARY: Jason Allen D. (D), a juvenile, contended that he had a bona fide right to enter a housing complex to visit his cousin and to stand on the sidewalk in front of a building in the complex, notwithstanding that no trespassing signs were posted there and that he had been arrested several times for the same conduct by police, so that a trial court sitting as a juvenile court erred in finding that he was guilty of delinquent trespass. The State (P) argued that the finding of delinquent trespass was warranted because Jason (D) had proper notice that he was not to trespass on the complex grounds but nevertheless did so.

RULE OF LAW

Where a trespass statute makes it a crime to enter, cross, or remain on private property after being notified by the owner or the owner's agent not to do so, but also provides that entering or crossing private property is not a crime where it is done under a bona fide claim of right, it being the intention of the statute "only to prohibit any wanton trespass upon the private land of others," a person is not guilty of the trespass crime set forth in the statute where the person enters, crosses, or remains on the property of another while holding an objectively reasonable belief that they have a claim of right to be there.

FACTS: The Frederick City Housing Authority owned a public housing complex known as the Sagner Housing Complex, portions of which were designated as no-trespassing areas, including the area in front of 153 Pennsylvania Avenue, one of the buildings in the complex. The Frederick Police Department was authorized to enforce the no-trespassing laws on behalf of the Housing Authority. In November 1996, a police officer found Jason Allen D. (D) standing by the building at 153 Pennsylvania Avenue, and, after ascertaining that Jason (D) was not a resident, issued a written notice to Jason (D) stating that Jason (D) was not permitted on the property. Then, almost a year later, in September 1997, a different officer arrested Jason (D) twice for trespassing on the same day. The first arrest did not occur on the property, nor did the arresting officer witness Jason (D) commit any offense on the property. After the officer transported Jason (D) to the police station, Jason (D) was processed, released to his parents, and instructed not to return to the property. Nonetheless, Jason (D) returned to the property, and again was found by the police, standing on a curb within the complex with several other people. Although the police failed to ascertain their relationship to Jason (D) or to the housing complex, the police arrested Jason (D), who was brought before a trial court sitting as a juvenile court. At trial, there was testimony that the Housing Authority's standard lease agreement permitted tenants to have guests, and that pursuant to Housing Authority policy, a non-resident who had received a no-trespass notice would not be allowed to return to the property, regardless of the lease provision regarding guests. However, no written policy was introduced into evidence, nor was it explained whether or how the Housing Authority informed its tenants of the policy, or how the Housing Authority made known to its tenants that a particular person was banned from the property as a consequence of receiving a no-trespassing notice. Brandon Morris, Jason's (D) cousin, had lived at the housing complex for 14 years, and had been present when Jason (D) was arrested, as Jason (D) was his guest at the time. Nevertheless, the evidence did not reflect that Brandon knew of the Housing Authority policy that automatically barred re-entry onto the property by any person who had received a no-trespassing notice. Jason (D) testified that in all his encounters with the police, the officers had told him that he could come back to the housing complex as long as he was with someone who lived there. The relevant state statute provided in pertinent part that (1) any person who remained upon, entered upon, or crossed the land, premises, or private property of the owner or owners, after having been duly notified by the owner or their agent not to do so, was considered guilty of a misdemeanor; (2) this rule applied to property used as a housing project and operated by a housing authority if a duly authorized agent of the housing authority gave the required notification; and (3) the statute did not apply where such entry or crossing was done under a bona fide claim of right, "it being the intention of this section only to prohibit any wanton trespass upon the private land of others." The court found that Jason (D) had proper notice that he was not to trespass in the complex, that he was in the complex at the time of his arrest, and that he was in fact hanging out with his friends who lived there. Accordingly,

Continued on next page.

the court convicted Jason (D) of delinquency as to trespass, a misdemeanor. Jason (D) appealed, and the state's intermediate appellate court granted review.

ISSUE: Where a trespass statute makes it a crime to enter, cross, or remain on private property after being notified by the owner or the owner's agent not to do so, but also provides that entering or crossing private property is not a crime where it is done under a bona fide claim of right, it being the intention of the statute "only to prohibit any wanton trespass upon the private land of others," is a person guilty of the trespass crime set forth in the statute where the person enters, crosses, or remains on the property of another while holding an objectively reasonable belief that they have a claim of right to be there?

HOLDING AND DECISION: [Judge not identified in the casebook extract.] No. Where a trespass statute makes it a crime to enter, cross, or remain on private property after being notified by the owner or the owner's agent not to do so, but also provides that entering or crossing private property is not a crime where it is done under a bona fide claim of right, it being the intention of the statute "only to prohibit any wanton trespass upon the private land of others," a person is not guilty of the trespass crime set forth in the statute where the person enters, crosses, or remains on the property of another while holding an objectively reasonable belief that they have a claim of right to be there. The use of the term "wanton" in the statute indicates that the legislature intended the offense of misdemeanor trespass to be a general intent crime. Applying the plain meaning of the terms "wanton" and "bona fide" to the facts, Jason (D) had a bona fide claim of right to enter the housing complex as a guest of a resident, and, thus, he did not act wantonly. The uncontroverted evidence established that, at the time of the second arrest, Jason (D) was at the complex with his cousin, Brandon Morris, a current and long-time resident of the complex. The State (P) did not dispute this. Rather, the State (P) argued that Brandon's invitation was ineffective to confer bona fide status upon Jason (D), either because Brandon was a minor, or because a tenant's right to invite a social guest was superseded by the Housing Authority's right to exclude non-residents. Moreover, the Housing Authority lease provided that tenants were entitled to have guests, and it did not specifically prohibit children of lessors from inviting their friends to the property. Nor was there evidence that either Brandon or Jason (D) knew of the automatic bar that supposedly applied, by "policy," to any person who received a no-trespass notice. Thus, Jason (D) held an objectively reasonable belief that he was allowed to return to the housing complex "as long as [he was] visiting somebody." Jason (D) had the burden of production regarding his bona fide claim of right defense, and he met that burden. Thereafter, the burden of persuasion shifted to the State (P) to convince the juvenile court, beyond a reasonable doubt, that Jason (D) lacked a bona fide claim of right. However, the State (P) failed to meet that burden because it never contested Jason's (D) claim that Brandon invited him as a social guest to the complex, and, although the land in issue was privately owned by the Housing Authority, a visitor who believed they were lawfully invited to the complex could reasonably perceive the sidewalk in front of 153 Pennsylvania Avenue as a "public" thoroughfare. In this regard, it is noteworthy that the United States Supreme Court has held that "the freedom to loiter for innocent purposes is part of the 'liberty' protected by the Due Process clause of the Fourteenth Amendment." *City of Chicago v. Morales*, 527 U.S. 41 (1999). Reversed.

ANALYSIS

The statute in this case expressly states that it is intended only to prohibit wanton trespass, thus reinforcing that the legislature intended the crime to be one of general intent. The requirement that the crime be wanton is markedly different from the standard applied to tortious trespass, which occurs regardless of whether a defendant commits the trespass wantonly, or unwittingly, or willfully. In the civil context, a trespass is committed even when a trespasser makes a mistake as to their right to be on the land, so it is immaterial whether the defendant trespassed willfully or not. In contrast to the intent required for a criminal trespass, the intent required as a basis for liability as a trespasser in tort is simply an intent to be at the place on the land where the trespass allegedly occurred, regardless of good faith, under the mistaken belief, however reasonable, that they are committing no wrong. In contrast, the knowledge requirement inherent in criminal trespass is designed primarily to exclude from criminal liability both the inadvertent trespasser and the trespasser who believes that they have received an express or implied permission to enter or remain.

Quicknotes

BONA FIDE In good faith.

BURDEN OF PERSUASION The duty of a party in a legal proceeding to introduce evidence to support a fact that is in dispute in an action; combines with the burden of production to constitute the burden of proof.

BURDEN OF PRODUCTION The duty of a party in a legal proceeding to come forward with enough evidence to support a particular fact proposition to establish a prima facie

Continued on next page.

case and have the issue decided by the trier of fact, rather than having the case dismissed if the burden is deemed unsatisfied as a matter of law; combines with the burden of persuasion to constitute the burden of proof.

BURDEN OF PROOF The duty of a party to introduce evidence to support a fact that is in dispute in an action; made up of the burden of production and the burden of persuasion.

DELINQUENCY In criminal law, acts or conduct of a juvenile that violate criminal law.

GENERAL INTENT The intent to conduct an act but without the intent to commit an unlawful act.

MISDEMEANOR A crime that does not constitute a felony; generally less severe than a felony and results in lesser punishment.

TRESPASS Unlawful interference with, or damage to, the real or personal property of another.

WANTON Characterized by extreme recklessness and utter disregard for the rights of others.

CHAPTER 15

Perjury and False Statements

Quick Reference Rules of Law

Bronston v. United States

Convicted perjurer (D) v. Federal government (P)

409 U.S. 352 (1973)

NATURE OF CASE: Petition for certiorari on federal question arising out of perjury conviction.

FACT SUMMARY: Samuel Bronston (D), sole owner of Samuel Bronston Productions, Inc., arranged for his corporation to enter bankruptcy proceedings. During the bankruptcy hearing, he testified in response to a question about his personal bank accounts. The testimony was literally true but implied a falsity. Bronston (D) was convicted of perjury and he petitioned for a writ of certiorari.

RULE OF LAW

A witness may not be convicted of perjury for an answer, under oath, that is literally true but not responsive to the question asked and that is arguably misleading by negative implication.

FACTS: Samuel Bronston (D) was the sole owner of Samuel Bronston Productions, Inc., which produces motion pictures in European countries. Bronston (D) opened and directed bank accounts in multiple European banks on behalf of the corporation. In 1962, for example, the corporation transacted with 37 bank accounts in 5 countries. The corporation petitioned for Chapter 11 bankruptcy protection. At the hearing, Bronston (D) gave the following testimony to questions asked by a creditor's attorney:

Q. Do you have any bank accounts in Swiss banks, Mr. Bronston?
A. No, sir.
Q. Have you ever?
A. The company had an account there for about six months, in Zurich.

Bronston (D) had a personal bank account in Geneva, Switzerland, for about five years. Prosecutors charged Bronston (D) with perjury under 18 U.S.C. § 1621 because his second answer, while literally truthful (i.e., the company did have an account in Zurich for about six months), implied that he did not ever personally have any Swiss bank accounts. The jury convicted Bronston (D) after being instructed in part that conviction was appropriate if the answer was not literally false but constituted a false statement in context. Bronston (D) appealed and the court of appeals affirmed his conviction. The United States Supreme Court accepted the case on a writ of certiorari to address the application of § 1621 to a nonresponsive and arguably misleading answer.

ISSUE: May a witness be convicted of perjury for an answer, under oath, that is literally true but not responsive to the question asked and that is arguably misleading by negative implication?

HOLDING AND DECISION: (Burger, C.J.) No. A witness may not be convicted of perjury for an answer, under oath, that is literally true but not responsive to the question asked and that is arguably misleading by negative implication. Bronston (D) asserted at trial and in his appeal that he could not be convicted of perjury because his answer was admittedly truthful. The trial court and the court of appeals held that perjury occurs when the truthful statement is intentionally given in place of a responsive answer as a means to lie by negative implication. Section 1621 cannot apply, however, to Bronston's (D) answer. The statute defines perjury as a willful statement not believed to be true. Bronston's (D) statement was believed by him to be, and was in fact, true. It was the examining lawyer's responsibility to note the evasiveness of Bronston's (D) answer and clarify whether Bronston (D) had personal Swiss bank accounts. It is not the place of the jury to determine whether Bronston (D) intended to mislead or deceive; the jury can only consider the actual answer given and whether the witness believed it to be true. Section 1621 must be read in its historical context as well. The French imposed capital punishment on perjurers because no witnesses for the accused were called and it was thus imperative that the truth be spoken on the stand by the accusers. The English tradition called for pillorying as the significantly lesser punishment for perjury because witnesses for both sides appeared and filled out the details of a case. This statute is in the Anglo-American tradition because the courts have other safeguards in place against false testimony. Congress did not intend § 1621 to cover false statements by negative implication. The witness must be made aware that their answer was misleading or nonresponsive and given an opportunity to correct the error. The remedy is a new question, not a perjury conviction. Reversed.

ANALYSIS

This case switches the responsibility for the "evasive" answer from the witness to the questioner. One result of the case was the belief that the witness could now lie with impunity if the answer was carefully crafted, but the

Continued on next page.

focused attorney should always catch a non-responsive answer and ask a follow-up question designed to get an affirmative response. A famous case that involved the so-called *Bronston* defense was the President Bill Clinton impeachment case, in which President Clinton invoked the defense to the perjury charges because his answers may have been evasive but technically true.

Quicknotes

CERTIORARI A discretionary writ issued by a superior court to an inferior court in order to review the lower court's decisions; the Supreme Court's writ ordering such review.

PERJURY The making of false statements under oath.

United States v. Moore

Federal government (P) v. False form-signer (D)

612 F.3d 698 (D.C. Cir. 2010)

NATURE OF CASE: Appeal from conviction for a false statement based on insufficiency of the evidence as to "materiality."

FACT SUMMARY: Moore (D) was convicted of making a materially false statement because he signed a false name on a United States Postal Service delivery form. While Moore (D) admitted he willfully signed a false name, he argued that no rational jury could have found the false name was "material" to warrant a conviction.

RULE OF LAW

A false statement is sufficiently material if it has a natural tendency to influence, or is capable of influencing, either a discrete decision or any other function of the agency to which it was addressed.

FACTS: As part of an investigation, inspectors from the United States Postal Service intercepted a package containing drugs addressed to a female at an address. A "controlled delivery" was made by an undercover postal inspector to the address. When no one answered, the inspector prepared to fill out a Postal Service form notifying the addressee that a parcel was waiting and could be obtained by picking it up or by arranging for another delivery. Moore (D) arrived before the form could be completed and accepted delivery of the package by signing a false name. Moore (D) admitted at trial that he signed the delivery form using a false name, but argued it was not a materially false statement. Moore (D) was convicted of making a materially false statement in violation of 18 U.S.C. § 1001(a)(2).

ISSUE: Is a false statement sufficiently material if it has a natural tendency to influence, or is capable of influencing, either a discrete decision or any other function of the agency to which it was addressed?

HOLDING AND DECISION: (Ginsburg, J.) Yes. A false statement is sufficiently material to have a natural tendency to influence, or is capable of influencing, either a discrete decision or any other function of the agency to which it was addressed. To prove Moore (D) made a statement in violation of the criminal code, the Government (P) must show he (1) "knowingly and willfully" (2) "[made] any materially false, fictitious, or fraudulent statement or representation" (3) in a "matter within the jurisdiction of the executive . . . branch of the Government of the United States." In determining whether a false statement is material, the issue is whether the statement has a tendency to influence a discrete decision of the body to which it was addressed. The evidence showed the name that Moore (D) signed was immaterial to the undercover postal inspector's decision to deliver the package to him. While the statement need not actually influence an agency in order to be material; it need only have "a natural tendency to influence, or [be] capable of influencing" an agency function or decision. Moore's (D's) false statement was capable of affecting the Postal Service's general function of tracking packages and identifying the recipients of packages entrusted to it. Moore's (D's) use of a false name also could have impeded the ability of the Postal Service to investigate the trafficking of narcotics through the mails. Affirmed.

ANALYSIS

The "materiality" element to support a conviction for making a false statement requires only a showing of a tendency to influence a discrete decision of the body to which it was addressed. Here, the effect on the undercover postal inspector was immaterial, as Moore's signing a false name on a delivery form would disrupt the general function of the Postal Service to tracking packages and identifying the recipients. Ironically, the court explained the false name given by Moore (D) was "material" because it could have prevented the Postal Service from identifying and locating him in pursuit of its investigation.

Quicknotes

MATERIAL FALSE REPRESENTATIONS A statement or conduct by one party to another that constitutes a false representation of a material fact.

MATERIALITY Importance; the degree of relevance or necessity to the particular matter.

Brogan v. United Sates

Union officer (D) v. Federal government (P)

522 U.S. 398 (1998)

NATURE OF CASE: Writ of certiorari to address federal question.

FACT SUMMARY: James Brogan (D), a union officer, accepted payments from a company whose employees he represented. Federal agents visited his home and asked him questions about the payments. Brogan (D) answered "no" when asked if he accepted payments from the particular corporation while he was a union officer.

RULE OF LAW

There is no exception to criminal liability for a false statement to a federal agency that consists of a mere denial of wrongdoing, the "exculpatory no."

FACTS: James Brogan (D) was a union officer in 1987 and 1988. JRD Management Corporation (JRD) was a real estate company whose employees the union represented. JRD gave cash payments to Brogan (D). The Internal Revenue Service and Department of Labor began investigating JRD. During the investigation, federal agents visited Brogan's (D) home and asked him several questions. Brogan (D) answered "no" when asked if he accepted payments from JRD while he was a union officer. Prosecutors charged Brogan (D) with, inter alia, making a false statement to federal agents in violation of 18 U.S.C. § 1001. The jury convicted Brogan (D) and the court of appeals affirmed his conviction. The United States Supreme Court granted certiorari on the federal question of whether the "exculpatory no" was an exception to the criminal offense in 18 U.S.C. § 1001.

ISSUE: Is there an exception to criminal liability for a false statement to a federal agency that consists of a mere denial of wrongdoing, the "exculpatory no?"

HOLDING AND DECISION: (Scalia, J.) No. There is no exception to criminal liability for a false statement to a federal agency that consists of a mere denial of wrongdoing, the "exculpatory no." Section 1001 covers "any" false statement and Brogan (D) concedes he is guilty of the literal reading of the statute. Brogan (D) asserts, however, that the Court should adopt the more expansive reading adopted by several circuits that permit the "exculpatory no" exception. The major premise is that § 1001 only criminalizes statements that pervert governmental functions. The minor premise is that simple denials of guilt to federal investigators do not pervert governmental functions. Therefore, Brogan (D) argues, the "exculpatory no" is an exception. These arguments fail completely. A federal investigation is a governmental function that depends on the truthfulness of its subjects, so the major premise fails. The minor premise is inaccurate because it arises out of the assumption that prosecutors will overzealously use § 1001 against persons who say "no" instead of remaining silent as a means of "piling on" offenses. Congress created this separate criminal offense with serious consequences. It is not the Court's place to second-guess that decision. The plain language of the statute supports Brogan's (D) conviction. Affirmed.

ANALYSIS

The "exculpatory no" doctrine was judicially created to limit the rather broad scope of § 1001. The Supreme Court flatly rejected the creation and focused on the plain language of the statute. Prosecutors, however, are advised not to pursue prosecutions for "exculpatory no" violations. *See* the United States Department of Justice's *Justice Manual*, at www.usdoj.gov. The practical result of the *Brogan* decision remains unseen.

Quicknotes

CERTIORARI A discretionary writ issued by a superior court to an inferior court in order to review the lower court's decisions; the Supreme Court's writ ordering such review.

Glossary

Common Latin Words and Phrases Encountered in the Law

A FORTIORI: Because one fact exists or has been proven, therefore a second fact that is related to the first fact must also exist.

A PRIORI: From the cause to the effect. A term of logic used to denote that when one generally accepted truth is shown to be a cause, another particular effect must necessarily follow.

AB INITIO: From the beginning; a condition that has existed throughout, as in a marriage that was void ab initio.

ACTUS REUS: The wrongful act; in criminal law, such action sufficient to trigger criminal liability.

AD VALOREM: According to value; an ad valorem tax is imposed upon an item located within the taxing jurisdiction calculated by the value of such item.

AMICUS CURIAE: Friend of the court. Its most common usage takes the form of an amicus curiae brief, filed by a person who is not a party to an action but is nonetheless allowed to offer an argument supporting their legal interests.

ARGUENDO: In arguing. A statement, possibly hypothetical, made for the purpose of argument is one made arguendo.

BILL QUIA TIMET: A bill to quiet title (establish ownership) to real property.

BONA FIDE: True, honest, or genuine. May refer to a person's legal position based on good faith or lacking notice of fraud (such as a bona fide purchaser for value) or to the authenticity of a particular document (such as a bona fide last will and testament).

CAUSA MORTIS: With approaching death in mind. A gift causa mortis is a gift given by a party who feels certain that death is imminent.

CAVEAT EMPTOR: Let the buyer beware. This maxim is reflected in the rule of law that a buyer purchases at their own risk because it is the buyer's responsibility to examine, judge, test, and otherwise inspect what they are buying.

CERTIORARI: A writ of review. Petitions for review of a case by the United States Supreme Court are most often done by means of a writ of certiorari.

CONTRA: On the other hand. Opposite. Contrary to.

CORAM NOBIS: Before us; writs of error directed to the court that originally rendered the judgment.

CORAM VOBIS: Before you; writs of error directed by an appellate court to a lower court to correct a factual error.

CORPUS DELICTI: The body of the crime; the requisite elements of a crime amounting to objective proof that a crime has been committed.

CUM TESTAMENTO ANNEXO, ADMINISTRATOR (ADMINISTRATOR C.T.A.): With will annexed; an administrator c.t.a. settles an estate pursuant to a will in which the administrator is not appointed.

DE BONIS NON, ADMINISTRATOR (ADMINISTRATOR D.B.N.): Of goods not administered; an administrator d.b.n. settles a partially settled estate.

DE FACTO: In fact; in reality; actually. Existing in fact but not officially approved or engendered.

DE JURE: By right; lawful. Describes a condition that is legitimate "as a matter of law," in contrast to the term "de facto," which connotes something existing in fact but not legally sanctioned or authorized. For example, de facto segregation refers to segregation brought about by housing patterns, etc., whereas de jure segregation refers to segregation created by law.

DE MINIMUS: Of minimal importance; insignificant; a trifle; not worth bothering about.

DE NOVO: Anew; a second time; afresh. A trial de novo is a new trial held at the appellate level as if the case originated there and the trial at a lower level had not taken place.

DICTA: Generally used as an abbreviated form of obiter dicta, a term describing those portions of a judicial opinion incidental or not necessary to resolution of the specific question before the court. Such nonessential statements and remarks are not considered to be binding precedent.

DUCES TECUM: Refers to a particular type of writ or subpoena requesting a party or organization to produce certain documents in their possession.

EN BANC: Full bench. Where a court sits with all justices present rather than the usual quorum.

EX PARTE: For one side or one party only. An ex parte proceeding is one undertaken for the benefit of only one party, without notice to, or an appearance by, an adverse party.

EX POST FACTO: After the fact. An ex post facto law is a law that retroactively changes the consequences of a prior act.

EX REL.: Abbreviated form of the term "ex relatione," meaning upon relation or information. When the state brings an action in which it has no interest against an individual at the instigation of one who has a private interest in the matter.

FORUM NON CONVENIENS: Inconvenient forum. Although a court may have jurisdiction over the case, the action should be tried in a more conveniently located court, one to which parties and witnesses may more easily travel, for example.

GUARDIAN AD LITEM: A guardian appointed by the court to represent a minor or incompetent person in a legal action.

HABEAS CORPUS: You have the body. The modern writ of habeas corpus is a writ directing that a person (body) being detained (such as a prisoner) be brought before the court so that the legality of their detention can be judicially ascertained.

IN CAMERA: In private, in chambers. When a hearing is held before a judge in their chambers or when all spectators are excluded from the courtroom.

IN FORMA PAUPERIS: In the manner of a pauper. A party who proceeds in forma pauperis because of their poverty is one who is allowed to bring suit without liability for costs.

INFRA: Below, under. A word referring the reader to a later part of a book. (The opposite of supra.)

IN LOCO PARENTIS: In the place of a parent.

IN PARI DELICTO: Equally wrong; a court of equity will not grant requested relief to an applicant who is in pari delicto, or as much at fault in the transactions giving rise to the controversy as is the opponent of the applicant.

IN PARI MATERIA: On like subject matter or upon the same matter. Statutes relating to the same person or things are said to be in pari materia. It is a general rule of statutory construction that such statutes should be construed together, i.e., looked at as if they together constituted one law.

IN PERSONAM: Against the person. Jurisdiction over the person of an individual.

IN RE: In the matter of. Used to designate a proceeding involving an estate or other property.

IN REM: A term that signifies an action against the res, or thing. An action in rem is basically one that is taken directly against property, as distinguished from an action in personam, i.e., against the person.

INTER ALIA: Among other things. Used to show that the whole of a statement, pleading, list, statute, etc., has not been set forth in its entirety.

INTER PARTES: Between the parties. May refer to contracts, conveyances, or other transactions having legal significance.

INTER VIVOS: Between the living. An inter vivos gift is a gift made by a living grantor, as distinguished from bequests contained in a will, which pass upon the death of the testator.

IPSO FACTO: By the mere fact itself.

JUS: Law or the entire body of law.

LEX LOCI: The law of the place; the notion that the rights of parties to a legal proceeding are governed by the law of the place where those rights arose.

MALUM IN SE: Evil or wrong in and of itself; inherently wrong. This term describes an act that is wrong by its very nature, as opposed to one which would not be wrong but for the fact that there is a specific legal prohibition against it (malum prohibitum).

MALUM PROHIBITUM: Wrong because prohibited, but not inherently evil. Used to describe something that is wrong because it is expressly forbidden by law but that is not in and of itself evil, e.g., speeding.

MANDAMUS: We command. A writ directing an official to take a certain action.

MENS REA: A guilty mind; a criminal intent. A term used to signify the mental state that accompanies a crime or other prohibited act. Some crimes require only a general mens rea (general intent to do the prohibited act), but others, like assault with intent to murder, require the existence of a specific mens rea.

MODUS OPERANDI: Method of operating; generally refers to the manner or style of a criminal in committing crimes, admissible in appropriate cases as evidence of the identity of a defendant.

NEXUS: A connection to.

NISI PRIUS: A court of first impression. A nisi prius court is one where issues of fact are tried before a judge or jury.

N.O.V. (NON OBSTANTE VEREDICTO): Notwithstanding the verdict. A judgment n.o.v. is a judgment given in favor of one party despite the fact that a verdict was returned in favor of the other party, the justification being that the verdict either had no reasonable support in fact or was contrary to law.

NUNC PRO TUNC: Now for then. This phrase refers to actions that may be taken and will then have full retroactive effect.

PENDENTE LITE: Pending the suit; pending litigation underway.

PER CAPITA: By head; beneficiaries of an estate, if they take in equal shares, take per capita.

PER CURIAM: By the court; signifies an opinion ostensibly written "by the whole court" and with no identified author.

PER SE: By itself, in itself; inherently.

PER STIRPES: By representation. Used primarily in the law of wills to describe the method of distribution where a person, generally because of death, is unable to take that which is left to the person by the will of another, and therefore the person's heirs divide such property between them rather than take under the will individually.

PRIMA FACIE: On its face, at first sight. A prima facie case is one that is sufficient on its face, meaning that the evidence supporting it is adequate to establish the case until contradicted or overcome by other evidence.

PRO TANTO: For so much; as far as it goes. Often used in eminent domain cases when a property owner receives partial payment for their land without prejudice to their right to bring suit for the full amount they claim their land to be worth.

QUANTUM MERUIT: As much as one deserves. Refers to recovery based on the doctrine of unjust enrichment in those cases in which a party has rendered valuable services or furnished materials that were accepted and enjoyed by another under circumstances that would reasonably notify the recipient that the rendering party expected to be paid. In essence, the law implies a contract to pay the reasonable value of the services or materials furnished.

QUASI: Almost like; as if; nearly. This term is essentially used to signify that one subject or thing is almost analogous to another but that material differences between them do exist. For example, a quasi-criminal proceeding is one that is not strictly criminal but shares enough of the same characteristics to require some of the same safeguards (e.g., procedural due process must be followed in a parole hearing).

QUID PRO QUO: Something for something. In contract law, the consideration, something of value, passed between the parties to render the contract binding.

RES GESTAE: Things done. In evidence law, this principle justifies the admission of a statement that would otherwise be hearsay when it is made so closely to the event in question as to be said to be a part of it, or with such spontaneity as not to have the possibility of falsehood.

RES IPSA LOQUITUR: The thing speaks for itself. This doctrine gives rise to a rebuttable presumption of negligence when the instrumentality causing the injury was within the exclusive control of the defendant, and the injury was one that does not normally occur unless a person has been negligent.

RES JUDICATA: A matter adjudged. Doctrine which provides that once a court of competent jurisdiction has rendered a final judgment or decree on the merits, that judgment or decree is conclusive upon the parties to the case and prevents them from engaging in any other litigation on the points and issues determined therein.

RESPONDEAT SUPERIOR: Let the master reply. This doctrine holds the master liable for the wrongful acts of their servant (or the principal for their agent) in those cases in which the servant (or agent) was acting within the scope of the master's authority at the time of the injury.

STARE DECISIS: To stand by or adhere to that which has been decided. The common law doctrine of stare decisis attempts to give security and certainty to the law by following the policy that once a principle of law as applicable to a certain set of facts has been set forth in a decision, it forms a precedent that will subsequently be followed, even though a different decision might be made were it the first time the question had arisen. Of course, stare decisis is not an inviolable principle and is departed from in instances where there is good cause (e.g., considerations of public policy led the Supreme Court to disregard prior decisions sanctioning segregation).

SUPRA: Above. A word referring a reader to an earlier part of a book. (The opposite of infra.)

ULTRA VIRES: Beyond the power. This phrase is most commonly used to refer to actions taken by a corporation that are beyond the power or legal authority of the corporation.

Addendum of French Derivatives

CHATTEL: Tangible personal property.

CY PRES: Doctrine permitting courts to apply trust funds to purposes not expressed in the trust but necessary to carry out the settlor's intent.

IN PAIS: Not pursuant to legal proceedings.

PER AUTRE VIE: For another's life; during another's life. In property law, an estate may be granted that will terminate upon the death of someone other than the grantee.

PROFIT A PRENDRE: A license to remove minerals or other produce from land.

VOIR DIRE: Process of questioning jurors as to their predispositions about the case or parties to a proceeding in order to identify those jurors displaying bias or prejudice.